Top-down,
Modular
Programming
in FORTRAN
with WATFIV

WINTHROP COMPUTER SYSTEMS SERIES

Gerald M. Weinberg, *editor*

Top-down, Modular Programming in FORTRAN with WATFIV

RAHUL CHATTERGY

University of Hawaii

UDO W. POOCH

Texas A&M University

WINTHROP PUBLISHERS, INC.
Cambridge, Massachusetts

Library of Congress Cataloging in Publication Data

Chattergy, R.
    Top-down, modular programming in FORTRAN with WATFIV.

    Bibliography: p.
    Includes index.
    1. FORTRAN (Computer program language) 2. Modular programming. I. Pooch, U. W. II. Title.
QA76.73.F25C43   001.6'424   79-20802
ISBN 0-87626-879-3

© 1980 by Winthrop Publishers, Inc.
  17 Dunster Street, Cambridge, Massachusetts   02138

10 9 8 7 6 5 4 3 2 1

To all of our ladies
  who made our work necessary
  yet worth the while

Contents

Foreword

It's become a cliché in computing that a new FORTRAN textbook must be justified in the light of the multitude of existing FORTRAN texts. Although I think the practice is sensible, *Top-down, Modular Programming in FORTRAN with WATFIV* needs no justification on those terms — neither from me nor the authors. Why? Because, as you'll notice, the book is "in FORTRAN," not "on FOR-TRAN." We don't have to justify a book being "in English," do we?

The book is in FORTRAN because a great many people "speak FORTRAN" and so wish to teach programming in that idiom. But the book is *about* programming, and that is what any such textbook should be about these days. We've long passed the time when we didn't know the difference between a language manual and a programming text.

At least we *should* have passed that time long ago, but many authors have not. Therefore, a book such as this — in which the authors pay scrupulous attention to style, design, and problem solving — is an extremely welcome addition to the textbook scene. The amount of care that Chattergy and Pooch have put into the choice and refinement of these examples is extraordinary. In their present state, the examples reflect many iterations of criticism and revision by students and colleagues — just what a hard-working textbook requires.

The choice of an introductory textbook always involves a great deal of personal taste on the part of the instructor or department. Students differ; schools differ; standards differ. But I'm confident that *Top-down, Modular Programming in FORTRAN with WATFIV* will strike a responsive chord in many places looking fo something beyond the run-of-the-mill FORTRAN language textbook — something that addresses both the instructor's needs and the students' needs in a unique style.

GERALD M. WEINBERG

Series Editor

Preface

The objective of this text is to show novice programmers general methods of program development, test, and modification using the FORTRAN language as a medium of expression. The language used is ANSI FORTRAN, with some features of the WATFIV version of FORTRAN incorporated into the earlier chapters to assist the novice programmer.

The spectrum of the FORTRAN language runs from ANSI FORTRAN to the various recently developed, structured versions of FORTRAN. To select the most useful version of FORTRAN, we considered some of the reasons for the popularity of FORTRAN in an age when much more powerful languages, such as PASCAL and PL/I, are readily available. We believe that one reason for this phenomenon is the existence of a large collection of FORTRAN programs in various areas of science and engineering. Another is the fact that FORTRAN is easy to learn and, consequently, has a large following among scientists, engineers, statisticians, and other numerical analysts. The versions of FORTRAN in use by these circles are very close to ANSI FORTRAN and nowhere near the structured versions of FORTRAN. FORTRAN '77 would have been our choice today if it had been invented in 1955. The time for structured FORTRAN has passed, since more powerful structured programming languages are already available. If structured programming were our goal, we would be wise to invest our time and efforts in learning PL/I or PASCAL and not tinker with yet another version of FORTRAN.

Then why write another text on FORTRAN? We find that FORTRAN is still the first programming language learned by many novice programmers. We also believe that bad programming habits picked up early have a very long half-life. We have seen many examples of this. One such case is that of a senior honors student in computer science who wrote a cross assembler for a microprocessor in FORTRAN where approximately every third statement was an arithmetic IF. Honors students in computer science presumably know everything about structured programming and other mathematical formalities of software engineering, but an arithmetic IF is still an old friend they can rely on in a pinch. Hence our purpose is to show that programs of reasonable quality can be written, even in ANSI FORTRAN, by following some general principles of program development. In the past, the FORTRAN language has absorbed more than its share of blame for the lack of discipline and organization of the programmers using it. The recent rejuvenation of FORTRAN is yet another reason for this book. It appears that while we have been waiting for FORTRAN to fade away like an old soldier, it has started to appear on personal computer systems. Because of limited resources, most versions of FORTRAN on these systems are subsets of ANSI FORTRAN and lack the constructs of structured programming languages. If the potential for the use of the personal computer systems is fully realized, there will be thousands of programmers who will learn to program in FORTRAN for the first time. We hope that this text will provide them with a better introduction to programming in FORTRAN than many other books currently available.

The method for program development we have used is the top-down, modular method. This general approach to problem solving has been utilized for years; empires have been built on the principle of divide and conquer. One of the most concise descriptions of this approach is given by Hoare: "Inside every large problem there is a small problem struggling to get out" (q.v. *Playboy,* August 1978, p. 25). This method is illustrated by examples and augmented by the top-down testing and modification of programs. The top-down, modular method is in no way bound to any specific programming language. It is a way of organizing one's thoughts, always keeping one's goal in focus. The ultimate code may be more structured in PL/I than in ANSI FORTRAN, but the thought process that leads to this code must be organized and independent of the programming language. Whenever psssible, we have pointed out general concepts useful in programming, such as the importance of data structures, the perils of sharing data rather than procedures, and the usefulness of the principle of information hiding. Most texts on FORTRAN do not discuss these ideas, but they are important since they show many of the limitations of FORTRAN. We have, however, omitted the important topic of proving programs correct, since the mathematical background of most novice programmers does not justify its inclusion. In summary, our emphasis is on teaching the programmer the techniques of program development as early as possible.

We would also like to emphasize that this text is aimed primarily at amateur programmers. According to Weinberg,† the greatest difference between an amateur and a professional programmer lies in the ultimate clientele of the programs developed. A professional programmer never knows who the user(s) may be. He/she must survey every conceivable requirement of the users and protect programs from all modes of misuse. The amateur, on the other hand, programs for a small group of users and very often only for him/herself. Thus the programming environment of an amateur programmer is quite different from that of a professional. Fortunately for us, the majority of programmers are amateurs. We also believe that the difference between an amateur and a professional programmer is only one of degree and not of kind. Most professional programmers start out as good amateur programmers. Thus, although we have emphasized some simple techniques of defensive programming (checks for bounds violation of arrays, checks for simple errors in subprograms,

†Gerald M. Weinberg, *The Psychology of Computer Programming* (Princeton, N.J.: Van Nostrand-Reinhold, 1971), p. 122.

etc.), we have by no means discussed everything a professional programmer should do to ensure foolproof programs.

Most of our examples are selected to demonstrate basic programming techniques, such as the pairwise comparison or the binary search. The numerical examples are chosen in such a way that the underlying ideas can be simply explained by graphical means. We caution the reader that this is not a text on numerical analysis. We have discussed the mechanics of sorting, since the concept of sorting can be easily grasped without any profound knowledge of mathematics. The basic sorting techniques of exchange, insertion, and selection are demonstrated with simple examples. These are followed by more advanced methods of Shell's decreasing increment sort and the Quick sort. References are cited for the reader interested in their mathematical analysis. Discussion of random number generation includes a set of guidelines for designing such generators, and two specific models are given with references to their origin.

Many FORTRAN texts are written in sections starting with introductory concepts and progressing to advanced concepts. After some experimentation with this approach, we rejected it for its disadvantages. We found that programs written with only "elementary" concepts have awkward structures and, as such, are poor programs. Individuals becoming proficient in writing such programs have a difficult time breaking bad habits and making full use of the "advanced concepts" at a later date. For example, instead of

$$\text{IF(ERROR .LT. 0.0) ERROR} = -\text{ERROR}$$
$$\text{IF(ERROR .LE. 0.0001) GO TO 100}$$
$$- -$$

100 STOP

we have used

$$\text{IF(ABS(ERROR) .LE. 0.0001) STOP}$$

A person who does not understand the meaning of a simple function such as ABS will not find it easier to do so if it is simply postponed as an advanced concept relating to built-in functions. Similarly, a person who can visualize the flow of control during the execution of a program can understand the meaning of

$$\text{IF(DATA .GT. 0.0) SUM} = \text{SUM} + \text{DATA}$$

when the flow of control is explained to him/her in the proper context. Treating such a statement as an advanced concept merely encourages the habit of branching at the least possible excuse.

We have omitted certain features of FORTRAN such as double precision, or complex and logical variables. Experience has shown that the beginner is rarely confronted with problems where these features are important and hence is not particularly motivated to learn them. We hope that when the need arises, the reader will be motivated to find these features in the FORTRAN manual published by his/her vendor.

If the reader has already visited the local computing center and fears for his/her sanity, these fears are fully justified. The computing center is a strange world of endemic chaos populated by demigods who speak the strange language of DD asterisks and DELETE, DELETEs. Unfortunately, the rituals vary from one center to the next and cannot be summarized in one text. It is on-the-job learning that the reader must acquire with whatever help is available. The reader will perhaps learn that computer science is somewhat like economics. The same computer print-out can be analyzed by different computer experts and result in different erroneous conclusions. The only note of encouragement that we can offer the reader is the motto of General Joseph W. Stilwell: "Illegitimati non Carborundum." Freely translated by the general, it means "Don't let the bastards grind you down."†

We will consider our efforts well spent if, at the end of this text, the reader comes to the following conclusions:

(i) The top-down, modular method is a wise approach to program development;
(ii) Programs of reasonable quality can be written even in ANSI FORTRAN; and
(iii) There is more to programming than can be discussed in a simple FORTRAN text.

If the reader does not share these views, let us disagree as friends and remember that this too shall pass.

RAHUL CHATTERGY
UDO W. POOCH

---

†Barbara Tuchman, *Stilwell and the American Experience in China* (New York: Macmillan Publishing Co., Inc., 1971), p. 5.

Top-down,
Modular
Programming
in FORTRAN
with WATFIV

1 Introduction to Digital Computers and Programming

Digital computers are widely used for solving problems in such areas as science, engineering, and business. This widespread use of computers is directly related to their ability to process rapidly and accurately enormous quantities of data following prespecified sequences of instructions. The process of creating these sequences of instructions is called *programming*, and the languages used for specifying these instructions are called *programming languages*. A complete sequence of data processing instructions considered as a single entity is called a *program*. In order to use a computer, we must have a thorough knowledge of at least one such programming language and the process of program development.

1.1 FUNCTIONAL DESCRIPTION OF A COMPUTER

The task of understanding what it means to program a computer and how it is programmed is simplified if we have some understanding of what a computer is and how it works. A detailed structural description of a computer is, however, beyond the scope of this text; fortunately it is not needed to program solution methods for computer applications. A functional description of a computer will be sufficient for our purpose (see Fig. 1.1). A computer contains a memory unit for storing information. A memory unit can be thought of as a linear arrangement of memory cells, each cell capable of storing information in coded form, using some internal computer code. The information stored in these cells consists of *instructions* and *data*. The processing unit consists of an arithmetic and logic unit and a control unit. It fetches instructions from the memory unit and executes them, in the process storing or fetching data in or out of the memory unit. The instructions normally specify, explicitly or implicitly, the locations of data in memory cells. The processor fetches instructions from *successive* memory cells, unless directed otherwise by special *branch instructions*. At this point, it is not necessary to know the details of the interactions among the pro-

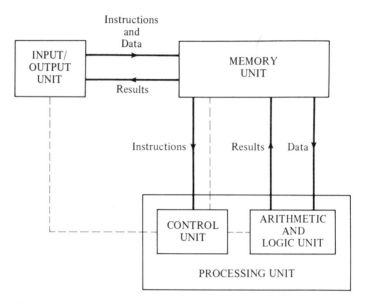

Fig. 1.1 Functional description of a digital computer. The dashed lines represent the flow of control signals.

cessing unit and the input/output unit. The control unit in the processor supervises the orderly operation of the whole system.

In the operation of a computer, a very important role is played by the process of storing and fetching information in and out of a memory cell. For this process, each memory cell is uniquely identified by a number, called its *address*. A functional description of a memory unit is shown in Fig. 1.2. The exact numerical address of a memory cell is often called its *absolute address*. In order to write a program, a programmer has to identify the memory cells into which instructions and data are stored. The use of absolute addresses for this purpose complicates the job of programming because the programmer now has to keep track of memory usage by different programs. To eliminate this problem, most programming languages allow a programmer to use symbols for addresses, and this method of addressing is called *symbolic addressing*. Figure 1.3 is a functional description of symbolically addressed memory cells. In order to program in most languages, it is necessary to understand this concept of symbolic addressing of memory cells. The details of all the other operations in a computer can be suppressed, at least for amateur programming.

1.2 PROGRAMMING LANGUAGES

Computers can be programmed in more than one programming language and these languages can be categorized into three classes. At one end of the language spectrum lie all the *machine languages*. Each computer has its own machine language, and

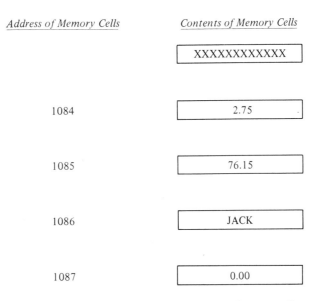

Fig. 1.2 Functional description of the organization of memory cells.

instructions in this language can be directly interpreted and executed by the control unit. Instructions stored in the memory unit are all in a machine language. A machine language uses only two symbols, commonly represented by a 0 and a 1. Hence machine language instructions are often long and difficult to comprehend strings of zeros and ones. The machine language representation of the HALT instruction of a Slobovian computer is shown below:

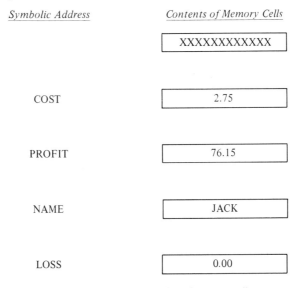

Fig. 1.3 Symbolic addressing of memory cells.

0001101001001110

Programs written in a machine language also require the use of absolute addresses. Clearly, programming in a machine language, unless done automatically with the aid of a computer, will be extremely error-prone. In order to be executed by a computer, however, instructions must somehow ultimately be written in that computer's own machine language.

In the middle of the language spectrum lie various *assembly languages*. These languages allow a programmer to use symbolic addresses for memory cells and mnemonic codes for instructions. An example of an assembly language instruction is

JMP   LOOP

which directs the control unit to fetch the next instruction from the memory unit, stored in a memory cell with symbolic address LOOP. Assembly languages are *machine-oriented* in the sense that each simple assembly language instruction has a one-to-one correspondence with an underlying machine language instruction. Assembly language programs are automatically translated into machine language programs (*object programs*) by special translating programs called *assemblers*.

At the other end of the language spectrum lie the various *high-level languages* or *problem-oriented languages*. These are languages which are carefully formatted to resemble natural languages such as English. Examples of such languages are PL/I, APL, COBOL, and FORTRAN. A typical example of an instruction in a high-level language is

IF DAMAGE > 100.00 THEN CALL INSURANCE
ELSE GO TO PAY

High-level languages are problem-oriented in the sense that most of them are designed to solve problems in specific areas. Hence they have built-in language features that reflect the special characteristics and needs of the problems in a particular area. For example FORTRAN (FORmula TRANslation) is primarily used for scientific data processing, and hence it has built-in trigonometric functions and structures for representing vectors and matrices. COBOL (COmmon Business-Oriented Language) has special structures for representing business records not found in FORTRAN.

Programs in high-level languages are written by using complex *statements* and not simple machine-oriented instructions. These statements are automatically translated into machine language instructions by a *compiler*. Each statement in a high-level language normally generates a sequence of several machine language instructions. Programs in a high-level language are easier to write, document, modify, and diagnose for errors. They are also largely machine-independent, i.e., the same program can be executed on different computers, which is not the case with machine or assembly language programs. This characteristic of a program is called *portability*, and it is important since large complex programs are costly to design from scratch.

1.3 COMPILERS

Application of high-level programming languages simplifies the task of programming but introduces a problem of translation. The processing units in most computers cannot directly interpret high-level language statements, and programs written in such high-level languages must be translated into machine languages before they can be executed by a computer. This translation process is normally achieved by systems called *compilers*. A compiler (or language translator) is a program which upon its execution translates a user's program written in a high-level language (*source language*) into a computer's machine language.

Most compilers do more than mere translations of a source language program into a machine language program. Clearly, if the programmer does not follow the rules of the source language, his/her program will contain errors and a compiler will not be able to translate it correctly. Most compilers are designed to detect such errors and to generate error messages. These are called *compile-time errors*. If these errors are severe in nature, the compiler will flag the program and prevent the program from entering the execution phase.

For every high-level language, there is more than one compiler. Some compilers are designed to perform extensive checks for errors in programs during the process of translation. Others are designed to produce efficient machine language programs. The efficiency of an object program is measured in terms of its speed of execution, or the number of memory cells needed to store it, or some combination of both.

High-level languages are practically useful to the extent that compilers can be found to translate them into machine languages. Since compilers are also designed by humans, a source language can be modified by designing a new compiler capable of translating the modified language. The modified source language can be thought of as a different version of the basic high-level language. Such modifications are often introduced to enhance ease of programming in a given source language. For example, the FORTRAN language has a nationally recognized standard form called ANSI (American National Standards Institute) FORTRAN. This standard form, however, is not always easy to program in, especially for a beginner. A modified form of the standard FORTRAN has been developed called the WATFIV version of FORTRAN. In order to use this version of the FORTRAN language, one needs a WATFIV compiler. This compiler has been designed by computer scientists at the University of Waterloo in Canada. In standard FORTRAN, the input and output of data must be formatted and the formatting instructions are often difficult for a beginner to use. The WATFIV version of FORTRAN allows unformatted input and output, thereby eliminating a learning bottleneck. WATFIV compilers also generate reasonably clear and extensive error messages. This feature of the WATFIV compiler is a great help to the novice programmer. This text starts with the WATFIV version of FORTRAN and evolves toward standard FORTRAN. We hope that this will help the novice to learn to program easily, and yet in standard FORTRAN to reap the benefits of such a standard language.

1.4 JOB CONTROL LANGUAGE

A computer system can provide a variety of information processing services. It can, for example, make a duplicate copy of a program on a storage medium, or compile one or more programs and store the machine language programs for future execution, or link several short programs together to form a long program. The list of capabilities is very long and it serves no purpose to list them all. Even with this large capability and flexibility, however, we cannot simply input a source language program into a computer and expect it to know what to do with the program. For example, we have to tell the computer which source language we are using. Since more than one compiler is normally available for each source language, we have to indicate which compiler should be used to translate the program. We may also want to specify such factors as the maximum amount of execution time and memory to be allocated to the program. We may be required to specify the account number which will be charged, the name of the programmer, etc. All this information is usually transmitted to the computer system using instructions in a *command language* or *job control language*. These languages are totally independent of the high-level programming languages used to compose programs for solving problems, but they are installation-dependent. The reader should ascertain from his/her own installation the necessary job control language instructions for compiling and executing FORTRAN programs.

1.5 COMMUNICATION WITH A COMPUTER

There are many different mediums for getting a program and data into a computer and receiving the results of computations. The most familiar medium is a *punched card*, shown in Fig. 1.4. Such a card is also known as a Hollerith card, named after Dr. Herman Hollerith who developed the earliest version of such a card in 1890. The eighty-column card dates back to 1930. The punched card is a cheap and versatile medium for both input and output. It has *eighty vertical columns* and can store eighty

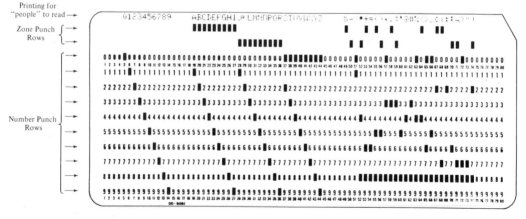

Fig. 1.4 Format of a Hollerith card showing some of the legal FORTRAN characters.

characters of information. The standard card has *ten rows* for representing the digits 0 to 9 as holes punched in corresponding rows. There are two *zone rows* on top of the ten numbered rows. Characters other than 0 to 9 are represented by multiple holes punched in a single column. As an input medium, a deck of punched cards containing a program and data is read into a computer system by means of a *card-reader*.

The most commonly used method of retrieving information from a computer is by means of a high-speed *line-printer*. These printers can print entire lines of up to 132 characters or more in a single operation, as opposed to typewriters, which print only one character at a time. Some of these printers can print 1200 lines per minute. Special formatted paper can be used with such printers for the high-speed printing of business data. The output of such devices is commonly known as *hard-copies*, since with reasonable care, the output can be made to last long after the end of the execution that produced it. The operation of running a program on a computer with a card-reader and line-printer is depicted in Fig. 1.5. In some modern time-sharing systems, the programmer may find not card-readers and line-printers but cathode-ray tube (CRT) terminals attached to keyboards, as shown in Fig. 1.6. The

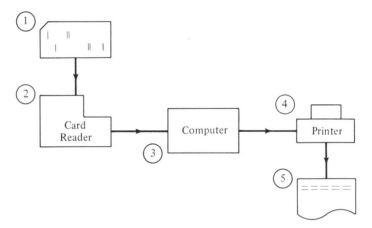

Fig. 1.5 Operations involved in running a program: ① deck of punched cards with program and data; ② card deck read by card-reader; ③ data processed by computer; ④ output printed by line-printer; ⑤ hard-copy received by the programmer.

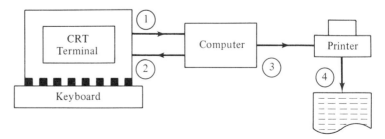

Fig. 1.6 Communication via a CRT terminal: ① program and data keyed in from CRT terminal; ② output from computer displayed on terminal (soft copy); ③ and ④ hard-copy generated upon request.

protocols and supporting programs for using these terminals vary from system to system and should be learned from the vendor-supplied manuals. The program and data are keyed in via the keyboard and are displayed on the CRT screen. Upon request, the program is executed by the computer and the result is displayed on the CRT screen. Hard-copies of outputs can also be created upon request.

2 Informal Introduction
to Fortran

This chapter provides an informal introduction to the FORTRAN language by means of examples. The main issues discussed are the structure of simple programs and the top-down method of composing programs. The reader will notice that the FORTRAN language is particularly easy to read and understand, even without a thorough knowledge of its syntax.

2.1 VARIABLES AND FUNCTIONS

Numerical problems and their solutions are commonly expressed in terms of *variables* and *functions*. In this section we briefly discuss these two concepts to the extent necessary for writing programs. For our purpose a *variable* is essentially a name, usually having some physical significance for the numerical problem being considered, to which unique numerical values can be assigned at any given time. For example, temperature, pressure, velocity, and position are variables whose values may characterize the state of a given physical system at any given time. Mean and variance are variables whose values characterize the statistical nature of a population. In a computer program, a variable is simply a name which is used as a label to identify

Labels or Names	*Contents of Memory Locations*
.	X X X X X X X X
HEIGHT	5.3
WEIGHT	125
AGE	18
.	X X X X X X X X

Fig. 2.1 Functional description of variables and their values stored in uniquely labeled memory locations.

a memory location into which the value of that variable is stored. For example, if a program uses the variables HEIGHT, WEIGHT, and AGE and at a given point during the execution of the program they have the following values 5.3, 125, and 18, respectively, we can functionally describe the representation of these variables in memory as shown in Fig. 2.1. Each time a new value is assigned to a variable, i.e., stored in the memory location representing that variable, the *old value* stored in the same memory location is *permanently destroyed*.

We define a *function* simply as a mathematical expression involving variables. The *value of a function* is obtained by performing the specified mathematical operations using the values of the variables involved in the expression. For example, a function named VOLUME of two variables named AREA and HEIGHT, respectively, is given by the following mathematical expression:

$$(AREA) \times (HEIGHT)$$

The complete description of the function is

$$VOLUME\,(AREA,\ HEIGHT) = (AREA) \times (HEIGHT)$$

The left-hand side of the above expression gives the *name of the function* and lists its variables. The right-hand side specifies the manner in which the value of the function is computed from the values of these variables. The sign of equality is interpreted as ''is assigned the value of'', i.e., compute the value using the right-hand side and assign this value to the name of the function on the left-hand side. The value of a function at any given time is stored in the memory in the same manner as the values of variables (see Fig. 2.2). A more abstract definition of a *function* is that it is the *name of a procedure* for computing a value from a given set of values of variables. The earlier and simpler definition of a function is a special case of this more abstract definition, where the entire procedure is given by a single mathematical expression.

2.2 PROBLEM SOLVING USING FORTRAN

In this section we discuss, using an example, the type of problems that can be efficiently solved using computer programs written in FORTRAN. These problems are often called scientific problems because they arise in science and engineering. Perhaps a more descriptive name is numerical problems, since their solutions involve almost exclusive use of numerical techniques. The name FORTRAN—derived from FORmula TRANslation—also indicates the nature of problems solved by the use of FORTRAN programs.

Suppose H_k denotes the height of the Kth person in a population. Then we can compute the average height for a population of N persons by the formula

Labels or Names	Contents of Memory Locations
.	X X X X X X X X
AREA	5.34
HEIGHT	10.10
VOLUME	53.934
.	X X X X X X X X

Fig. 2.2   Functional description of the storage of values of a function and its variables in memory.

$$H_{\mathrm{av}} = \frac{(H_1 + H_2 + \ldots + H_N)}{N}$$

If we use a computer, we can write a program for the computer in FORTRAN to compute H_{av} using the above formula. For this program the values of $H_1, \ldots, H_N$, and N become the input data, and the value of H_{av} is the output data. To obtain a clearer picture of how a computer program can be used to solve a problem, let us write the method of computation of the value of H_{av} in more detail. We describe this method by the following sequence of instructions:

(i) Obtain the value of N.

(ii) Create a variable, called COUNTER, and assign the value of N as its initial value.

(iii) Create a variable, called SUM, and set its initial value to zero.

(iv) Obtain a value of HEIGHT and increment the value of SUM by this value.

(v) Decrement the value of COUNTER by one.

(vi) If the value of COUNTER is greater than zero, go to step (iv). Else go to step (vii).

(vii) Divide the value of SUM by the value of N and assign this value to a variable called HAV.

Sequences of instructions, such as the one shown above, are commonly called *algorithms*. An algorithm consists of some initial data, a set of processing instructions which are executed repeatedly, and some criterion for stopping this repeated execution. In the algorithm for computing the value of H_{av}, the initial data are obtained and organized in steps (i) to (iii). Instructions in steps (iv) and (v) are repeatedly executed until the stopping condition given in step (vi) is satisfied. Step (vii) contains a final instruction before the output value can be obtained. This algorithm, when written in FORTRAN, becomes a FORTRAN program for computing the average height of a population.

The FORTRAN compiler, in the process of translating this program, assigns

N	3
COUNTER	3
SUM	0
HEIGHT	X X X X X X X X
HAV	X X X X X X X X

(a)

N	3
COUNTER	2
SUM	1
HEIGHT	1
HAV	X X X X X X X X

(b)

N	3
COUNTER	1
SUM	8
HEIGHT	7
HAV	X X X X X X X X

(c)

N	3
COUNTER	0
SUM	12
HEIGHT	4
HAV	X X X X X X X X

(d)

N	3
COUNTER	0
SUM	12
HEIGHT	4
HAV	4

(e)

Fig. 2.3

memory locations for storing the values of the variables N, COUNTER, SUM, HEIGHT, and HAV. If the value of N is assumed to be 3, then after the execution of the instructions in steps (i), (ii), and (iii), these memory locations contain the values shown in Fig. 2.3 (a).

If $H_1 = 1$, then the values of these variables become those shown in Fig. 2.3(b) after the execution of the instructions in steps (iv) and (v) for the *first time*.

The results of the second and third executions of steps (iv) and (v) are shown in Figs. 2.3(c) and (d), where we have assumed that $H_2 = 7$ and $H_3 = 4$. Note that as new values are stored in HEIGHT, the old values are destroyed.

After the end of the third execution, the value of COUNTER becomes zero. According to the stopping condition given in step (vi), the computer now executes step (vii); the final results are shown in Fig. 2.3(e).

2.3   PERIOD OF A PENDULUM

Let us consider the problem of computing the period of oscillation of a pendulum as shown in Fig. 2.4. The period of oscillation is the time taken by the pendulum to

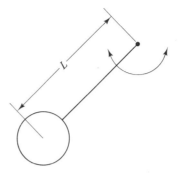

Fig. 2.4 A swinging pendulum of length *L*.

swing from one end to the other and back to the starting position. The period is a function of the length of the pendulum and is given by the formula

$$T = 2 \, \Pi \left(\frac{L}{g}\right)^{1/2} \tag{2.1}$$

Where *T* and *L* denote the period and the length, respectively, $\pi = 3.14159 \ldots$ is a constant, and *g* is the gravitational constant with the value of 32 ft/sec². The FORTRAN program developed below is based on this formula.

2.4   FORTRAN PROGRAM FOR THE PERIOD

In the FORTRAN program, we use PERIOD to denote the period *T* and PLNGTH to denote the length *L* of the pendulum. The constant π is denoted by PI and the gravitational constant *g* is GCONST. FORTRAN allows us a maximum of six characters for naming variables, and we make the best use of this rule to select descriptive variable names.

Equation (2.1) translated into FORTRAN becomes

PERIOD = 2.0 *PI* SQRT (PLNGTH/GCONST)   (2.2)

Obviously * and / denote the multiplication and the division operations in FOR-TRAN. Parentheses are used in FORTRAN in the same manner as in algebra.

Equation (2.1) involves the computation of a square root. Since this is a very common operation in numerical computation, FORTRAN provides a special function for the *automatic* computation of square roots. The name of this function is SQRT (SQuare RooT), and to use this function we simply write its name followed by the expression in parentheses whose square root is to be computed. Note that we need not concern ourselves with the procedure for computing the square root. This is done automatically by the SQRT function. Such functions are called *built-in functions*, and FORTRAN provides a set of such commonly used functions to simplify the task of programming. Built-in functions are concrete examples of our abstract definition of functions as names of procedures for computing values where the exact nature of these procedures is of no concern to the programmer.

Now in order to execute the FORTRAN statement given by Eq. (2.2), the computer must have the values of the variables PI, PLNGTH, and GCONST. Suppose the length of a particular pendulum of interest is 5.2 ft. Then the values of these variables can be assigned by the following FORTRAN statements:

$$PI = 3.14159 \hspace{4cm} (2.3a)$$
$$GCONST = 32.0 \hspace{3.6cm} (2.3b)$$
$$PLNGTH = 5.2 \hspace{3.8cm} (2.3c)$$

Combining all our FORTRAN statements, we have the following program segment:

$$
\begin{aligned}
&PI = 3.14159 \\
&GCONST = 32.0 \hspace{4cm} (2.P1)\\
&PLNGTH = 5.2 \\
&PERIOD = 2.0\,*PI*\,SQRT\,(PLNGTH/GCONST)
\end{aligned}
$$

Note that the computer will execute these statements strictly in a *top-to-bottom sequence*. Hence every instruction in a program has its proper place. An out-of-place instruction in a program may terminate its execution or generate incorrect results. For example,

$$
\begin{aligned}
&PI = 3.14159 \\
&GCONST = 32.0 \\
&PERIOD = 2.0\,*PI*\,SQRT\,(PLNGTH/GCONST) \\
&PLNGTH = 5.2
\end{aligned}
$$

will either terminate during the execution of the third statement or generate wrong results, since PLNGTH is assigned its correct value of 5.2 only *after* the execution of this statement.

2.5 OUTPUT FROM THE PROGRAM

If the Program (2.P1) is executed on a computer, it will compute the value of PERIOD and store it in memory, but not generate any output. To obtain the value of PERIOD as output, we need to add a specific output instruction to our program. There are several instructions for generating outputs, but for the moment we use the simplest:

$$PRINT, PERIOD$$

This FORTRAN statement instructs the computer to print the computed value of the variable PERIOD as output.

Obviously, the proper place for this statement in our program is after the statement that computes the value of PERIOD. Note that some FORTRAN compilers may not translate such a statement since this is not a standard FORTRAN statement but belongs to the WATFIV version of FORTRAN. Program (2.P1) now becomes

```
PI = 3.14159
GCONST = 32.0                                          (2.P2)
PLNGTH = 5.2
PERIOD = 2.0 *PI* SQRT (PLNGTH/GCONST)
PRINT, PERIOD
```

2.6 VARIATIONS OF INPUT DATA

Program (2.P2) can only be used to compute the period of oscillation of a specific pendulum of length 5.2 ft. If the length of the pendulum is changed, then the third statement PLNGTH = 5.2 in the program must be changed appropriately. A better approach is not to assign a specific value to PLNGTH in the program itself as is done in (2.P2), but to read this value as input data during the execution of the program. The simplest FORTRAN statement for reading input data is

READ, PLNGTH

We replace the third statement of (2.P2) by this READ statement. Now that we are reading the value of PLNGTH as input data, our program must be followed by a *data card* with the value of PLNGTH on it. To ensure that this value on the data card is correct, we follow the read statement with an "echo check" print statement

PRINT, PLNGTH

The modified program is as follows:

```
PI = 3.14159
GCONST = 32.0                                          (2.P3)
READ, PLNGTH
PRINT, PLNGTH
PERIOD = 2.0 *PI* SQRT (PLNGTH/GCONST)
PRINT, PERIOD
```

Another reason for using the statement PRINT, PLNGTH is that it allows us to see and establish a relationship between the input data and the corresponding output data. Without this statement, the value of PERIOD printed by itself may not be very meaningful.

2.7 TERMINATION OF EXECUTION

In our program (2.P3) we have not instructed the computer what to do after executing PRINT, PERIOD. Presumably, we want it to terminate the execution of our program since we have our answer. In FORTRAN this is done by the statement

STOP

We also add an END statement to mark the physical end of our program. The END statement is used by the compiler to terminate the translation of our program. The END statement is not translated by the compiler into an instruction for execution by the computer during the execution of our program. The complete program appears as follows:

PI = 3.14159
GCONST = 32.0   (2.P4)
READ, PLNGTH
PRINT, PLNGTH
PERIOD = 2.0 *PI* SQRT (PLNGTH/GCONST)
PRINT, PERIOD
STOP
END

Figure 2.5 provides a functional description of the execution of this program. Typical output obtained from the execution of this program is

0.5200000E 01
0.2532831E 01

Since PRINT, PLNGTH is executed first, the *first* number in the output is the value of the length of the pendulum. The *second* number, generated by PRINT, PERIOD,

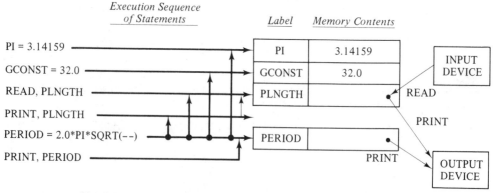

Fig. 2.5 Functional description of the execution of Program (2.P4). Arrows on the left point to the memory locations involved during the execution of each statement. Arrows on the right show the execution of the input/output instructions.

is the value of the time period of oscillation. These values are printed out in the *exponent format* or E format. To convert these values to a more familiar form, we note that the two digits following the letter E denote an exponent or power of ten. Next we multiply the digits on the left-hand side of E by the specified power of ten as shown below:

$$0.5200000E\ 01 = 0.52 \times 10^1 = 5.2$$
$$0.2532831E01 = 0.253281 \times 10^1 = 2.532831$$

We can now test this computed output against the value of the period of oscillation of a pendulum 5.2 ft long computed by hand.

2.8 MULTIPLE VALUES OF INPUT DATA

Program (2.P4) computes the period of oscillation of a single pendulum. The length of the pendulum is no longer fixed but can be changed prior to the execution of the program. Suppose we want to examine the periods of oscillation of several pendulums before selecting one for use. Then (2.P4) has to be executed many times, once for each value of PLNGTH. This repeated execution of (2.P4) can be done manually by feeding the card deck to the card-reader again and again with the data card replaced by a new one each time. A better approach is to instruct the computer to repeat the execution of (2.P4) *automatically* without manual intervention.

The computer executes the statements of a program such as (2.P4) in a strict top-to-bottom sequence. Thus, after executing PRINT, PERIOD it encounters the STOP statement and quits execution. In order to execute (2.P4) repeatedly, we have to break this strict top-to-bottom flow of control of the computer and instruct it to go back and repeat the execution of a section of a program. Two things are needed to achieve this goal: first, a means of identifying individual statements in a program, and secondly, a statement to instruct the computer to go to a particular statement and continue execution from there.

In FORTRAN, statements are *uniquely identified* by positive integers called *statement numbers*. A statement number is written next to a statement on the left-hand side. No two distinct statements use the same number. Only those statements which must be identified for the transfer of control need be identified by statement numbers.

The transfer of control is achieved by a GO TO statement followed by the statement number of the statement to which we wish to transfer control. For example,

GO TO 200

instructs the computer to go to statement numbered 200 and to continue execution from that point on in a top-to-bottom sequence.

Using a GO TO statement, Program (2.P4) can be modified to

```
50      PI = 3.14159
        GCONST = 32.0
        READ, PLNGTH
        PRINT, PLNGTH
        PERIOD = 2.0 *PI*SQRT (PLNGTH/GCONST)
        PRINT, PERIOD
        GO TO 50
        STOP
        END
```

Now after every execution of PRINT, PERIOD, the computer will encounter the GO TO 50 instead of the STOP and automatically reexecute the program starting at statement numbered 50, i.e., PI = 3.14159.

Recall that during the execution of this program, the values of PI and GCONST are not destroyed. There is therefore no need to repeat the execution of the first two statements. We can improve the speed of execution of our program if we modify it as follows:

```
        PI=3.14159
        GCONST = 32.0
50      READ, PLNGTH
        PRINT, PLNGTH                                              (2.P5)
        PERIOD = 2.0 *PI* SQRT (PLNGTH/GCONST)
        PRINT, PERIOD
        GO TO 50
        STOP
        END
```

Every time READ, PLNGTH is executed in (2.P5), a *new* value of PLNGTH is read from a *new* data card. This value is then stored in the memory, thereby *destroying* the *old* value of PLNGTH. In order to execute (2.P5), we provide a *set of data cards* (a data deck) at the end, with each card containing a distinct value of PLNGTH. Note also that we have *indented* some of the statements in (2.P5) to identify easily the section that is executed repeatedly.

2.9 TERMINATION OF A LOOP

An execution of Program (2.P5) generated the following output:

```
UNNUMBERED EXECUTABLE STATEMENT ENCOUNTERED AFTER A TRANSFER
        0.5200000E 01
        0.2532831E 01
        0.4700000E 01
        0.2407983E 01
        0.3500000E 01
        0.2077966E 01
        ILLEGAL CHARACTER SEQUENCE IN INPUT DATA.
        THE FIRST EIGHTY CHARACTERS ARE → //.
```

Let us now try to understand what this output means. First of all, the numbers printed out are the values of PLNGTH and the corresponding values of PERIOD. By consulting (2.P5), the reader should determine on his/her own the relationship of these values to the variables. Perhaps this effort will convince the reader of the necessity of attaching *labels* or *headings* to output data.

Now the first message tells us that (2.P5) has an unnumbered executable statement after a statement that transfers control. The only statement that transfers control in (2.P5) is GO TO 50. Following this, we have STOP which is an executable statement with no statement number. What this means is that the STOP statement is never executed during the execution of (2.P5). Control always passes to the statement numbered 50 before reaching STOP.

This is an example of a *permanent loop* in a program, which in principle will execute forever. However, every execution of this loop reads a *new* data card for PLNGTH, and eventually all the genuine data cards are read and processed. The computer then proceeds to read the last card in the deck which is a job control card with two slashes on it. Since there is no numerical value on this card, the computer cannot use its contents as a value of PLNGTH. It therefore terminates execution of (2.P5) with the message shown at the end of the output.

Although (2.P5) is thus terminated, it is obviously an improper termination. Our intention was to terminate (2.P5) by the STOP statement, but because of the structure of the loop, this statement is never executed. What we need here is a method for ascertaining the end of the data deck and terminating execution upon reaching it. A commonly used method is to supply data at the end of the deck which are obviously improper for the computations being carried out in the program. Then within the loop, before any computation begins, we test the input data for these improper values. Once these improper values are detected, we terminate execution of the program.

In FORTRAN, tests are carried out by means of *logical expressions*, whereby a logical expression can be thought of as a *question* to which an unambiguous yes or no answer can be given. For example, suppose the last data card in (2.P5) contains a negative number. This is obviously an improper value for PLNGTH since the length of a pendulum cannot be negative. Now after the READ, PLNGTH is executed, we want to test the value of PLNGTH to see whether it is negative. In FORTRAN, we use a logical expression, such as

PLNGTH .LT. 0.0

which can be thought of as an abbreviation of the question: Is the value of PLNGTH less than zero? Here .LT. is obviously a symbol used to mean ''less than.'' If the answer to this question is yes, then we direct the computer to stop. In FORTRAN we express this direction as

IF (PLNGTH .LT. 0.0) STOP

This is called a *logical* IF statement. If the answer to the question following the IF is *yes*, then the computer executes the statement on the *right*. Otherwise, it executes the statement that *follows* the logical IF. Adding this logical IF statement after the READ, PLNGTH in (2.P5) we have

```
              PI = 3.14159
              GCONST = 32.0
       50     READ, PLNGTH                                    (2.P6)
                IF (PLNGTH .LT. 0.0) STOP
              PRINT, PLNGTH
              PERIOD = 2.0 *PI* SQRT (PLNGTH/GCONST)
              PRINT, PERIOD
              GO TO 50
              END
```

Execution of (2.P6) generated the following output:

```
              0.5200000E 01
              0.2532831E 01
              0.4700000E 01
              0.2407983E 01
              0.3500000E 01
              0.2077966E 01
```

2.10   PROGRAM STRUCTURES

Program (2.P4) represents the simplest useful program structure. It consists of a set of instructions in FORTRAN that is executed only once. Program (2.P6) is more complex in structure, containing a *loop* which is executed repeatedly until a test condition is satisfied. More examples of FORTRAN programs follow, illustrating this basic structure of simple programs. The reader should have no difficulty in understanding these programs, since the FORTRAN statements are similar to those we have already discussed. From this point on, he/she may also start to read concurrently the syntax of FORTRAN given in Sec. 3.1 – 3.9. In summary, the basic structure of a simple program for processing a set of input data is as follows:

   (i)   Initialize variables;
  (ii)   Read input data;
 (iii)   Test input data for termination of execution;
  (iv)   Print input data;
   (v)   Process input data;
  (vi)   Print results;
 (vii)   Go to step (ii).

2.11   GROCERY BILL

The purpose of this section is to show a commonly used technique for adding numbers in a program by using a loop and a variable for storing partial sums. The need for such a technique has already been demonstrated by the algorithm presented in Sec. 2.2. The problem is to write a FORTRAN program to compute the total cost from the costs of the individual purchases listed in a grocery bill. The algorithm is shown below, where each step is immediately followed by the FORTRAN statements used to implement it.

(i) Create a variable, called TOTAL, and set its initial value to zero.

   TOTAL = 0.0

(ii) Read a value of COST. If negative, then go to step (v).

   20 READ, COST
   IF (COST .LT. 0.0) GO TO 50

(iii) Else increment the value of TOTAL by the value of COST.

   TOTAL = TOTAL + COST

(iv) Go to step (ii).

   GO TO 20

(v) Print the value of TOTAL and stop.

   50 PRINT, TOTAL
   STOP
   END

The FORTRAN statement used in step (iii) needs further clarification. If we interpret the equal sign in

$$TOTAL = TOTAL + COST$$

as in algebra, then subtracting the common value of TOTAL from both sides, we have

$$0.0 = COST$$

which does not make sense for our program. In FORTRAN such equal signs are always interpreted as "is assigned the value of." The values of the variables on the right-hand side are used to compute a *new* value which is then *assigned to* the variable on the left-hand side. This FORTRAN statement stands for:

New value of TOTAL = (Current value of TOTAL) + (Current value of COST)

Figures 2.6(a) and (b) show the values of TOTAL and COST in memory prior to and after the execution of

$$TOTAL = TOTAL + COST$$

COST	3.75	COST	3.75
TOTAL	4.25	TOTAL	8.00

(a)   (b)

Fig. 2.6 (a) Memory contents prior to the execution of TO-TAL = TOTAL + COST. (b) Memory contents after the execution of TO-TAL = TOTAL + COST.

The complete FORTRAN program is shown below.

```
C          *** TOTAL COST OF A GROCERY BILL
C          *** INITIALIZE TOTAL
      TOTAL = 0.0
C          *** READ A VALUE OF COST FROM GROCERY BILL
C          *** AND PRINT IT AS OUTPUT
C   20 READ, COST
      PRINT, COST
C          *** NEGATIVE VALUE OF COST SIGNALS END
C          *** OF DATA.  GO TO 50 AND PRINT TOTAL              (2.P7)
      IF (COST .LT. 0.0) GO TO 50
C          *** ADD COST OF PURCHASE TO TOTAL
      TOTAL = TOTAL + COST
C          *** GO TO 20 AND READ NEXT VALUE OF COST
      GO TO 20
C          ***PRINT VALUE OF TOTAL AND STOP
   50 PRINT, TOTAL
      STOP
      END
```

In addition to the regular FORTRAN statements, Program (2.P7) contains several additional lines starting with the letter C. These are called *comments*. Such comments are used by the programmer to explain the purposes of the program and the individual FORTRAN statements. Any line of characters starting with a C is treated by the compiler as a comment and is not translated into machine language. We have prefixed all our comments with *** since it is one of those sequences of characters that never appear at the beginning of any regular FORTRAN statement. This is our convention for ease of separation of comments from FORTRAN statements; by no means is it universal. We have also indented every line of comment to have it stand apart from the regular FORTRAN statements.

As far as possible, comments should explain the purpose behind the use of a statement in a program. For example,

```
      C       ***IF COST LT 0 GO TO 50
      IF (COST .LT.0.0) GO TO 50
```

is a worthless comment since the FORTRAN statement itself says as much. Similarly,

```
C          *** READ NEXT DATA CARD
        GO TO 20
```

is a misleading comment since a GO TO statement does not read a data card.

Note also that this program uses more than one statement number and that these statement numbers are in *ascending* order, i.e., statement 50 appears after statement 20. Although this is not required in FORTRAN, it is a good convention to adhere to when many statement numbers are used in a program. A typical output from this program is shown below:

$$0.4250000E\ 01$$
$$0.3750000E\ 01$$
$$0.2680000E\ 01$$
$$0.2000000E\ 01$$
$$0.1068000E\ 02$$

The reader should try to ascertain the presence of a negative value in the output. How can we eliminate this negative value from the output?

2.12   TOP-DOWN COMPOSITION OF PROGRAMS

We have presented two examples of FORTRAN programs and discussed their general structural features, and will now develop a logical, step-by-step procedure for composing such programs. The procedure we recommend is known as the *top-down, modular* programming technique. With this approach, we compose programs in levels. At the highest level, we list the alternate ways of solving a given problem in general terms. In many cases, of course, we can find only one method of solution, but the point is to search consciously for alternate methods. Finding alternate methods for solving a problem is also a test of the programmer's depth of understanding of the problem. If we have not found alternate solutions, then perhaps we have not considered the problem long enough.

In the next lower level, we select a specific method on the basis of a criterion, such as speed of execution on a computer, memory requirements, accuracy of the computed results, or ease of programming, and describe it in more detail. From this point on, each lower level becomes a refined and more detailed extension of the corresponding higher level until, at the lowest level, a detailed FORTRAN program is obtained.

In the higher levels of the top-down approach, we do not use any specific programming language such as FORTRAN. Instead, we try to find the best way to implement logically some part of the method of solution. Thus we use expressions that are relevant to this method, even though we may not be able to translate them directly into FORTRAN statements. We design each lower level as a refinement and extension of its immediate higher level, adding more specific details. In the process we ensure that each level contains a complete set of instructions for solving the problem, as free of errors as possible. This means that if we had a processor that could interpret a natural language, we could program it to solve the problem using one of the higher level descriptions alone.

Let us consider the advantages of the top-down programming technique as described above. At the highest level, we try to list alternate ways of solving a given problem. For complex problems, the effort spent in generating this list greatly increases our understanding of the problem. When alternate methods are available, we select one on the basis of its speed of execution, economy of storage, ease of modification, or simplicity of logic. Thus we force ourselves to make a conscious decision between perhaps a fast, difficult to-comprehend, special purpose program and a slow, but easy-to-understand and-modify, general purpose program.

Avoidance of a programming language such as FORTRAN at the higher levels helps us to concentrate on simplifying program logic. Efforts to eliminate errors at each level reduce the chance of introducing difficult-to-locate logical errors in the final program. In the next section, we illustrate the top-down approach with an example.

2.13 SMALLEST OF FOUR VALUES

The problem is to write a FORTRAN program that can find the smallest of four values supplied as input data. In searching though the literature on FORTRAN programs, we found the following program that purports to solve this problem. Study this program for two or three minutes, then move on, even if you do not understand it, for it is a poor example of problem solving.

```
        READ, A, B, C, D
        PRINT, A, B, C, D
        IF (A .GT. B) GO TO 55
        IF (A .GT. C) GO TO 70
        IF (A .GT.D) GO TO 41
        PRINT, A
        STOP                              (2.P8)
41      PRINT, D
        STOP
70      IF (C .GT. D) GO TO 41
        PRINT, C
        STOP
55      IF (B .GT.C) GO TO 70
        IF (B .GT. D) GO TO 41
        PRINT, B
        STOP
        END
```

In the program above, .GT. is an abbreviation in FORTRAN for "greater than." The program shown has too many branches, jumping both forward and backward, and this feature is a prime cause of the difficulty in understanding the logic of this program. With a little thought and the top-down approach, we can write a better program than the one shown above.

Level 1

We store any one of the four values in a variable called MIN. Then we compare the value stored in MIN with each of the other three values in succession and, at the end of each such comparison, store the smaller of the values compared in MIN. Thus, at the end of each comparison, the variable MIN stores the smallest of the values inspected *so far*, and at the end of the process, it stores the smallest of the four values.

Level 2

We use the names VALUE1, VALUE2, VALUE3, and VALUE4 for the four values given as input data, and VALMIN for the variable MIN introduced in Level 1. The process of a compare and store described in Level 1 can be done in FORTRAN by statements similar to the one given below:

IF (VALUE3 .LT. VALMIN) VALMIN = VALUE3

If the value of VALUE3 is *not* less than that of VALMIN, then the computer will execute the statement *following* this logical IF. Suppose, however, that the answer to the question "is VALUE3 less than VALMIN?" is yes. Then the computer executes VALMIN = VALUE3, but *what does it do after that*? According to the rules of FORTRAN, the computer then *proceeds to the statement after this logical IF*. This execution sequence is shown in Fig. 2.7.

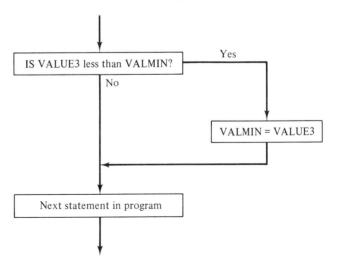

Fig. 2.7 Execution of IF (VALUE .LT. VALMIN) VALMIN = VALUE3.

Level 3

```
C          ***FIND THE SMALLEST OF FOUR VALUES
C          ***READ THE FOUR VALUES AS INPUT DATA
      READ, VALUE1, VALUE2, VALUE3, VALUE4
      PRINT, VALUE1, VALUE2, VALUE3, VALUE4
C          ***INITIALIZE VALMIN WHICH STORES THE
C          ***SMALLEST VALUE FOUND SO FAR                    (2.P9)
      VALMIN = VALUE1
C          ***COMPARE VALMIN WITH VALUE 2 AND
C          ***STORE THE SMALLER OF THE TWO IN VALMIN
      IF (VALUE2 .LT. VALMIN) VALMIN = VALUE2
C          ***COMPARE VALMIN WITH VALUE3 AND STORE
C          ***THE SMALLER OF THE TWO IN VALMIN
      IF (VALUE3 .LT. VALMIN) VALMIN = VALUE3
C          ***COMPARE VALMIN WITH VALUE 4 AND STORE
C          ***THE SMALLER OF THE TWO IN VALMIN
      IF (VALUE4 .LT. VALMIN) VALMIN = VALUE4
C          ***VALMIN NOW STORES THE SMALLEST OF
C          ***THE FOUR VALUES.  PRINT VALMIN AND STOP
      PRINT, VALMIN
      STOP
      END
```

Typical output of this program is shown below:

> 0.1750000E 00   −0.2170000E 01   0.4720000E 00   0.1260000E 01
> −0.2170000E 01

2.14 EXERCISES

2.1 Some *approximate* formulae for converting measurements from the FPS system to the metric system are given below:

Temperature: Celsius $= \dfrac{\text{(Fahrenheit)}}{2} - 16.$

Length: Centimeters $= 2.5$ inches
         Kilometers $= 1.6$ miles

Weight: Kilograms $= 0.45$ pounds.

Write a program for converting measurements according to the above rules.

2.2 A data card is prepared for each student in a class, containing three test scores. Write a program to compute the average score of each student.

2.3 A data card is prepared for each student in a class, containing a test score. Write a program to compute the class average.

2.4   A salesperson is assigned a commission on the following basis:

Sales	Commission
$0.00 – $400.00	2.5% of sales
$400.01 – $600.00	3.5% of sales

A data card is prepared for each salesperson, containing the amount of sale in dollars, which lies in the range $(0, 600)$. Write a program to compute the commission of each salesperson.

2.5   Write a program to compute the volumes of cylinders of height H and radius R.

2.6   Each card in a data deck contains the age of a person. Write a program to compute the number of persons over age 35. How should the program be modified if the age limit (in this case 35) is supplied on the first card of the data deck?

2.7   Write a program to find the smallest of 2000 values. Will your program generate the correct answer if by chance the data deck contains 1977 or 2005 values?

2.8   If Q is an estimate of the square root of a number X, then a better estimate P can be obtained as follows: $P = 0.5(Q + X/Q)$. We can use $0.5(X + 1)$ as an initial estimate of the square root of X. An estimate P is considered to be sufficiently accurate if $|P^2 - X|/X \le 0.0001$. Write an *algorithm* based on this method to compute a sufficiently accurate estimate of the square root of X.

2.9   Using the algorithm developed in Exercise 2.8, write a program to compute a sufficiently accurate estimate of the square root of X. Test your program for $X = -16.0$ and $X = 0.0$.

2.10 As a continuation of Exercise 2.2, suppose a student obtains a passing grade if his/her average score exceeds 65. Modify the program to find the total number of students with passing grades.

3 FORMAL DISCUSSION OF FORTRAN

In Chap. 2 we discussed the structure of simple programs and the top-down method of program development. The reader should by now have some idea of what a FORTRAN program looks like and the meaning of some simple FORTRAN statements. In this chapter we discuss FORTRAN statement formats and the syntax of the language in detail.

3.1 FORMATS OF STATEMENTS

The format of FORTRAN statements is based on the eighty-column cards commonly used as input medium. Each statement consists of at most four fields, although not all statements utilize all of the fields. These fields are:

Field	Columns on Card
Label	1–5
Continuation Indicator	6
Statement	7–72
Identification	73–80

Labels are used to identify FORTRAN statements so that they can be referenced by other FORTRAN statements. In FORTRAN these labels are positive integer numbers.

A statement can be continued or extended to a follow-up card by punching any character other than zero in column six. A FORTRAN statement or its continuation must be inclusively within columns seven through seventy-two.

The last eight columns on a card containing a FORTRAN statement are ignored by all FORTRAN compilers. Normally these columns are used to identify the position of a card in a card deck by using a sequence number for each card from an increasing sequence of positive integer numbers.

FORTRAN programs also allow comments for the purpose of documentation. A card containing a line of comment starts with the letter C in column one.

3.2 ARITHMETIC OPERATORS

FORTRAN is used primarily for solving numerical problems. It has specific symbols for representing the five arithmetic operators used with numerical data. These are listed below, in their order of priority, from top to bottom:

**	Exponentiation
*,/	Multiplication and Division
+,−	Addition and Subtraction

In FORTRAN, sets of nested parentheses, for the explicit specification of priorities of operation, follow the same convention as in algebra. In the case of nested parentheses, computation proceeds outward from the innermost parentheses. The sequence of execution of successive operators of *equal priority* can be specified by means of nested parentheses. In the absence of such explicit directions, operators of equal priority are executed in the left-to-right order, except for exponentiations, which are executed from right to left. For example, as far as exponentiation is concerned,

$$(A**B**C)$$

represents

$$A ** (B^C) = A^{(B^C)} \quad \text{and not} \quad (A^B)^C$$

Thus, if A, B, and C were given the values of 2, 3, and 4, respectively, a right-to-left evaluation would result in $2^{3^4} = 2^{81}$, while a left-to-right evaluation would result in $(2^3)^4 = (8)^4 = 4096 = 2^{12}$, radically different answers.

3.3 CONSTANTS

We now consider the data on which these operators operate. The simplest form of such numerical data is a constant. In FORTRAN there are two main types of constants, called REAL and INTEGER. An integer constant does not have a decimal point. Examples are:

$$1231 \quad -573 \quad 0 \quad 237$$

Note that commas cannot be used in integer constants. The constant 2,147,483,647 (or 2**31 − 1), which happens to be the largest integer constant that can be used in many computers, must be written as 2147483647 in FORTRAN.

A real constant has a decimal point in it. The integer constants shown in the above example become real constants when written as:

$$1231. \quad -573. \quad 0. \quad 237.$$

Other examples of real constants are:

$$-31.24 \quad 0.0021 \quad 0.425E-2$$

The last real constant is given in the exponent form. This is the FORTRAN equivalent of the scientific notation used to write very large or very small constants. In scientific notation, 0.00017 is written as 1.70×10^{-4} and 112735.3 becomes 1.127353×10^5. Notice that the scientific notation has one significant digit to the left of the decimal point, while in the exponent form of FORTRAN, all digits are to the right of the decimal point. Thus the corresponding constants between scientific notation and the FORTRAN exponent notion are as follows:

Real Constant	Scientific Notation	FORTRAN Exponent Notation
0.00017	1.70×10^{-4}	0.17E−03
112735.3	1.127353×10^5	0.1127353E 06
0.00425	4.25×10^{-3}	0.425E−02

Note that commas cannot be used in real constants either.

3.4 VARIABLES

In FORTRAN a variable is a symbolic name used to identify a memory location in which values can be stored. Such a symbolic name can have six characters at most, with the *first* character required to be a letter of the English alphabet.

The other characters can be either letters of the alphabet or digits 0 through 9. Examples of symbolic names are:

$$\text{TIME, INCMNT, SUM1, SUM2, SUM3, PAY, COST}$$

Because of their six-character length, FORTRAN variable names can be made descriptive of the physical variables that they represent, with long names suitably abbreviated. An example of such an abbreviation is the variable name INCMNT. This FORTRAN name represents a variable called increment. A rule of thumb for abbreviation can be stated as follows: eliminate all vowels from the name except the first letter. If more than six characters remain, continue the process of elimination in a judicious manner so as to retain as much of the original sound of the name as possible. Examples of this procedure are:

> INCREMENT–INCRÉMÉNT–INCŔMNT–INCMNT
> ACCELERATION–ACCÉLÉRÁTIØN–ACĆLRTN–ACLRTN

Note that names are essentially a matter of personal taste and the rules of thumb should not be followed slavishly. Try to be consistent *within* a program at least.

As with constants, FORTRAN has two types of variables, called REAL and INTEGER. REAL and INTEGER variables assume values that are real and integer constants, respectively. The type of variable is communicated by *declaration* statements. There are two modes of declaration in FORTRAN, *implicit declaration* and *explicit declaration*. In the implicit declaration mode, the first letter of the name of the variable is used to indicate the corresponding type. In this mode, all names starting inclusively with the letters I through N are considered integer variables. All other variables are considered to be real variables. Examples of integer variables are:

> NAME, KOUNT, JSUM, MASS, K24, INCMNT

Examples of real variables are:

> XMASS, COUNT, SUM, AK37, TIME, PAY, COST

Note that a real variable SUM becomes an integer variable when written as JSUM. Similarly, an integer variable KOUNT becomes a real variable when written as COUNT.

In the explicit declaration mode, the type of variable is explicitly declared via a REAL or INTEGER declaration statement. Examples of REAL declaration statements are:

> REAL MASS, INCMNT, K24
> REAL MIN, MAX, MID

In the implicit declaration mode, the above listed variables would be considered integer variables. Here, however, we have explicitly declared them to be real variables. Examples of INTEGER declaration statements are:

> INTEGER TIME, DISTNC, SUM
> INTEGER COUNT, F64, ERROR

All type declaration statements must precede the first executable statement in a program.

3.5 ARITHMETIC EXPRESSIONS

In FORTRAN, an arithmetic expression is an expression involving constants and variables connected by arithmetic operators. Examples of such expressions are:

> VELCTY * TIME + DISTNC
> (3.124 * R**2 + 2.76)/X14
> KOUNT + INCMNT
> (I + J + K)/3 + MASS

Successive arithmetic operator symbols must be separated by constants, variables, or parentheses. For example, we must write x^{-3} as X**(−3) and not as X**−3. As a consequence of the two types of variables and constants, we have two corresponding types of arithmetic expressions. For example, an arithmetic expression involving only real variables and real constants is called a *real arithmetic expression*. The first two examples of the arithmetic expressions shown above are real arithmetic expressions, while the last two examples involving only integer variables and constants are called *integer arithmetic expressions*.

Arithmetic expressions involving variables and constants of both types are called *mixed mode expressions*. We should try to avoid obvious mixed mode expressions, which are easy to detect, because the careless use of mixed mode expressions can lead to computational errors. For example, 314.0*10.0**(−1) = 31.4, while 314.0*10**(−1) = 0. It should also be remembered that the result of an integer division, where the denominator is greater than the numerator, is zero. Thus 10**(−1) = 1/10 = 0, while 10.0**(−1) = 1.0/10.0 = 0.1, and furthermore, J/(J + 1) is always zero for J ≥ 0, whereas X/(X + 1.0) is not. Thus it is a good habit to avoid integer division in the computation of such quantities as averages and percentages.

Mixed mode expressions are not allowed in standard FORTRAN. To convert the *value* of a variable from the real mode to the integer mode, FORTRAN provides a function called IFIX or INT. If PAY is a real variable with the value of 75.39, then

> IFIX(PAY)

generates the integer 75 for its value, which can be assigned to any integer variable. Note that PAY still remains a real variable with a value of 75.39. For a similar conversion of a value from the integer mode to the real mode, the FORTRAN function FLOAT is available. Given that INCMNT is an integer variable with a value of 15,

> FLOAT(INCMNT)

returns the value 15.0 in the real mode.

3.6   EVALUATION OF ARITHMETIC EXPRESSIONS

For programming convenience, most FORTRAN compilers allow the use of mixed mode expressions. In the process of evaluating such an arithmetic expression, sub-expressions involving only integer variables and constants are evaluated first using integer arithmetic operations. These integer results are then converted to the real mode and the remainder of the expression is evaluated using real arithmetic operations. When using nested parentheses, the evaluation proceeds outward from the innermost parentheses. Priorities of arithmetic operators have already been discussed in Sec. 3.2. The reader should verify each of the following examples:

$$((3 + 5 - 6) ** 3/10) + 5 = 5$$
$$((3 + 5 - 6) **3/10.0) + 5 = 5.8$$
$$5/10 - 5.0/10 + 5/10.0 - 5.0/10.0 = -0.5$$
$$(4.0* 2.0/10.0* 0.5) ** 2 = 0.16$$
$$(4.0* 2.0/10.0 ** 0.5) ** 2 = 6.4$$

It should be noted that exponentiations such as $Z ** 1.7$ that involve real exponents are carried out by computing the natural logarithm of Z. Since the natural logarithm function is undefined for negative values of Z, the process of exponentiations with real exponents will fail in such cases. If the exponent does not have a fractional part, it is recommended that the exponent be expressed in the integer mode for reasons of accuracy.

3.7   ASSIGNMENT STATEMENTS

Assignment statements are used in FORTRAN to assign values to variables. The general form of an assignment statement is shown below:

Variable Name = Arithmetic Expression

The sign of equality used in the above expression has a different meaning in FORTRAN than that attributed to it in algebra. In an assignment statement, the value of the expression on the right-hand side is computed and this value is assigned to the variable on the left-hand side. Thus the sign of equality means ''is assigned the value of.'' We often use such a statement to increment the value of a variable. For example,

KOUNT = KOUNT + INCMNT

means

$$(KOUNT)_{new} = (KOUNT)_{current} + INCMNT$$

i.e., add to the current value of KOUNT the value of INCMNT and assign the sum of that value to KOUNT as its new value. The current value of KOUNT is obviously replaced by the sum and hence lost.

3.8   LOGICAL EXPRESSIONS

In most programs, a logical determination (test) is made at various points in the program to determine what sequence of instructions needs to be followed. Simple examples of this notation were illustrated in the programs discussed in Chap. 2. Frequently such tests are formulated in terms of logical expressions, which consist of arithmetic expressions connected by relational operators. A logical expression does not have a numerical value; it can be thought of as a question, the answer to which is either yes or no. A list of the relational operators is given below.

FORTRAN *Operator*	*Algebraic* *Symbol*	*Meaning*
.GT.	$>$	Greater Than
.GE.	$\geq$	Greater Than or Equal
.EQ.	$=$	Equal
.NE.	$\neq$	Not Equal
.LE.	$\leq$	Less Than or Equal
.LT.	$<$	Less Than

These operators are binary operators which use two arithmetic expressions as operands; the result of the binary operation is always a logical value of true or false. For example, let us consider

$$(X + Y)**2 \ .LT. \ (B - C)$$

Here we have two arithmetic expressions, $(X + Y)**2$ and $(B - C)$, connected by the relational operator .LT.. The value of this logical expression is true if the value of $(X + Y)**2$ is less than the value of $(B - C)$; otherwise the value is false.

Simple logical expressions may be combined by means of logical operators to form complex logical expressions..Two of the most commonly used logical operators are .AND. and .OR.. Let L1 and L2 be two logical expressions which are combined by the .AND. operator to form L3. Then the value of L3 is true if L1 *and* L2 are both true; otherwise L3 is false. Suppose L1 and L2 are combined by the .OR. operator to generate the value of L3. Then L3 is true *either* if L1 is true, *or* if L2 is true, *or* if *both* L1 and L2 are true; otherwise its value is false.   Applications of logical expressions are discussed in the following section.

3.9 TRANSFER OF CONTROL

While executing a program, a computer always follows the sequence of statements in the linear order in which they are written, i.e., in a sequential manner. Often it becomes necessary to break this linear transfer of control from one statement to its immediate successor by using transfer of control statements.

The simplest form of such a transfer of control statement is called *an unconditional transfer*. To achieve an unconditional transfer, the target statement must be identified by a unique statement number (positive integer constant), and then a GO TO command must be used as shown in the format below:

GO TO *n*

In the above statement, *n* is a statement number of a statement to which control is transferred. Examples of such statements are:

GO TO 23
GO TO 121
GO TO 575

An alternate form to transfer control is called the *conditional transfer* of control statement. One method of achieving conditional transfer is to use a logical IF statement in the form illustrated below:

IF (Logical Expression) GO TO 75
GO TO 59

If the logical expression is true, control is transferred to statement numbered seventy-five; on the other hand, if the logical expression is false, control is transferred to statement numbered fifty-nine. Note that the statement on the right-hand side of the logical IF statement is required to be any executable statement except another logical IF or DO statement. Hence we can write

IF (X .GT. 0.0) SUM = SUM + X
GO TO 125

In the above case when X is positive, the value of the SUM variable is incremented by the value of X *and then the control is transferred to the statement immediately following the logical IF statement* (GO TO 125). When X is less than or equal to zero, control is transferred to the statement numbered one hundred twenty-five via the GO TO 125 transfer statement.

Suppose that when X is in the range of $[-7.1, 4.3]$ we want to follow one course of action, and otherwise we want to follow a different course of action. This test can be implemented as follows:

IF (X .GE. −7.1 .AND. X .LE. 4.3) GO TO 51
GO TO 23

Alternatively, we can use

IF (X .LT. −7.1 .OR. X .GT. 4.3)GO TO 23
GO TO 51

A logical IF statement provides the capability to branch to one of two alternate statements in a program. If any one of these statements precedes the logical IF statement, a loop is created. An alternate method of achieving a conditional transfer of control is to use an arithmetic IF statement. The arithmetic IF statement is of the form

$$\text{IF}\left(\begin{array}{c}\text{arithmetic}\\\text{expression}\end{array}\right) \text{SN1, SN2, SN3}$$

where the transfer condition in FORTRAN is essentially a three-way branch based upon the arithmetic value of the given expression, which could be less than zero, equal to zero, or greater than zero. It should be noted that the expression being tested can be any *valid* arithmetic expression, and that SN1, SN2, and SN3 are FORTRAN statement numbers that represent valid executable FORTRAN statements. For example,

IF(B**2 − 4.0 *A*C) 20, 10, 30

⋮

20   D = B + C

⋮

30   D = B

⋮

40   D = C

will transfer control to statement 20 if the value of the expression (B² − 4AC) is negative, transfer control to statement 10 if the value of the expression is zero, and finally transfer control to statement 30 if the value of the expression is positive.

A comparison of arithmetic and logical IF statements is illustrated below for equal situations.

Arithmetic IF	*Logical IF*
(a) IF (X− Y) 1, 1, 2	IF (X.LE.Y) X = X*20.
1 X = X*20.0	DO 3 I = 1, 25
2 DO 3 I = 1, 25	
(b) IF (B− 50.0) 3, 4, 3	IF (B.EQ.50.0) STOP
3 INCR = INCR + 1	INCR = INCR + 1
GO TO 2	GO TO 2
4 STOP	

On occasion a branch to more than two or three alternate statements is needed. For such multiple branches, a COMPUTED GO TO statement is used in the format shown below:

$$\text{GO TO } (n_1, n_2, \ldots, n_k), \text{ INT}$$

In the above statement, $n_1, \ldots, n_k$ are k statement numbers and INT is any integer variable. The transfers of control based on the value of INT are shown below.

$$\text{INT} = \begin{cases} 1, & \text{Transfer to statement } n_1 \\ 2, & \text{Transfer to statement } n_2 \\ \cdot & \cdot \\ \cdot & \cdot \\ \cdot & \cdot \\ k, & \text{Transfer to statement } n_k \end{cases}$$

An application of the COMPUTED GO TO statement is shown in the next chapter.

3.10 DO LOOP

In Chap. 2, programs were illustrated with loops where the repeated execution of a loop is terminated by the satisfaction of a general test condition. An alternate way of controlling a loop is by means of a counter. The counter is provided with a test value and an increment value, and set to a starting value prior to the execution of the loop. After every execution of the loop the counter is incremented, and as long as the countervalue is less than or equal to the test value, the execution of the loop is repeated. When the countervalue becomes greater than the test value, an exit from the loop occurs. An example of such a scheme for controlling a loop is shown below:

```
C          ***Start = STARTING VALUE, TEST = TEST VALUE;
C          ***INCMNT = INCREMENT, LOOPK = LOOP COUNTER.
           INTEGER LOOPK, START, TEST, INCMNT
C          ***INITIALIZE VARIABLES START, TEST AND INCMNT
           START = (Starting value)
           TEST = (Test value)
           INCMNT = (Increment)
C          ***INITALIZE COUNTER BEFORE ENTERING LOOP
           LOOPK = START
      20   ... (First statement in loop) ......
                    .
                    .
                    .
      80   ... (Last statement in loop) ......
           LOOPK = LOOPK + INCMNT
           IF(LOOPK .LE. TEST) GO TO 20
     100   ...... (Statement outside loop) ......
```

Notice that the test for the termination of the execution of the loop (LOOPK .LE. TEST) is made at the bottom of the loop. Such loops are very frequently used, and hence to reduce the programming effort, a special statement called the DO statement is provided. The same loop formed by a DO statement is illustrated below for comparative purposes:

```
          INTEGER LOOPK, START, TEST, INCMNT
          START = (Starting value)
          TEST = (Test value)
          INCMNT = (Increment)
          DO 80 LOOPK = START, TEST, INCMNT
   20     (First statement in loop)
   80     (Last statement in loop)
  100     (Statement outside loop)
```

A loop formed by a DO statement is called a DO loop. The general form of such a DO statement is

$$\text{DO } n \text{ I} = \text{J,K,L}$$

In this statement, n denotes the statement number of the last statement in the loop, called the *object* of the DO loop. I acts as a counter for the loop and is called the *index* of the DO loop. J, K, and L are, respectively, the starting value, the test value, and the increment of the counter, and are called the *parameters* of the DO loop.

The index of the DO loop must be an integer variable. The parameters can be unsigned positive integer constants or variables but *not* arithmetic expressions. In standard FORTRAN, the value of TEST must always be greater than or equal to the value of START. Some FORTRAN compilers allow the value of TEST to be less than the value of START, in which case the DO loop is executed only once.

The range of a DO loop begins with the statement immediately following the DO statement and ends with the object statement. The range of a DO loop can be entered only via the DO statement, although an exit from the range is allowable even before the value of the index variable exceeds the test value. Consider the following as illustrations of these concepts:

```
          DO 30 I = 5,M,3
              . . . (Statement in the range of DO loop) . . .
              If(X .LE. Y) GO TO 100
   30     (Object of DO loop)
  100
```

These statements terminate either when the value of I becomes greater than the value of M, or when the value of X becomes less than or equal to the value of Y.

The values of the parameters of a DO loop cannot be altered within the range of the DO loop. If the increment of a DO loop is one, then it may be suppressed. For example, in

$$\text{DO } 75 \text{ I} = \text{J,100}$$

the starting value of the index equals the value of J, the test value is 100, and the increment is one. Given the values of J, K, and L with $K \geq J$, a DO loop is executed $[(K - J)/L] + 1$ times where [] denotes truncation.

In some programs, it becomes necessary to branch conditionally from one statement within the range of a DO loop to other statements also in the range of the DO loop. In such cases, it often becomes difficult to select a unique object for the DO loop. For this reason we shall always use a CONTINUE statement as the standard object of all our DO loops. A CONTINUE statement instructs the control unit to proceed with the *usual* control sequence at that point in a program. If the usual sequence at that point happens to be top-to-bottom, then the presence of the CONTINUE statement alters nothing (i.e., it is a do nothing statement). If, however, the usual sequence is a possible transfer to the beginning of the range of a DO loop, then the computer follows such a transfer after reaching the CONTINUE statement. An example of such a DO loop is illustrated below:

```
DO 50 I = J,K,L
    . . . . . . . . . . . . . . . . . . . . . . . . . . .
    . . . . . . . . . . . . . . . . . . . . . . . . . . .      FORTRAN statements that are
                                                               within the range of the DO loop
    . . . . . . . . . . . . . . . . . . . . . . . . . .
50    CONTINUE
```

Note that the range of a DO loop, if indented as shown above, can provide an easy identification in a program. DO loops are extremely useful for programming with arrays and will be used frequently in Chap. 5. In programs it often becomes necessary to nest DO loops, i.e., to use a DO loop within the range of another DO loop. When nesting DO loops, their ranges must not be allowed to intersect. An example of nested DO loops with intersecting ranges, which is illegal in FORTRAN, is illustrated below:

```
        DO 50 I = 3,100
            . . . . . . . . . . . . . . . . . . . . . . . . . . . . . . . .
            DO 20 J = 2,M,3
                . . . . . . . . . . . . . . . . . . . . . . . . . . . . . .
        50    CONTINUE
                . . . . . . . . . . . . . . . . . . . . . . . . . . . . . .
        20        CONTINUE
```

The following examples are legal nestings of DO loops:

```
        DO 50 I = 3,100
            . . . . . . . . . . . . . . . . . . . . . . . . . . . . . . . .
            DO 20 J = 2,M,3
                . . . . . . . . . . . . . . . . . . . . . . . . . . . . . .
        20        CONTINUE
                . . . . . . . . . . . . . . . . . . . . . . . . . . . . . .
        50    CONTINUE
        DO 80 K = 3,37,5
            . . . . . . . . . . . . . . . . . . . . . . . . . . . . . . . .
            DO 80 L = J,20
                . . . . . . . . . . . . . . . . . . . . . . . . . . . . . .
        80    CONTINUE
```

It should be noted that we cannot use a conditional or unconditional branch statement within the range of the outer DO loop that is controlled by index K that branches to 80 CONTINUE. Since this CONTINUE statement is part of the range of the inner DO loop controlled by index L, such a branch will constitute an illegal branch within the range of a DO loop.

3.11 DATA OUTPUT

The two ways of obtaining data (or output) from a program are the unformatted and the formatted output. By format we mean a set of instructions to produce a specific arrangement of data during output. In case of the unformatted output, the format is controlled by the computer system (actually the compiler). Not all FORTRAN compilers allow unformatted output. With the WATFIV compiler, the statement

PRINT, List of variables separated by commas

can be used to obtain output in a computer controlled format. To print out character strings, we can use

PRINT, 'Character string'

to output the character string within quotation marks.

For formatted output, it becomes necessary to specify the format of the output via a FORMAT statement. A FORMAT statement is identified by a statement number which is referenced in the PRINT statement. An example of a formatted output statement is illustrated:

PRINT 200, List of variables separated by commas
200   FORMAT (List of format codes separated by commas)

Before discussing the format codes in detail, let us consider a more flexible instruction for obtaining output. Until now, we have been concerned with printing data on paper (hard-copy) by using a line-printer. The PRINT statement is sufficient for that purpose. In general, however, we have to consider the possibility of generating output to various media such as magnetic tapes, punched cards, CRT displays, etc. In standard FORTRAN this can be achieved by using a WRITE statement:

WRITE (N1,N2) List of variables separated by commas

N1 represents an integer constant, called the *unit number,* which identifies the device to be used for obtaining output. For example, in many systems, N1 = 6 represents the line printer and N1 = 7 represents the card punch. N2 represents the statement number of the associated FORMAT statement that is to be used to output the data. A specific example of such a WRITE statement is

WRITE (6,200) List of variables separated by commas
200 FORMAT (List of format codes separated by commas)

With the assumption that N1 = 6 represents the line-printer, this WRITE statement is equivalent to

PRINT 200, List of variables separated by commas

From now on, to follow standard practice, we shall always use the WRITE statement in our programs.

The first format code that is listed in a FORMAT statement for displaying data is used to control the line spacing of the line printer. The various spacing codes called the carriage control codes of the line printer are given in Table 3.1.

Table 3.1. List of carriage control codes

Code	Resulting Line Spacing
1H𝒷	Single space. 𝒷 denotes blank
1H0	Double space.
1H1	Top of next page.
1H+	Overprint previous line.

Next consider the format code for printing values of integer variables. The general form of the format is Iw where I specifies "integer," and where w is an integer constant which specifies the number of print positions allowed for the value of the integer variable (called the *field width*). As an example, consider the following statements:

K = −23
WRITE (6,40) K
40 FORMAT (1H0,I5)

The output of the WRITE statement will be a double space and on that current line, two blanks followed by −23. A list showing the different forms of the output of the value of K for different values of w in Iw is given below.

Iw	Output
I7	𝒷𝒷𝒷𝒷−23
I5	𝒷𝒷−23
I2	**

The value of K is printed right-justified in the given output field. Note that the negative sign takes up a print position. Obviously a field width of two (I2) is too small for printing three characters (−23) and therefore two asterisks are printed out, indicating an incorrect length specification. Whenever asterisks are printed out in the I*w* format, the value of *w* should be increased.

If more than one value is to be printed out on one line, we may wish to control the spacing between these values, even if only for readability. This can be done by using the format code *n*X, where *n* is an integer constant which determines the number of blank print positions between the values that are printed out. Consider the following statements:

$$K1 = 23$$
$$K2 = -54$$
$$\text{WRITE (6,75) K1, K2}$$
$$75 \quad \text{FORMAT (1H0,I3,3X,I5)}$$

Examples of output for different values of *n* are shown below.

*n*X	Output
2X	b̸ 23 b̸b̸b̸b̸− 54
3X	b̸ 23 b̸b̸b̸b̸− 54
5X	b̸ 23 b̸b̸b̸b̸b̸b̸− 54

The character b̸ denotes a blank print position, while the underlined blanks are produced by the corresponding *n*X code.

There are two format specifications for printing values of real variables. The simpler of the two formats uses the form F*w*.*d*. Here *w* specifies the field width and *d* specifies the number of digits after the decimal point. The following example shows the use of the F format:

$$X = -23.17$$
$$\text{WRITE (6,90) X}$$
$$90 \quad \text{FORMAT (1H ,F8.1)}$$

Sample output formats for different choices of *w* and *d* follow.

F*w*.*d*	Output
F10.3	b̸b̸b̸− 23.170
F8.1	b̸b̸b̸− 23.2
F7.4	******

Note that the negative sign and the decimal point each uses up a print position of its own. The displayed value is printed out right-justified within the field. If the value of *d* is larger (F10.3) than the number of digits after the decimal point in the value of X, extra zeros are added to the right. On the other hand, if the value of *d* is smaller (F8.1), the value of X is rounded. If the field width *w* (F7.4) is too small, a string of

w asterisks is printed out. In this case, as with the integer format, the value of w should be increased. The value of w should be larger than $d + 2$ to start with.

For very large and very small values of real variables, the E$w.d$ format is used, where w specifies the field width and d specifies the *number of significant digits in the value* to be printed out. As an example, consider

$$X = -0.0003596$$
$$\text{WRITE (6,80) X}$$
$$80 \quad \text{FORMAT (1H , E12.3)}$$

For various choices of values of w and $d,$ the corresponding output formats are as follows.

E$w.d$	*Output*
E14.5	̶b̶b̶b̶b̶0.35960E−03
E12.3	b̶b̶b̶b̶0.360E−03
E10.4	0.3596E−03
E8.4	********

The exponent (of ten) is printed out right-justified in the field preceded by the letter E. The exponent can be a two-digit integer; thus the exponent 3 is printed as 03. The print position to the immediate right of E is used to print the sign of the exponent. If the exponent has a negative value, then a minus sign will be printed out, while for other exponent values a blank is used. The value of X is printed out in the normal form with the decimal point positioned at the extreme left. If the value of d is larger (E14.5) than the number of digits in the value of X, zeros are added to the right. If d is smaller (E12.3), the value of X is rounded. If the field width w is too small (E8.4), then a string of w asterisks is printed. The value of w should be larger than $d + 7$, since seven positions are used up by the exponent, sign, leading zero, and the decimal point.

A string of characters can be printed out by using the Hollerith format code nH followed by the character string that is to be displayed, where n denotes the number of characters in the string, including blanks. For example,

$$\text{WRITE (6,100)}$$
$$100 \quad \text{FORMAT (1H1,30X,23H RESULTS OF COMPUTATION)}$$

will print on top of the next page, thirty blank spaces followed by the character string "RESULTS OF COMPUTATION".

We can use different format codes separated by commas in a single FORMAT statement; however, the format codes must match the types of the corresponding variables listed in the WRITE statement using that FORMAT. For example,

```
              X = -3.4127
              Y = 0.000051
              K = 371
              WRITE (6,100)
     100   FORMAT (1H1,50X, 8H RESULTS)
              WRITE (6,150) X,K,Y
     150   FORMAT(1H0,40X,F8.3,4X,I4,2X,E11.3)
```

will print on top of the next page, fifty blanks followed by

RESULTS

and then after skipping two lines, forty blanks followed by

ƀƀ-3.413ƀƀƀƀƀ371ƀƀƀƀƀ0.510E-04

Note that the types of the format codes F8.3, I4, and E11.3 matched the (implicit) types of the corresponding variables X, K, and Y listed in the second WRITE statement.

If we need to repeat format codes several times in groups, we can avoid explicit repetition by using *group counts* as illustrated below:

```
              WRITE (6.350) I,X,J,Y,K,Z
     350   FORMAT (1H0,3(I8,5X,E16.7))
```

Here the values of the integer and the real variables are paired together, separated by five blanks and grouped to repeat three times to account for all the variables. A special case of the group count occurs when a single format code is repeated many times. For example,

```
              WRITE (6,350) I,J,K,L,M
     350   FORMAT (1H ,5I7)
```

Here the same format code I7 is repeated five times for the five variables I, J, K, L, and M. The number 5 before I7 is then called a *replication factor*.

In FORTRAN FORMAT statements, the slash (/) is used to indicate the end of one FORTRAN record and the start of a new one. A record for printed output means a line of output, while a record for card input means a card image of input. This means that a single FORMAT statement can be used to specify the format of more than one line of output. For example,

```
              X = -15.2
              Y = 0.001
              I = 15
              J = -9
              WRITE (6,200) X,Y,I,J
     200   FORMAT (1H1,50X,8H HEADING /1H0,50X,2F7.2,2I4)
```

will produce on top of the next page, after fifty blank spaces,

HEADING

ƀ− 15.20ƀƀƀ0.00ƀƀ15 ƀƀ− 9

with double spacing between HEADING and the next line. The ''/'' following HEADING in FORMAT statement 200 indicates the end of the first line of output and a second line is started after double spacing (because of carriage control 1H0). Consecutive slashes may be used to skip over several blank lines in the output. The format codes discussed so far are summarized in Table 3.2.

Table 3.2.   Format codes for data output

Format Code	*Use*
Iw	Integer values.
nX	Blank spaces.
F$w.d$	Real values.
E$w.d$	Real values (very large or small) in exponent form
/	Separation of records.

FORMAT statements can be placed anywhere in a FORTRAN program. We shall follow a convention, however, of placing all FORMAT statements in a program at the end of that program, just before the END statement.

A format code, assigned to a variable in a WRITE statement, must match the type of the variable it is assigned to. Normally, the total number of format codes within a FORMAT statement should equal the total number of variables in the WRITE statement referencing that FORMAT statement. In the case where more format codes are specified than are strictly necessary, the extra format codes are ignored. In the case where not enough format codes are specified, the codes are repeated from the rightmost set of inner parentheses, including any group count that may be present. For example,

WRITE (6,500) A,B,C,D
500   FORMAT (1H0,5X,F10.3,5X,F10.3)

will produce two double-spaced lines of output by repeating the format codes starting with 1H0. However,

WRITE (6,500) A,J, B,C,K
500   FORMAT (1H0,5X,F10.3,(5X,I5,5X,F10.3))

will repeat the format codes only within the rightmost set of inner parentheses for the variables C and K. Thus C will be assigned a format code of I5, and if not defined to be an integer variable, the output operation will fail and an error message will be generated.

A compiler does not translate format codes but simply stores them for future use by the input/output processor. Strictly speaking, therefore, format codes can be specified at execution time of the program. The format codes are read as character data (see Sec. 3.13) into a one-dimensional array (see Chap. 5) and then referenced by using the name of the array, rather than a statement number, by the WRITE statements.

3.12 DATA INPUT

The simplest and most straightforward way of assigning input data to variables in a FORTRAN program is by means of the assignment statements. However, input data assigned in this manner (see Chap. 2) cannot be changed from one execution of the program to the next without changing statements within the program itself. Input data can be broadly classified into two categories: those that do not change from one execution of the program to the next, and those that do change. Input data in the first category can be assigned to the variables by the FORTRAN compiler during the translation of the FORTRAN program. This is done by means of a nonexecutable FORTRAN statement, called DATA, which is normally inserted at the beginning of a FORTRAN program along with other declaration statements. As an example of the use of a DATA statement, consider the following:

DATA ALPHA/−2.9/,BETA/5.3/,INCMNT/6/

This statement will cause the compiler to initialize the variables ALPHA, BETA, and INCMNT to the values −2.9, 5.3, and 6, respectively. In addition to the above, the DATA statement can also be written as follows

DATA ALPHA, BETA, INCMNT/−2.9,5.3,6/

with the same effect. The same data value can be repeatedly assigned by using a replication factor.

DATA TOTAL1, TOTAL2, TOTAL3/3*0.0/

will initially assign three zeros to the three listed variables. The values listed in a DATA statement must match the type of variables to which they are assigned.

The DATA statement is only used to initialize variables at compile time. During the execution of the program, input data in the second category can be read in by using either the unformatted or the formatted form of the READ statement. The unformatted READ statement is an extension to the standard FORTRAN language and found in the WATFIV version of FORTRAN. The unformatted READ consists of the instruction READ followed by a list of variables whose values are to be read, for example,

READ,A,B,C,I,J,K

In the data cards prepared for such a READ statement, the values of the variables need to be punched in the same order in which the variables themselves are listed, and furthermore, the values need to be separated by means of at least one blank column. Every time a READ statement is executed, the computer starts to read a *new* data card and continues to read data cards until it finds a value for every variable listed in the READ statement.

Consider the two READ instructions shown below:

READ, A,B,C
READ, I,J

Since each READ statement starts with a *new* data card, the values of the set of variables A, B, C and the set of variables I, J must be placed on at least two separate data cards. If we put more values on a data card than there are variables listed in the READ statement, the computer will ignore all extra values on that card once each listed variable has been assigned a value. Since the computer continues reading data cards until it finds values for all the variables listed in the READ statement, the values of the variables A, B, and C can be arranged in any one of the following ways:

(a) all three values on one card,

(b) only two values on one card and the third one on a separate card, or

(c) each value on a separate data card.

The formatted READ statement, part of standard FORTRAN, is of the form

READ(N1,N2) List of variables separated by commas

N1 is an integer constant, called the *unit number,* which identifies the device to be used for obtaining input data; again, in many systems N1 = 5 represents the card reader. N2 represents the statement number of the associated FORMAT statement. The format codes listed in the FORMAT statement of a formatted READ divide the eighty columns of the data card into several fields. For example,

READ (5,100)I,J,K,L
100   FORMAT (5(I5,5X))

divides the first fifty columns of the data card into ten fields as illustrated below.

Data Fields	Separator Fields (blanks)	Columns
1		1–5
	1	6–10
2		11–15
	2	16–20
3		21–25
	3	26–30
4		31–35
	4	36–40
5		41–45
	5	46–50

Columns 51–80 of the data cards are ignored by the computer. Each data field is five columns wide, and the fields are separated from each other by separator fields of five blank columns each. The values of the variables I, J, K, and L must be punched within fields 1, 2, 3, and 4, respectively; field five is not used at all in this particular case. All *blank columns* within a data field are considered to be *zeros,* and consequently integer values must be punched right-justified into their appropriate fields. If an integer value is not right-justified, it will be multiplied by a power of ten for each blank column to its right within the designated field. For the last READ statement, suppose a data card was prepared as shown below

Columns:	1	2	3	4	5	6	7	8	9	10	11	12	13	14	15
		–	2	3	9		5	1				6	3	5	

and there were blanks in all other columns. Then the number -239 is read in as the value of variable I. This number has been punched right-justified in its designated field on the card. Since the number 51 is punched within a separator field separating two data fields, it is ignored. Nothing should have been punched into the separator field. The number 635 is punched in the second data field, but it is not right-justified. There is one blank column to the right of the number within its field. Thus the value associated with the variable J is 635×10. Since blank columns are interpreted as zeros, the values of K and L are read in as zeros.

The values of real variables can be read with two different formats. As an example of the simpler of the two formats, using the F$w.d$ format, consider the following statements:

$$\text{READ (5,100)X,Y,Z}$$
$$\text{100 \quad FORMAT (3F10.5)}$$

The above READ statement divides the columns of the data card into the three data fields shown below.

Data Fields	Columns
1	1–10
2	11–20
3	21–30

The format code F10.5 requires that the last five columns of each field contain the fraction part of the value that is punched. This default declaration is overridden, however, by *explicitly* punching the decimal point into the data card at its proper place. When the decimal point appears explicitly on the card, the computer ignores the "*d*" part of an F*w.d* code and reads the number as it appears on the data card. In addition, if the decimal point is punched explicitly, there is no longer any need to right-justify the value in the appropriate data field. Thus the safest thing to do when using the F*w.d* format for real variables is to punch the decimal point explicitly into the card and to put the value anywhere within its corresponding field. Some examples of input data punched using the F10.5 format for the variable X follow.

				Data Field							Value of X
Columns:	1	2	3	4	5	6	7	8	9	10	
			−	3	5	6	1	2			−35.612
			←	3	5	6	1	2			−3.5612
	2	.	1	5	3						2.153
								9	2	6	0.00926
				−				9	2	6	−0.926

Values for real variables can also be read using the E*w.d* format. This format is used when the value is either very small or very large. For example, the number -0.157×10^{-3} can be punched and then read using the E16.7 format as

$$\not{b}\not{b}\not{b}\not{b}\not{b}\not{b}-0.157E-03$$

The last two columns in the field are used for the exponent, and hence it is necessary to right-justify the number in order to avoid multiplying the exponent by subsequent factors of ten. The letter E is punched explicitly into the card to separate the exponent from the rest of the number. The decimal point is also punched explicitly into the card to avoid any confusion as to its position.

There are various other forms in which a number can be punched using the E format. For example, the letter "E" may be omitted or the decimal point may not be punched explicitly. These are all unnecessary complications and are not discussed here because they do not have any advantage over the given simple approach.

The slash format "/" discussed with the WRITE statement can also be used with the READ statement. Using the slash the computer will skip to the next data card or record or skip over several data cards or records. For example,

```
            READ (5,100) N,M,A,B,C,V,W
      100   FORMAT (2I5/3F10.4//2F10.5)
```

will cause the computer to read the values of N and M from the first data card, skip to the second data card for the values of A, B, and C, then skip over the third data card (//), and finally read the values of V and W from the fourth data card. If the list of variables is omitted, then the READ statement skips over the next card in the data deck. Since FORMAT statements can again be placed anywhere within a FOR-TRAN program, the convention that will be followed is to put all FORMAT statements at the end of the program, just before the END statement.

3.13   INPUT AND OUTPUT OF CHARACTER DATA

Occasionally it is necessary to read in and write out data in FORTRAN programs consisting of strings of characters, for example, names of persons. Character strings can be stored either in integer or in real variables, with the number of characters that are stored in a single variable varying from one system to another. Suppose that in a computer system, eight binary digits are used to represent a character and that the values of integer variables are represented by thirty-two binary digits. An integer variable can then store four characters at most. The format code for character strings in data is of the form Aw, where w denotes the number of characters in the string and A denotes that Alpha strings are processed. As an example, for the computer system mentioned earlier, we can use

```
            READ (5,200) NAME1, NAME2
      200   FORMAT (2(A4,2X))
```

to read in two names of four characters (maximum) each. A data card is prepared as shown below:

```
      Columns:  1  2  3  4  5  6  7  8  9  10 11 12 13
                J  A  C  K        B  A  R  B  A  R  A
```

The variable NAME1 will represent the character string JACK. The variable NAME2, however, will only represent BARB since it can store four characters at most. The string ARA is lost in the process. If we now use

```
            WRITE (6,300) NAME2, NAME1
      300   FORMAT (1H0,2(A4,4X))
```

we get the following output:

```
                  BARBbbbbJACKbbbb
```

3.14 DETECTING THE END OF A DATA DECK

The simplest method for detecting the end of a data deck is by placing a data card at the end with some inappropriate values for the variables. By testing for these values, the end of a data deck can be detected. An example of this approach follows:

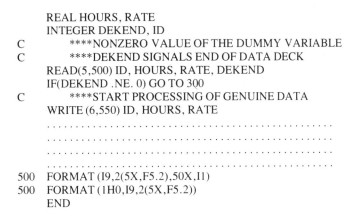

In many programs, it is difficult to make up values which are inappropriate for those variables. When using formatted input, it is possible to resort to another simple method based on the use of a dummy variable in the list of the input variables. Let us assume that the last column of each data card can be freely used by the programmer. The following example illustrates the method described above.

```
          REAL HOURS, RATE
          INTEGER DEKEND, ID
C              ****NONZERO VALUE OF THE DUMMY VARIABLE
C              ****DEKEND SIGNALS END OF DATA DECK
          READ(5,500) ID, HOURS, RATE, DEKEND
          IF(DEKEND .NE. 0) GO TO 300
C              ****START PROCESSING OF GENUINE DATA
          WRITE (6,550) ID, HOURS, RATE
          .............................................
          .............................................
          .............................................
          .............................................
500   FORMAT (I9,2(5X,F5.2),50X,I1)
500   FORMAT (1H0,I9,2(5X,F5.2))
          END
```

Note that FORMAT 500 specifies that the last column of each data card contains a value for DEKEND. In all data cards except for the last card, this column is left blank and consequently DEKEND is assigned the value zero. We add an extra card at the end of the data deck, which is entirely blank except for the last column. Any digit other than a zero is punched into the last column. Thus when the value of DEKEND becomes nonzero, the end of the data deck has been reached.

Some computer systems can automatically detect the end of a data deck. The card image after the last data card read by the system contains some characters pertaining to the job control language. In many systems, the processor can detect this card and take some action specified by the READ statement. A READ statement in such a system would look as follows:

READ (N1,N2,END = N3) List of variables separated by commas

Let us now consider the use of the feature END = N3. This feature is used to detect the end of the input data to a program, otherwise known as the end of file. N3 is a statement number used in the program. When the computer detects the end of the input data file, it transfers control to the statement numbered N3 in the program. For example,

100   READ (5,100,END = 600) A,B,C
 .
 .
 .
       GO TO 100
600   STOP
       END

has a permanent loop starting with the READ statement. When the last data card is processed, the GO TO 100 causes the READ statement to be executed again, and this time, the end of file card is read. The computer recognizes this as the end of the input data and branches to the STOP statement numbered 600.

3.15 EXERCISES

3.1 Write the FORTRAN expressions for the following:

(i) $\dfrac{A}{B+C}$

(ii) $\dfrac{B}{B \times C}$

(iii) $\dfrac{A}{B} + C$

(iv) $\dfrac{-B+C}{-A}$

(v) $A^B \, C^D$

(vi) $\left(\dfrac{AB}{C+D}\right)^2$

(vii) $\dfrac{A}{B+C} - \dfrac{EG}{F}$

(viii) $\dfrac{AX^2}{B+X} - \dfrac{CX}{D-X}$

3.2 Write the algebraic expressions for the following:
(i) A**2*B
(ii) A*B**2
(iii) A + B*C + D
(iv) (A + B)*C + D
(v) A**B**2
(vi) A/B/C
(vii) A/B*3 + A
(viii) (A + B)**2/(C − D) + E

3.3 Compute the values of A, K, and B given A = −3.5, K = 2, and B = 4.3:

(i) A = B*K
(ii) A = B**K
(iii) K = K + K
(iv) K = K/K + K
(v) K = K/(K + K)
(vi) A = (A + B)*K

3.4 Indicate the actions taken after the execution of each of the following logical IF statements (A = 5.2, B = −3.4, C = 2):
(i) IF(A .LE. B) GO TO 200
A = A − B
(ii) IF(B .LE. 0.0) B = −B
GO TO 200
(iii) IF(A**2 − B .GT. C − B) B = B + C
A = (A − B)/C
(iv) IF(B .LE. 0.0) STOP
STOP
(v) IF(A .GT. C .AND. B .EQ. C) GO TO 100
A = B + C
(vi) IF(A .EQ. B .OR. B .LT. C) A = C
GO TO 100

3.5 Find the errors in the following statements:
(i) IF(A**2 + B**2) C = C/D
(ii) IF(A ≤ B) GO TO 100
(iii) IF(A .LT. B . A .LT. C) GO TO 50
(iv) IF(A .LT. B) A = B, GO TO 200

3.6 Replace the following loops, if possible, by DO statements:
(i) LOOPK = START
20 IF(LOOPK .GT. TEST) GO TO 50

LOOPK = LOOPK = INCMNT
GO TO 20
(ii) LOOPK = START
50 --

LOOPK = LOOPK − INCMNT
IF (LOOPK .GE. TEST) GO TO 50

3.7 Which of the following DO statements are correct?
(i) DO 50 I = 5, 20, 1
(ii) DO 50 I = 5, 20.1
(iii) DO 50 I = 5, 20
(iv) DO 50 I = 20, 5, − 1
(v) DO 50 I = (M + 1), N
(vi) DO I50 = 5, 20
(vii) DO 50 I = 0, 20, 2
(viii) DO 50 I = 5, 20, 3

3.8   Show the output formats for the following statements given:

$$X = -51.23$$
$$J = 27000$$
$$P = 0.00032$$

WRITE(6,600) X, J, P

(i)   600   FORMAT(1H0, 50X, 8H RESULTS/1H0, 40X, F8.3, 5X, I3, 5X, E10.3)

(ii)   600   FORMAT(1H0, F5.2, 2X, I6, 2X, E16.7)

(iii) 600   FORMAT(1H0, 2(E16.7, 5X, I5))

(iv)   600   FORMAT(1H0, E10.4, 6X, I4, 2X, F5.2)

3.9   Show the output from the following code segments:

(i)   DO 500 I = 30, 37, 2
```
        WRITE(6,700) I
500     CONTINUE
700     FORMAT(1H0, 10X, I4)
```

(ii)   WRITE(6,600)
```
     DO 100 L = 1, 5, 2
       J = L*L - L
       WRITE(6,650) L, J
100     CONTINUE
600     FORMAT(1H0, 10X, 17H VALUES OF L AND J)
650     FORMAT(1H0, 5X, I3, 5X, I1)
```

3.10   Write the outputs for the following code segments:

(i)   SUM = 0.0
```
     DO 50 I = 1, 10
       SUM = SUM + FLOAT(I)
50      CONTINUE
        WRITE(6,100) SUM
100     FORMAT(1H0, F6.2)
```

(ii)   DO 50 I = 1, 10
```
       SUM = 0.0
       SUM = SUM + FLOAT(I)
50      CONTINUE
        WRITE(6,100) SUM
100     FORMAT(1H0, F6.2)
```

4 SIMPLE FORTRAN PROGRAMS

This chapter contains six programs in FORTRAN, each derived by the top-down approach. The purpose of this chapter is to familiarize the reader with the techniques of writing simple programs by actual demonstration of program development. Before starting this chapter, the reader should re-read Sec. 3.1–3.9 at least once. From that point on, every time the reader encounters a new statement, he/she should consult the appropriate sections in Chap. 3. In addition to the statements covered in Sec. 3.1– 3.9, these programs use such statements as the DO, DATA, and the COMPUTED GO TO; the later ones also use FORMAT statements with READ and WRITE for data input and output. Some basic algorithms such as the *pairwise comparison* technique for obtaining the maximum and the minimum values and the *binary search* technique are illustrated with examples. The reader is also introduced to the mechanics of simple numerical techniques such as linear interpolation, extrapolation, and least-square curve fitting.

4.1 LINEAR INTERPOLATION

To interpolate means to compute intermediate values of a function within a set of known values. Let us consider an example to illustrate the process of interpolation. Suppose we have collected data on the average blood pressure of a population as a function of age at intervals of ten years. These data can be represented as a discrete set of points as shown in Fig. 4.1(a). Our problem is to estimate the average blood pressure at ages which lie within the ten-year intervals of measurement.

This is a problem of interpolation and a simple graphical solution is shown in Fig. 4.1(b). We draw a smooth curve passing through the points in Fig. 4.1(a) and use this curve as a guide for estimating the desired values. If the values of the average blood pressure do not fluctuate wildly within each ten-year interval, the values read off this curve are reasonable estimates. The problem of linear interpolation is a spe-

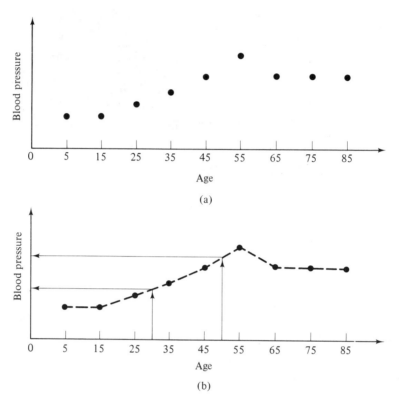

Fig. 4.1 (a) Discrete data on average blood pressure as a function of age. (b) Graphical interpretation using a smooth curve passing through all the points.

cial case of the above problem where the curve used for interpolation is a straight line.

Problem Description

Given that a function f of variable x has the values A and B for $x = a$ and $x = b$, respectively [see Fig. 4.2(a)], and *assuming* that f is approximately linear between $[a, b]$, find a straight-line approximation of f in (a, b).

Problem Solution

Level 1

If we assume that f is approximately linear in $[a, b]$, then it is reasonable to approximate it by a straight line passing through the points P_1 and P_2 shown in Fig. 4.2(a). Note that outside $[a, b]$ this straight line may not be a good approximation of

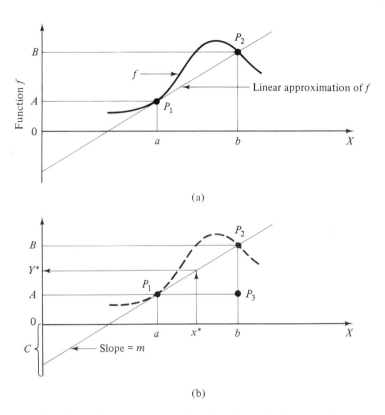

Fig. 4.2 (a) Graphical representation of f and its straight-line approximation over $[a, b]$. (b) Computation of slope m using the triangle $P_1P_2P_3$.

f. In addition, if our assumption of f being linear within $[a, b]$ is incorrect, then the straight line will be a poor approximation of f even within $[a, b]$. This error in approximation may be tolerable, however, if $(b - a)$ is sufficiently small.

Level 2

The general form of the equation of a straight line is $y = mx + c$, where m is the slope of the line and c is its intercept on the vertical axis. Using the triangle $P_1P_2P_3$ shown in Fig. 4.2(b), the slope m is easily obtained as

$$m = \frac{(B-A)}{(b-a)}$$

Substituting this value of m and $x = b$, $y = B$ in the equation of the straight line, we have

$$c = B - \frac{b(B-A)}{(b-a)}$$

These values of m and c completely specify the straight line and consequently solve the problem of linear interpolation of f in $[a, b]$. If $a < x^* < b$, then using linear interpolation [see Fig. 4.2(b)], our estimated value of f is $y^* = mx^* + c$, where m and c have the values shown above.

Level 3

(i) Read and print the values of a, b, A, and B.
(ii) Compute

$$m = \frac{(B-A)}{(b-a)}$$

$$\text{and} \quad c = B - \frac{b(B-A)}{(b-a)}$$

(iii) Print the values of m and c and stop.

The program shown at the next level uses the names LOWVAL, HGHVAL, LOW-FUN, and HGHFUN for a, b, A, and B, respectively.

Level 4

```
C
C          *** LINEAR INTERPOLATION PROGRAM. FUNCTION ***
C          *** VALUES ARE LOWFUN AND HGHFUN
C          *** CORRESPONDING TO LOWVAL AND HGHVAL
C          *** VALUES OF INDEPENDENT VARIABLE
C
       REAL LOWVAL,HGHVAL,LOWFUN,HGHFUN,SLOPE,INRCPT
C
       READ, LOWVAL,HGHVAL,LOWFUN,HGHFUN
       PRINT, 'LOWER LIMIT = ',LOWVAL,' HIGHER LIMIT = ',HGHFUN
       PRINT, 'LOW FCN VALUE = ',LCWFUN,' HIGH FCN VALUE = ',HGHFUN
C
C          *** COMPUTE SLOPE OF STRAIGHT LINE                          (4.P1)
C
       SLOPE=(HGHFUN-LOWFUN)/(HGHVAL-LOWVAL)
C
C          *** COMPUT INTERCEPT OF STRAIGHT LINE ***
C
       INRCPT=HGHFUN-SLOPE*HGHVAL
C
C          *** OUTPUT SLOPE AND INTERCEPT VALUES ***
C
       PRINT, 'SLOPE OF LINE = ',SLOPE,' INTERCEPT = ',INRCPT
       STOP
       END
```

A typical output obtained from this program is

```
LOWER LIMIT =       0.5170000E 00   HIGHER LIMIT =      0.1510000E 01
LOW FCN VALUE =     0.8123000E 00   HIGH FCN VALUE =    0.1510000E 01
SLOPE OF LINE =     0.9265601E 00   INTERCEPT =     0.3332691E 00
```

A more general problem of linear interpolation is described at the end of this chapter and left as an exercise to the reader.

4.2 RANGE OF HEIGHT DISTRIBUTION OF A POPULATION

Problem Description

A set of numbers is given representing heights of people in a population. Compose a FORTRAN program to compute the range of the distribution of these values where range is defined as the difference between the maximum and the minimum values.

Problem Solution

Level 1

The main problem here is to find the maximum and the minimum values of a set of numbers where the number of elements in the set is known only at the time of execution of the program. In addition, the number of elements in the set may change from one execution of the program to the next. In FORTRAN we can use the built-in functions AMAX1 and AMIN1 to find the maximum and the minimum values of a known and finite set of real variables. For example, suppose W = 0.5, X = −1.7, Y = 2.3, and Z = −0.3. Then AMAX1 (W, X, Y, Z) produces the value 2.3 and AMIN1 (W, X, Y, Z) returns −1.7. There is no way, however, to apply these functions directly to an unknown number of values of a variable such as height. To circumvent this problem, we use the pairwise comparison discussed at the next level.

Level 2

We discuss the *pairwise comparison* process only in the context of finding the maximum value. Similar arguments apply for finding the minimum value.

Suppose we have ten values for the variable height as shown in Fig. 4.3(a). By some yet to be specified inspection scheme, we have found the largest of the first five values and stored it in a variable called MAXIMUM-HEIGHT. Now we read the sixth value of height, compare it with the value stored in maximum-height, and store the larger of the two values in maximum-height. At the end of this process (a comparison of a pair of values), maximum-height contains the largest of the values of height found *so far*.

If we repeat this process until *all* the values of height have been read and compared, then maximum-height will contain the largest value of height. A little reflec-

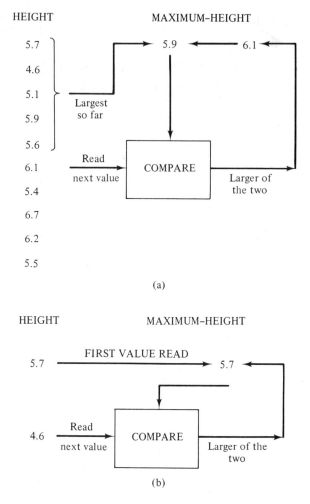

Fig. 4.3 (a) Pairwise comparison keeps track of the largest value of all the values read so far. (b) To start pairwise comparison, store the first value of height in MAXIMUM-HEIGHT.

tion will now clearly indicate that the unspecified inspection scheme at the start is really not necessary. We can start the process by simply storing the first value of height in maximum-height [see Fig. 4.3(b)].

Level 3

The pairwise comparison process described is implemented in FORTRAN by combining the AMAX1 and the AMIN1 functions with assignment statements as shown on the following page:

$$\text{HGTMAX} = \text{AMAX1 (HEIGHT, HGTMAX)}$$
$$\text{HGTMIN} = \text{AMIN1 (HEIGHT, HGTMIN)}$$

Clearly HGTMAX and HGTMIN represent the maximum-height and the minimum-height variables, respectively. The AMAX1 function compares the *current* values of HGTMAX and HEIGHT, and returns the larger of the two, which is then assigned as the new value of HGTMAX. In other words, we have

$$(\text{HGTMAX})_{\text{new}} = \text{AMAX1 (HEIGHT, (HGTMAX)}_{\text{current}})$$

A similar sequence of operations updates the value of HGTMIN.

Level 4

```
C          *** RANGE OF HEIGHT DISTRIBUTION  ***
C
      REAL HEIGHT,HGTMAX,HGTMIN,RANGE
C
      PRINT,' '
      PRINT, '                        HEIGHT DISTRIBUTION'
      READ,HEIGHT
      PRINT, ' '
      PRINT, '                          ',HEIGHT
C
C          *** INITIALIZE HGTMAX & HGTMIN
C          *** WITH THE FIRST VALUE OF HEIGHT
      HGTMAX=HEIGHT
      HGTMIN=HEIGHT
C
C          *** READ NEXT VALUE OF HEIGHT
  50  READ,HEIGHT
C          *** NEGATIVE VALUE OF HEIGHT SIGNALS
C          END OF DATA. GO TO RANGE COMPUTATION
      IF (HEIGHT.LT.0.0) GOTO 100                           (4.P2)
      PRINT, ' '
      PRINT, '                          ',HEIGHT
C          *** PAIR-WISE COMPARISON AND SELECTION
      HGTMAX=AMAX1(HEIGHT,HGTMAX)
      HGTMIN=AMIN1(HEIGHT,HGTMIN)
C
C          *** HGTMAX AND HGTMIN STORES THE MAX
C          *** AND MIN VALUES OF HEIGHT FOUND SO
C          *** FAR. GO TO 50 AND READ NEXT DATA CARD.
C
      GOTO 50
C          *** COMPUTE RANGE OF VALUES OF HEIGHT
 100  RANGE=HGTMAX-HGTMIN
      PRINT, ' '
      PRINT, 'MAXIMUM= ',HGTMAX,'   MINIMUM= ',HGTMIN
      PRINT, 'RANGE  = ',RANGE
      STOP
      END
```

Typical output of this program is shown on the following page.

```
                         HEIGHT DISTRIBUTICN

                         0.5460000E 01

                         0.6310000E 01

                         0.4250000E 01

                         0.5360000E 01

                         0.6670000E 01

                         0.7210000E 01

                         0.6270000E 01

    MAXIMUM=     0.7210000E 01    MINIMUM=        0.4250000E 01
    RANGE   =    0.2960000E 01
```

4.3 BALANCE OF A FIXED-TERM LOAN

Problem Description

A person borrows x dollars at r percent monthly interest for a fixed period of m months. The interest is computed on the unpaid balance at the beginning of each month. The person pays y dollars each month. The problem is to prepare a month-by-month breakdown of the balance of the loan and the total payment made.

Problem Solution

Level 1

First of all, we note that with loans of fixed duration, the payment for the last month, often called a balloon payment, is not necessarily the same as the other monthly payments. If the value of y is not much larger than the interest for the first month, then the last month's payment will be much larger than y and almost as large as the original loan.

Secondly, the value of y is not related in any manner to the values of x, r, or m in the problem description given above. Hence, if the value of y is sufficiently large, it is possible that the loan will be paid up long before the last month is reached. The program for solving this problem should therefore test for the occurrence of this situation. With these two clarifications attached to the problem statement, we proceed to the next level of solution.

Level 2

For a given value of y, compute and print the month-by-month balance of the loan and the amount paid either until the $(m - 1)$st month is reached or until the balance becomes less than the value of y.

The first case is the normal termination for this problem when the last month's payment must be computed separately. The second case may occur when the value of y is sufficiently large, as mentioned in Level 1. The next month's payment is then less than the value of y and the loan is completely paid up before the last month is reached.

The month-by-month balance of the loan can be computed as follows:

(Balance at the start of a month) = (Balance of the previous month) + (Interest),
(Balance at the end of a month) = (Balance at the start) − (Value of y).

No matter how the program terminates, the last payment is always the balance at the start of the month, i.e., the sum of the balance of the previous month and interest on it.

Level 3

(i) Read the values of loan, interest rate, duration, and monthly payment.
(ii) Initialize balance to loan and total paid to zero.
(iii) Enter a loop which is executed once for every month of the duration of the loan. The maximum number of executions is given by the value of ($m -$ 1). In the range of the loop, compute balance at the start of a month. If this value is less than the value of y, then *exit* from the loop and go to step (iv). Else compute the balance at the end of the month and increment total amount paid by the value of y. Print the values of balance and month.
(iv) We arrive at this step either after the loop in step (iii) has executed ($m -$ 1) times or when the balance at the start of some month is less than the value of y. In the first case we compute the balance at the start of the last month, which is the last payment. In the second case the balance at the start of the current month is the last payment. The program terminates after printing the values of the last payment and the total payment.

Level 4

```
C       *** COMPUTATION OF MONTH BY MONTH BALANCE ***
C       *** AND TOTAL AMOUNT PAID TOWARDS A LOAN ***
        REAL BALANC,LOAN,LAST,FAYMNT,RATE,TOTAL
        INTEGER DURATN,MONTH,LIMIT
C
C       *** READ AMOUNT OF LOAN, INTEREST RATE,
C       *** DURATION OF LOAN & MCNTHLY PAYMENT
C
        READ,LOAN,RATE,DURATN,PAYMNT
        PRINT,'AMOUNT OF LOAN = ',LOAN,' INTEREST RATE = ',RATE
        PRINT,'LOAN DURATION',DURATN,'MONTHS',' MONTHLY PAYMNT',PAYMNT
        PRINT,'BALANCE AT THE END OF ','    ','BALANCE'
C
C       *** INITIALIZE BALANCE, TOTAL PAID, AND LIMIT ***        (4.P3)
C
        BALANC=LOAN
        TOTAL=0.0
        LIMIT=DURATN-1
C
```

```
C          *** COMPUTE MONTH BY MONTH BALANCE ***
C
       DO 100 MONTH=1,LIMIT
C
C          *** BALANCE AT THE START OF THE MONTH ***
C
       BALANC=BALANC*(1.0+RATE/100.0)
C
C          *** EXIT FROM LOOP IF BALANCE IS LESS
C          *** THAN THIS MONTH'S PAYMNT ***
C
       IF (BALANC.LT.PAYMNT) GOTO 200
C
C          *** BALANCE AT THE END OF A MONTH ***
C
       BALANC=BALANC-PAYMNT
C
C          *** UPDATE TOTAL AMOUNT PAID ***
C
       TOTAL=TOTAL+PAYMNT
       PRINT,' ',MONTH,'          ',BALANC
100    CONTINUE
C
C          *** AT THIS POINT THE LAST MONTH HAS BEEN REACHED
C          *** COMPUTE LAST PAYMNT ***
C
       LAST=BALANC*(1.0+RATE/100.0)
C
C          *** STATEMENT 200 ALLOWS FOR THE CASE WHEN THE
C          *** BALANCE IS LESS THAN THE PAYMENT ***
C
200    IF(BALANC.LT.PAYMNT) LAST=BALANC
       PRINT, 'LAST PAYMENT =',LAST
C
C          *** UPDATE TOTAL AMOUNT PAID ***
C
       TOTAL=TOTAL+LAST
       PRINT,'TOTAL AMOUNT PAID = ',TOTAL
       STOP
       END
```

Two sets of output obtained under different conditions are shown below. The first set shows the case where the last month has been reached. The second set corresponds to the case where the exit from the loop via GO TO 200 has occurred. Since the program can terminate in two possible ways, both cases should be tested separately.

Case 1

```
AMOUNT OF LOAN =       0.5000000E 03  INTEREST RATE =      0.1000000E 02
LOAN DURATION            5 MONTHS  MONTHLY PAYMNT    0.1000000E 03
BALANCE AT THE END OF        BALANCE
               1           0.4499995E 03
               2           0.3949990E 03
               3           0.3344985E 03
               4           0.2679480E 03
LAST PAYMENT =    0.2947424E 03
TOTAL AMOUNT PAID =     0.6947424E 03
```

Case 2

```
AMOUNT OF LOAN =       0.5000000E 03   INTEREST RATE =      0.1000000E 02
LOAN DURATION          5 MONTHS  MONTHLY PAYMNT    0.3000000E 03
BALANCE AT THE END OF           BALANCE
               1                0.2499995E 03
LAST PAYMENT =     0.2749993E 03
TOTAL AMOUNT PAID =     0.5749993E 03
```

Note that the two sets of output verify our intuitive feeling that if we pay more per month, we end up paying less for the loan at the end.

4.4 PAYROLL PROCESSING

Problem Description

Every employee of a company is identified by a social security number (nine-digit integer), and every week a data card is prepared for each employee containing his/her social security number, hours worked, and the regular hourly rate of pay. For each employee, compute his/her gross pay, net pay, and taxes withheld. The first card of the data deck contains the total number of employees to be processed. The limit on the regular working hours in a week is assumed to be forty.

Problem Solution

Level 1

For each employee, weekly gross pay equals the sum of the regular pay plus the overtime pay, if any. Overtime hourly rate is 50% more than the regular hourly rate. Federal income tax and social security tax are computed at fixed percentages of gross pay. The federal income tax rate is assumed to be 20% and the social security tax rate is 5% of gross pay. Net pay is obtained by subtracting taxes withheld from the gross pay.

Level 2

    (i) Initialize federal tax rate and social security tax rate, limit of regular working hours, and overtime factor. Since the values of these variables are assumed to be constants, initialization is done during compilation using the DATA statement in FORTRAN.

   (ii) Read the number of persons to be processed.

  (iii) Enter a DO loop where the index counts the number of cards processed and the test value is given by the number of persons to be processed.
Read the social security number, hours worked, and the regular hourly rate of a person.
Compute regular pay = (minimum of (hours worked, limit)) *Regular hourly rate.

Set overtime pay to zero.

If hours worked is less than the limit, then compute gross pay as shown below. Else overtime rate = overtime factor *regular hourly rate and, overtime pay = (hours worked − limit) * overtime rate.

Gross pay = regular pay + overtime pay.

Total taxes withheld = (gross pay) * (sum of tax rates).

Net pay = (gross pay) − (total taxes withheld).

Print social security number, gross pay, taxes withheld, and net pay.

(iv) Upon exit from DO loop stop, write "end of list" and stop.

Level 3

```
C
C          *** PAYROLL PROCESSING ***
C
      REAL FDRATE,GRSPAY,HOURS,NETPAY,OVRATE,OVRPAY,RGRATE,REGPAY,SSRATE
      REAL FACTOR,LIMIT
      INTEGER CARD,PERSNS,SOCSEC
      DATA FDRATE,SSRATE/0.2,C.05/,LIMIT/40.0/,FACTOR/1.5/
C
C          *** WRITE HEADINGS OF OUTPUT ***
C
      WRITE(6,200)
C
C          *** GET NUMBER OF PERSCNS ON PAYROLL ***
C
      READ(5,250) PERSNS
C
C          *** PROCESS EACH PERSONS CARD IN A DO LOOP ***
C
      DO 100 CARD=1,PERSNS
      READ(5,300) SOCSEC,HOURS,RGRATE
      WRITE(6,325) SOCSEC,HOURS,RGRATE
C
C          *** COMPUTE REGULAR PAY ***
C
      REGPAY=AMIN1(HOURS,40.0)*RGRATE
C
C          *** SET OVERTIME PAY TC ZERO ***
C
      OVRPAY=0.0
C
C          *** TEST FOR OVERTIME; IF NO OVERTIME
C          *** GO TO 50 FOR GROSS PAY COMPUTATION ***
C
      IF(HOURS.LE.LIMIT) GCTO 50
C
C          *** ELSE COMPUTE OVERTIME RATE ***
C
      OVRATE=FACTOR*RGRATE
C
C          *** COMPUTE OVERTIME PAY ***
C
      OVRPAY=(HOURS-LIMIT)*OVRATE
C
C          *** COMPUTE GROSS PAY ***
C
50    GRSPAY=REGPAY+OVRPAY
C
```

(4.P4)

```
C            *** COMPUTE TOTAL TAXES WITHHELD ***
C
             TAXES=GRSPAY*(FDRATE+SSRATE)
C
C            *** COMPUTE NETPAY ***
C
             NETPAY=GRSPAY-TAXES
             WRITE(6,350) GRSPAY,TAXES,NETPAY
100     CONTINUE
        WRITE(6,375)
        STOP
200     FORMAT(1H1,20X,
       1'ID NUMBER    HOURS    RATE    GROSS PAY    TAXES    NETPAY')
250     FORMAT(I4)
300     FORMAT(I9,6X,F5.2,5X,F5.2)
325     FORMAT(1H0,20X,I9,2(3X,F5.2))
350     FORMAT(1H0,46X,3(3X,F7.2))
375     FORMAT(1H0,12H END OF LIST)
        END
```

Output from this program is shown below.

ID NUMBER	HOURS	RATE	GROSS PAY	TAXES	NETPAY
565746828	10.00	1.00			
			10.00	2.50	7.50
345221976	50.00	1.00			
			55.00	13.75	41.25

END OF LIST

4.5 PAYMENTS FOR A FIXED-TERM LOAN

Problem Description

Let us reconsider the problem of a fixed-term loan discussed in Sec. 4.3. This time, we want to find the value of the monthly payment y that will result in zero balance at the end of m months.

Problem Solution

Level 1

·The value of balance *at the end of m months* as a function of the monthly payment y is shown in Fig. 4.4. When the value of y is zero, the terminal balance is a positive number larger than the amount of the loan. When the value of y equals the sum of the loan and the first month's interest, the terminal balance is negative. This is because the entire loan with interest is paid at the end of the first month. As the value of y is gradually increased from zero, the value of the terminal balance decreases and

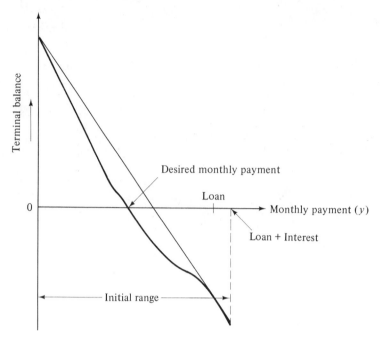

Fig. 4.4 Terminal balance as a function of monthly payment.

crosses the zero value at some point. This point, shown in Fig. 4.4, is the solution to our problem.

A simple method of solution is to compute the terminal balance for $y = 1, 2, 3,$ $\ldots$, until it becomes negative for the *first* time. This method can locate the required value of y to within one unit. A more efficient approach is to start with an estimate of the range of values of y containing the desired solution. This range is then reduced systematically until the desired solution is located. One such approach, called the *binary search* or the method of bisection, is discussed at the next level.

Level 2

To start with, the initial range of the allowable values of y begins at zero and ends at the amount of loan plus the first month's interest. We take the midpoint of this interval as an estimate of the correct value of y.

Next we compute the terminal balance for this value of y. If this balance is zero, we are finished. If this balance is positive, any value of y smaller than the selected midpoint will result in an even higher positive value for the terminal balance (see Fig. 4.4). We can therefore limit the range of values of y to *begin* at this midpoint.

On the other hand, if the terminal balance is negative, any value of y higher than the midpoint will result in an even smaller negative value for the terminal balance. Thus we can limit the range of values of y to *end* at the midpoint (see Fig. 4.5).

Note that we either throw away the left half or the right half of the initial range and thus, in effect, reduce the range by half. We can now repeat the entire procedure

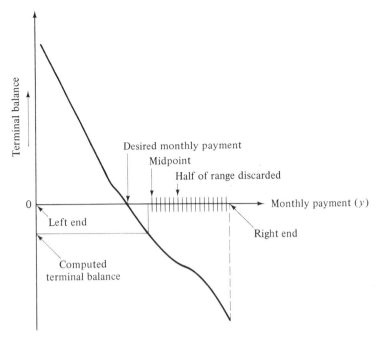

Fig. 4.5 Binary search used to discard half of initial range.

with this new range. Since the range is halved every time, the method is known as the method of bisection or binary search.

Level 3

We expect that due to computational errors, the value of balance will never be exactly equal to zero. We have therefore compared the absolute value of the balance with unity by using a greater than (.GT.) relational operator.

  (i) Read the values of loan, interest rate, and duration in months.
 (ii) Compute the right-end point of the range of values of payment by adding the first month's interest to the loan.
(iii) Initialize the left-and the right-end points of the range.
 (iv) Compute the midpoint of the range of values of payment and the corresponding terminal balance.
  (v) If the terminal balance is positive, assign the midpoint as the new left-end point. If it is negative, assign the midpoint as the new right-end point.
 (vi) If the absolute value of balance is greater than unity, go to step (iv). Else print the value of the midpoint and stop.

Level 4

```
C
C          *** COMPUTATION OF MONTHLY PAYMENT ***        (4.P5)
C          *** ON A FIXED TERM LOAN ***
```

```
C
        REAL BALANC,LOAN,LEFT,MIDPNT,RATE,RIGHT
        INTEGER DURATN,MONTH
C
C         *** READ AMOUNT OF LOAN, INTEREST RATE
C         *** AND DURATION IN MONTHS ***
C
        READ, LOAN,RATE,DURATN
        PRINT, 'AMOUNT OF LOAN=',LOAN,' INTEREST RATE=',RATE
        PRINT, 'DURATION OF LOAN=',DURATN,' MONTHS'
C
C         *** COMPUTE AND INITIALIZE RIGHT-END POINT ***
C
        RIGHT=LOAN*(1.0+RATE/100.0)
C
C         *** INITIALIZE LEFT-END POINT ***
C
        LEFT=0.0
50      BALANC=LOAN
C
C         *** COMPUTE MIDPOINT OF THE RANGE ***
C
        MIDPNT=(LEFT+RIGHT)/2.0
C
C         *** COMPUTE TERMINAL BALANCE ***
C
        DO 100 MONTH=1,DURATN
C
C            *** BALANCE AT THE START OF A MONTH ***
C
            BALANC=BALANC*(1.0+RATE/100.0)
C
C            *** BALANCE AT THE END OF A MONTH ***
C
            BALANC=BALANC-MIDPNT
100     CONTINUE
C
C         *** ELIMINATE RIGHT HALF IF TERMINAL BALANCE IS NEGATIVE
C
        IF(BALANC.LT.0.0) RIGHT=MIDPNT
C
C         *** ELIMINATE LEFT HALF IF TERMINAL BALANCE IS POSITIVE
C
        IF(BALANC.GT.0.0) LEFT=MIDPNT
C
C         *** REPEAT IF MAGNITUDE OF BALANCE EXCEEDS UNITY
C
        IF(ABS(BALANC).GT.1.0) GOTO 50
C
C         *** PRINT VALUE OF MONTHLY PAYMENT
C
        PRINT, 'MONTHLY PAYMENT= ',MIDPNT
        STOP
        END
```

Typical output from this program is as follows:

```
AMOUNT OF LOAN=      0.2000000E 04  INTEREST RATE=      0.1000000E 02
DURATION OF LOAN=            24  MONTHS
MONTHLY PAYMENT=      0.2225980E 03
```

4.6 COUNTING STUDENTS IN A CLASS

Problem Description

A FORTRAN class has four sections, each section containing some male and some female students. A data card is prepared for each student containing his/her social security number, a digit denoting the section number (1, 2, 3, 4), and a sex code (1 for a male and 0 for a female). We want to compute the total number of male and female students in each section.

Problem Solution

Level 1

For each section we use two counters, one for the male students and one for the female students. Each card is first tested to determine the section to which that person belongs. Then depending on the sex code value on that card, the proper counter for that section is incremented by one.

Level 2

We use the following technique for detecting the end of the data deck discussed in Chap. 3. We use an additional integer input variable called DEKEND in our READ statement. An integer value is read into this variable from the last column of each blank data card. We add an extra card at the end of the data deck. This card is entirely blank except for the last column. Any digit other then a zero is punched in the last column. Thus with formatted input, a nonzero value of DEKEND indicates the end of the data deck. Recall that in the case of formatted input, blanks are regarded as zeros.

The program contains four blocks of code; each block tests the value of the sex code and increments the proper counter by one. Depending on the value of the section variable, we branch to one of these four blocks of code. In FORTRAN we have implemented this multiple branch by using the COMPUTED GO TO statement as shown below:

GO TO (100, 200, 300, 400), SECTION

Obviously, SECTON is the name of the variable (integer) used to store the value of section. Errors may occur if by mistake the value of SECTON falls outside the range from one to four. For this reason, we have added extra code to test the value of SECTON before we attempt to branch. If the value of SECTON is outside the proper range, it prints out an error message and proceeds to read the next card.

The value of the SEX variable given on a data card may also be wrong. The program should therefore be designed to detect such errors as well. We have left this as an exercise for the reader. Some hints on error detection are also given at the end of this section.

Level 3

   (i) Initialize all counters to zeros.
  (ii) Until the last data card is processed, read the next data card and test the value of the section variable. If this value is not in the proper range, print input data and error message. Else using the value of section as an index, branch to the appropriate block of code. Within the selected block, test the value of the sex variable and increment the appropriate counter.
 (iii) Print results and stop.

Level 4

```
C
C          *** COUNTING TOTAL NUMBER OF MALE AND
C          *** FEMALE STUDENTS IN EACH OF FOUR ***
C          *** SECTIONS OF A CLASS ***
C
      INTEGER CARD,DEKEND,FEMAL1,FEMAL2,FEMAL3,FEMAL4,
     1     MALE1,MALE2,MALE3,MALE4,SECTON,SEX,SOCSEC
C
C          *** INITIALIZE COUNTERS & CHARACTER STRING LAST ***
C
      DATA FEMAL1,FEMAL2,FEMAL3,FEMAL4,MALE1,MALE2,MALE3,
     1     MALE4/8*0/
C
C          *** READ A DATA CARD ***
C
50    READ(5,550) SOCSEC,SECTON,SEX,DEKEND
C
C          *** NONZERO VALUE CF DEKEND SIGNALS END OF DATA
C          *** STATEMENT 500 PRINTS OUTPUT RESULTS ***
C
      IF(DEKEND.NE.0) GOTO 500
C
C          *** TEST VALUE OF SECTION. IF OUTSIDE
C          *** RANGE GO TO 450 FOR ERROR MESSAGE ***
C
      IF(SECTON.LT.1) GOTO 450
      IF(SECTON.GT.4) GOTO 450
C
C          *** BRANCH TO PROPER BLOCK OF CODE
C          *** USING VALUE OF SECTION ***
C
      GOTO(100,200,300,400), SECTON
C
C          *** TEST SEX FOR SECTION ONE.
C          *** INCREMENT APPROPRIATE COUNTER. ***
C
100   IF(SEX.EQ.1) MALE1=MALE1+1
      IF(SEX.EQ.0) FEMAL1=FEMAL1+1
C
C          *** GO TO 50 AND READ NEXT DATA CARD
C
      GOTO 50
C
C          *** SIMILAR COMMENTS APPLY TO ALL OTHER SECTIONS ***
C
```

(4.P6)

```
200     IF(SEX.EQ.1) MALE2=MALE2+1
        IF(SEX.EQ.0) FEMAL2=FEMAL2+1
        GOTO 50
300     IF(SEX.EQ.1) MALE3=MALE3+1
        IF(SEX.EQ.0) FEMAL3=FEMAL3+1
        GOTO 50
400     IF(SEX.EQ.1) MALE4=MALE4+1
        IF(SEX.EQ.0) FEMAL4=FEMAL4+1
        GOTO 50
C
C          *** ERROR IN VALUE OF SECTION. OUTPUT
C          *** ERROR MESSAGE AND GO TO READ NEXT DATA CARD ***
C
450     WRITE(6,600) SOCSEC,SECTON,SEX
        GOTO 50
C
C          *** OUTPUT RESULTS WITH HEADINGS ***
C
500     WRITE(6,650)
        WRITE(6,700) MALE1,FEMAL1,MALE2,FEMAL2,MALE3,
       1             FEMAL3,MALE4,FEMAL4
        STOP
550     FORMAT(I9,2(2X,I1),61X,I1)
600     FORMAT(1H0,23H ERROR IN SECTION VALUE/1H0,I9,2(3X,I1))
650     FORMAT(1H0,20X,34H DISTRIBUTION OF MALES AND FEMALES/
       1        1H0,30X,17H IN FOUR SECTIONS/1H0,10X,
       2       8H SECTION,4H NO.,5X,6H MALES,5X,8H FEMALES)
700     FORMAT(1H0,13X,1H1,13X,I2,11X,I2/1H0,13X,
       1   1H2,13X,I2,11X,I2/1H0,13X,1H3,13X,I2,11X,I2/1H0,
       2   13X,1H4,13X,I2,11X,I2)
        END
```

Typical output from the execution of this program is as follows:

```
ERROR IN SECTION VALUE

565746823   7   0

ERROR IN SECTION VALUE

530284219   0   1

                 DISTRIBUTION OF MALES AND FEMALES

                      IN FOUR SECTIONS

        SECTION NO.        MALES        FEMALES

            1                8              1

            2                1              1

            3                1              1

            4                1              1
```

Let us now note one of the deficiencies of the above program. Suppose that the value of the SEX variable is punched incorrectly in one of the data cards. Then the corresponding person is not counted, which is acceptable. However, no indication of this error is printed out. In essence, that person simply disappears from the output without a trace and that is a serious deficiency of Program (4.P6). The program can be easily modified to eliminate this problem and the reader should do so as an exercise. As an additional check on errors, it is also a good idea to count and print out the number of data cards processed successfully and the total number of data cards read.

4.7 EXERCISES

4.1 *Linear interpolation:* A function can be approximated by a sequence of straight lines as shown in Fig. 4.6. Given a set of function values and the corresponding values of the independent variable, compute and print the slopes the intercepts of all the straight lines.

4.2 *Binary search:* A model deposits $50 into her savings account at the beginning of every month. The bank adds a 6% interest to the savings at the end of every month. After a year, the model wants to vacation in Hawaii and needs $575 for the vacation. Using the method of binary search, find the number of months required to build up the required savings to within ± $10.

4.3 *Linear least-square curve fitting:* As shown in Fig. 4.7, we can often approximate the relationship between two variables x and y by fitting a straight line through a set of measured values containing random observational errors. We cannot hope to pass a single straight line through all these randomly observed points and only attempt to obtain a "best" fit. In one such approach, called the least-square curve fitting, the slope and the intercept of the straight line are given by

$$D = N \sum x_i^2 - (\sum x_i)^2$$
$$\text{Slope} = [N \sum (x_i y_i) - (\sum x_i)(\sum y_i)]/D$$

and

$$\text{Intercept} = [(\sum y_i)(\sum x_i^2) - (\sum x_i y_i)(\sum x_i)]/D$$

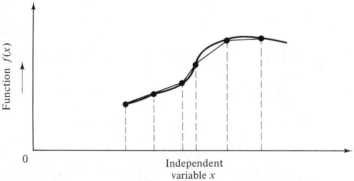

Fig. 4.6 A set of straight lines used to approximate a nonlinear function by linear interpolation.

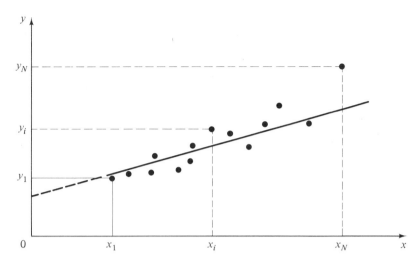

Fig. 4.7 A straight line used to approximate the relationship between x and y from a randomly observed set of values.

There are N observed values of pairs of variables (x_i, y_i) as shown in Fig. 4.7. Write a program to find the straight line that fits a given set of randomly observed data.

4.4 *Linear extrapolation:* To extrapolate means to estimate the values of a function outside a known range of values by passing a curve through the known values. When this curve is a straight line, we have linear extrapolation. Figure 4.8 shows the altitude of a jet interceptor as a function of time given by the equation $H(t) = (At^2)/2$; t denotes the intercept time and H is the maximum altitude attained. If we use a straight line through the points O and A, our extrapolated estimate of H is H_1. If we use straight lines through points A and B or B and C, then our estimates are H_2 and H_3, respectively. Clearly, as we use more and more recently computed values of $H(t)$ in our linear extrapolation scheme, our estimate of H improves. Write a program to compute the estimates H_1, H_2, and H_3 from the given equation of $H(t)$. Print H_1, H_2, H_3, and H for the purpose of comparing the accuracy of the estimates.

4.5 To update the customer accounts of a bank, a vice-president prepares input data for each customer. The first card, called the master input card, contains a customer's social security number, bank account number, and current balance. Each subsequent card contains the details of a transaction in the form of the customer's bank account number and the amount of the transaction in dollars. If the transaction amount is positive, it is a deposit and is credited to the customer's account. If it is negative, it is debited from the account. The customer is charged 10¢ per transaction up to a maximum of $1.00. Every transaction that overdraws the customer's account is penalized $2.00. Write a program to update accounts showing all transactions.

4.6 The real estate tax rate of a county is based on land-use classifications.

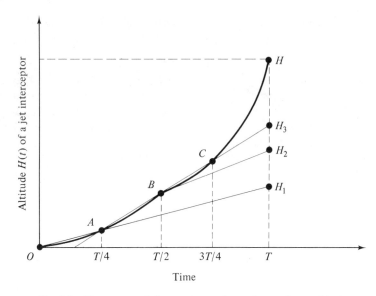

Fig. 4.8 Linear extrapolation used to estimate the maximum altitude attained by a jet interceptor.

Land-Use Classification	Tax Rate ($/sq. ft)
1 Agricultural	0.14
2 Single unit, Residential	0.19
3 Multiple unit, Residential	0.23
4 Commercial	0.29
5 Resort	0.32

Each data card contains a parcel number, land-use classification code, and length and width of the parcel in feet. For each land-use classification, find the number of parcels, total square feet, total tax assessment, percentage of all land, and the percentage of total real estate tax assessed.

4.7   At the end of a semester in a FORTRAN language class, each student scores between zero and one hundred. Each student's social security number and score are punched on a data card. Find the maximum, minimum, and average score of all students, and the number of students in each of the following categories:

    (i)   Score ≥ 75,

    (ii) $50 \leq$ score < 75,

    (iii) $30 \leq$ score < 50, and

    (iv) $0 \leq$ score < 30.

4.8   A population consists of three ethnic groups and the rate of yearly growth of each group is known. Given the present size of the population and the size of each group as a percentage of that population size, find the size of the population and the size of each ethnic group at intervals of one year for twenty years. Assume that the rate of yearly growth of each group is a function of the size of the group at the beginning of the year.

4.9   Gas meters are used by a company to find the volume of gas consumed by its customers, where the volume is given by the difference in two successive readings of a meter. The volume consumed is multiplied by a thermal factor to find the amount of heat used, which forms the basis for billing the customer. The customer is charged a fixed installation cost and the cost of the heat used on a sliding scale.

Amount of Heat Used	Price
0–50 units	$1.00/unit
51–150 units	$0.90/unit
151–300 units	$0.80/unit
More than 300 units	$0.70/unit

Write a program for preparing bills for the customers.

4.10   A theater showing X-rated movies sells 120 tickets a day at $2.50 per ticket. The operating cost of the theater is 80¢ per person at the current level of 120 persons a day. Each reduction in price of a ticket by 10¢ increases the number of tickets sold per day by 15. Each new patron over the current 120 a day also increases the operating cost by 4¢ per person. Compute the profits or losses in each case if the price of a ticket is reduced from $2.50 to $1.00 in steps of 10¢ at a time.

4.11   The program developed in Sec. 4.6 showed and discussed various methods for guarding against errors in input data. Obviously, guarding against erroneous input data is very important in payroll processing. Think about possible sources of errors in the payroll data and suggest methods for detecting such errors.

4.12   A simple method for computing the area under a curve is shown in Fig. 4.9. The total area is approximated by the sum of the areas of the rectangles of width h. The

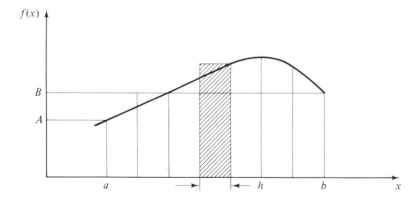

Fig. 4.9   Approximating the area under a curve by rectangles.

relevant formula is

$$\text{Area} = \sum_{i=1}^{n} f(x_i)h \text{ (approximate)}$$

Given the equation of $f(x) = 3.5x^2 + 2x$, write a program to compute the values of Area for $0 \le x \le 2$ and $h = 0.2, 0.1$, and 0.05.

4.13 A 200-gallon tank contains 100 gallons of water in which 50 pounds of salt are dissolved. Water, containing 0.6 pounds of salt per gallon, runs into the tank at the rate of 5 gallons per minute. The contents of the tank run out at the rate of 4 gallons a minute. Write a program to determine when the tank will overflow, to within a minute. What will be the concentration of salt in the tank at that time, measured in pounds per gallon?

4.14 A truck is moving along a straight line with a constant velocity V_1 (see Fig. 4.10). A missile is fired from the point M along a 60° line and moves with a constant velocity V_2. Write a program to compute the value of D for different values of V_1 and V_2 such that the truck can be hit.

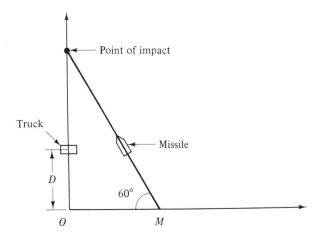

Fig. 4.10 Intercepting a truck with a missile.

5 Arrays

The FORTRAN programs that we have composed so far contain only simple variables, by which we mean any variable that can have only one value at a time. In this chapter we introduce a more complex form of FORTRAN data structure, called an *array*, which is an ordered set of values identified by a *single* variable name. Figure 5.1 shows examples of simple variables and their values stored in the memory of a computer, while Fig. 5.2(a) shows a simple linear array called COST along with its values.

	X X X X
SUM	5.71
	X X X X
DATA	−3.257
COUNTER	35
INDEX	16
	X X X X

Fig. 5.1 Functional diagram showing simple FORTRAN variables and their values stored in the memory of a computer.

	COST		PROFIT
	X X X X		X X X X
	1.75		3.89
	0.25		0.25
	3.89		1.75
	2.37		2.37
	X X X X		X X X X
	(a)		(b)

Fig. 5.2 Functional diagrams showing two linear arrays called COST and PROFIT and their associated values.

The most important characteristic of an array is that its values form an *ordered set* and not merely a *set*. The array called PROFIT, shown in Fig. 5.2(b), is not the same as the array COST, although the two *sets* of values shown in Fig. 5.2 are identical. For an ordered set of values, it makes sense to refer to the first value, the second value, and so on. The first and the third values stored in COST and PROFIT are different, and this is why COST and PROFIT are not identical.

In some problems, the order in which the values are stored in an array is important, and in such cases the array is often called a *vector*. In other problems, the ordering of values may not be important, but FORTRAN programs always recognize the existing order of values in an array. The individual memory locations which store the values of an array are called *elements* of the array.

5.1 SINGLE SUBSCRIPTED VARIABLES

Suppose we measure the distance of a satellite from earth as a function of time, starting at launch time. These measurements, taken at discrete instants of time, can be displayed by a graph as shown in Fig. 5.3. The time instants when distance measurements are taken are denoted by $t_1, t_2, t_3, \ldots, t_k, \ldots$ with corresponding values of the distance variable denoted by $d_1, d_2, d_3, \ldots, d_k, \ldots$. This is a simple example of the use of subscripted variables in the description of data. The time variable has a single name "t" with many values; each specific instance of its value is denoted by attaching an appropriate subscript to the name, such as t_k. Similarly, the distance variable is given the name "d" and instances of its values are denoted by subscripts such as $d_1, d_2, \ldots, d_k, \ldots$.

Subscripted variables are represented in FORTRAN by arrays. The value of t_k of the time variable in Fig. 5.3 can be represented in FORTRAN as TIME(K) and the

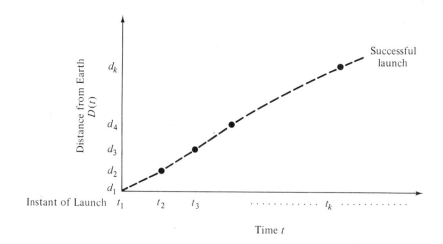

Fig. 5.3 Graph showing measured distance from earth as a function of time for a successful launch of a satellite.

value of the distance variable d_k by DISTNC(K). The names of the variables in FORTRAN are TIME and DISTNC, respectively. These variables are not simple variables since each has an ordered set of values associated with it. Such variables are called vectors in numerical analysis and one-dimensional arrays in FORTRAN. The letter K within parentheses, next to the names of TIME and DISTNC, is called an *index* and represents the subscript k used in Fig. 5.3. An array such as this can be thought of as strings of values attached to a single name, as shown in Fig. 5.4. The value of the index variable K specifies the location of a value in this string; any of these values can be obtained by using the name of the array followed by the appropriate index values in parentheses. TIME(K) and DISTNC(K) are called the Kth elements of the corresponding arrays. The index K can be an integer constant, an integer variable, or an integer arithmetic expression, and can only take positive values, *excluding zero*. Allowable expressions in standard FORTRAN are of the form: I, I$\pm$J, L*I$\pm$J.

5.2 DIMENSION DECLARATION

The name of an array has to observe the same FORTRAN conventions as those satisfied by the name of a simple variable. We are, however, currently storing a string of values under a single name, and we must therefore tell the computer the maximum length of this string so that arrangements for storage can be made. This can be done by means of the DIMENSION statement. Suppose in Fig. 5.3 we have two hundred values of time and distance at most. Then we include the following dimension statement at the beginning of any FORTRAN program that uses these data:

$$\text{DIMENSION TIME (200), DISTNC(200)} \qquad (5.1)$$

A dimension statement is another example of a declaration statement, similar to the type of declaration statement used earlier. If an array stores only integer values, its name should be declared to be an integer variable. Otherwise it should be declared to be a real variable. For example,

INTEGER TIME
REAL INCMNT
DIMENSION TIME (171), INCMNT (12)

TIME	0.0, 1.3, 2.1, 3.2, 4.1, 5.2, ...
DISTNC	0.0, 2.9, 4.7, 7.3, 12.5, 16.2, ...

TIME(5) = 4.1, DISTNC(6) = 16.2

Fig. 5.4 One-dimensional array as a string of values stored under a single name. The index is used to pick specific values from the string.

For convenience, the type and dimension declarations can be combined into one statement:

$$\text{INTEGER TIME (171)} \qquad (5.2)$$
$$\text{REAL INCMNT (12)} \qquad (5.3)$$

Statement (5.2) declares TIME to be the name of a one-dimensional integer array containing one hundred and seventy-one values at most and statement (5.3) declares INCMNT to be the name of another one-dimensional real array containing twelve values at most. Since almost all FORTRAN programs begin with the type declaration statements REAL and INTEGER, it is rarely necessary to use an explicit DIMENSION statement to declare the dimensions of arrays. We have mentioned the DIMENSION statement explicitly to inform the reader of its existence and purpose in the event he/she encounters a program that uses it.

Notice that in order to use an array in a FORTRAN program, the programmer must select a specific number to be used to declare its dimension. In some problems, the number of values to be stored in an array is specified and the declaration of dimension can be exact. In other cases, however, such information may not be available at the time the program is composed. The programmer must then make a guess and hope to overestimate his storage requirements. When a large computer is used, a small amount of overestimation of the storage requirements is not a serious problem. If, however, the programmer underestimates his storage requirements, he will then have to modify his dimension declarations and recompile his program. Since most amateur programs are compiled every time they are executed, underestimation of storage requirements is only a minor irritation.

5.3 SALESPERSONS OF THE MONTH

Arrays have an important use other than the representation of subscripted variables in FORTRAN programs. In many problems it is necessary to have *all* of the input data available *throughout the execution* of a program. Simple variables are not ideally suited for this purpose since new values read in always destroy the old values stored in them. Arrays provide a convenient means for storing all input data repeatedly used by a program during its execution. The solution of the following problem illustrates this point.

Problem Description

An automobile dealer has twenty-seven salespersons. The dealer decides to give bonuses each month to the persons who sold the largest number of automobiles that month. Every month the dealer prepares a set of cards, each containing a salesperson's social security number and the number of automobiles sold by that person. Write a program to find the salespersons of the month who receive the bonuses.

Problem Solution

Level 1

We store the input data consisting of the social security numbers and the number of automobiles sold in two one-dimensional arrays called ID and AUTO, respectively. Next we search the AUTO array for the largest number of automobiles sold. We then compare this value with the values stored in AUTO one at a time, and whenever the two values match, we print the social security number of the corresponding salesperson from the ID array.

Notice that the problem solution described above finds the ID numbers of *all* the persons who have sold the largest number of automobiles. To achieve this goal, the use of the two arrays ID and AUTO are *absolutely essential*. The largest number of automobiles sold can be found without storing the data in AUTO. However, in order to find the IDs of all the salespersons who qualify for the bonus, it is necessary to search the data on the automobiles sold for a second time. If these data and the corresponding IDs are not permanently stored in arrays during the execution of the program, it will be necessary to read the data again from a second set of data cards.

Level 2

To secure storage for our data, we use the following declaration statements in FORTRAN:

INTEGER AUTO (30), ID (30)

Notice that ID is implicitly declared to be an integer name, but we make use of the integer declaration to declare its dimension rather than using a separate dimension statement. The maximum number of values that can be stored in either array is thirty. Of course, according to the problem specification, twenty-seven is perfectly adequate for our storage needs. With a dimension of thirty, if the dealer hires a few more salespersons (no more than thirty, of course), he/she need not alter the program. On the other hand, if the dealer fires some salespersons, the program will be using more memory than necessary. On a large computer there is not much incentive for optimizing storage requirements at this low level. A totally outrageous demand (for this problem) of a hundred thousand memory locations for each array can, however, cause our program to have low priority of execution.

Next we read in the data using a DO loop. We first read the exact number of salespersons the dealer has (PERSNS) and then proceed to read the pertinent data for each. PERSNS must be declared to be an integer variable:

```
      READ (5,100) PERSNS
      DO 20 I = 1, PERSNS
          READ (5,200) ID(I), AUTO(I)
 20   CONTINUE
```

In the DO loop above, the READ instruction is executed PERSNS times, each execution of the READ reading a new card. During the first execution of the DO loop, the value of the index I is one, and hence the social security number and the number of automobiles sold read from the first card are stored in ID(1) and AUTO(1), respectively. Similarly during the *k*th execution of the loop, I=K and the data read from the *k*th card are stored in ID(k) and AUTO(k), respectively. This data storage scheme is illustrated in Fig. 5.5.

At this point let us consider a common problem which often arises during the execution of programs that use arrays. What will happen if due to error, the value read into PERSNS exceeds thirty? Our declaration statement has obtained for us thirty memory locations for storing the values of each array. If the value of PERSNS exceeds thirty, we are clearly going beyond our established bounds of storage for both arrays. Some compilers insert extra code for checking such bounds violations with arrays during execution, but most do not do so. In general, therefore, the program itself should always check for possible violations and terminate with a proper error message if such a violation occurs. The following modified section of FORTRAN code incorporates such a check. We have also added two output statements to print the input data in order to verify later the proper execution of the program:

```
        READ(5,100) PERSNS
C           ***CHECK FOR ARRAY BOUNDS VIOLATION
        IF(PERSNS.GT.30) WRITE(6,400) PERSNS
        IF(PERSNS.GT.30) STOP
C           ***WRITE OUTPUT HEADING
        WRITE(6,500)
        DO 20 I=1, PERSNS
            READ(5,200) ID(I), AUTO(I)
            WRITE(6,500) ID(I), AUTO(I)
20      CONTINUE
```

Fig. 5.5 Data stored in the memory after the third execution of the DO loop in Level 2 of Sec. 5.3.

Next we find the largest value stored in AUTO by a pairwise comparison process. First we store the value of AUTO(1) in a variable called AUTOMX. Then we compare the value in AUTOMX with the value in AUTO(K) for successive values of K from 2 to PERSNS, always storing the larger of the two values in AUTOMX (see Fig. 5.6). When the comparison ends, we have the largest of the values stored in AUTO in AUTOMX:

```
        AUTOMX = AUTO(1)
        DO 40 I = 2, PERSNS
            AUTOMX = MAX0(AUTOMX,AUTO(I))
     40     CONTINUE
```

Here we have used another built-in FORTRAN function MAX0. Given a finite set of integer variables such as J1, J2, J3, etc., MAX0(J1, J2, J3) obtains the largest value stored in J1, J2, and J3. For example, if J1=−3, J2=0, J3=−2, then MAX0(J1, J2, J3) produces the value zero. Next we use another DO loop to compare AUTOMX with each value stored in AUTO, printing the corresponding social security number stored in ID whenever a match is found:

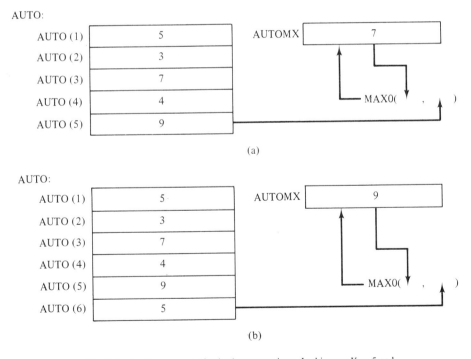

(a)

(b)

Fig. 5.6 (a) The process of pairwise comparison. In this case K = 5 and AUTOMX = 7, the largest value found so far in searching through AUTO(1), . . . , AUTO(4). The MAX0 function selects the larger of the two values stored in AUTOMX and AUTO(5) respectively. (b) Now K = 6, the MAX0 function has compared and found the larger of the two values stored in AUTOMX and AUTO(5) and this has been assigned to AUTOMX. It is now comparing the values in AUTOMX and AUTO(6).

```
            DO 60 I = 1, PERSNS
                IF(AUTOMX.EQ.AUTO(I)) WRITE(6,300) ID(I)
        60  CONTINUE
```

Level 3

The complete program can now be combined.

```
C
C           *** SALES PERSON OF THE MONTH ***
C
        INTEGER AUTO(30),ID(30),AUTOMX,PERSNS
        READ(5,100) PERSNS
C
C           *** CHECK FOR ARRAY BOUNDS VIOLATION ***
C
        IF(PERSNS.GT.30) WRITE(6,400) PERSNS
        IF(PERSNS.GT.30) STOP
C
C           *** WRITE OUTPUT HEADINGS ***
C
        WRITE(6,500)
        DO 20 I=1,PERSNS
            READ(5,200) ID(I),AUTO(I)
            WRITE(6,600) ID(I),AUTO(I)
        20  CONTINUE
C
C           *** AUTOMX STORES THE LARGEST VALUE IN AUTO
C           *** FOUND SO FAR ***                                (5.P1)
C
        AUTOMX=AUTO(1)
C
C           *** DO LOOP CARRIES OUT PAIRWISE COMPARISON PROCESS ***
C
        DO 40 I=2,PERSNS
            AUTOMX=MAX0(AUTOMX,AUTO(I))
        40  CONTINUE
C
C           *** AUTOMX STORES THE LARGEST VALUE IN AUTO
C           *** DO LOOP SEARCHES FOR IDS OF PERSONS FOR
C           *** BONUS BY COMPARING AUTOMX WITH VALUES IN AUTO ***
C
        DO 60 I=1,PERSNS
            IF(AUTOMX.EQ.AUTO(I)) WRITE(6,300) ID(I)
        60  CONTINUE
        STOP
        100 FORMAT(I3)
        200 FORMAT(I9,10X,I5)
        300 FORMAT(1H0,10X,I9)
        400 FORMAT(1H0,20X,23H ARRAY BOUNDS VIOLATION,I5)
        500 FORMAT(1H0,29X,10H ID. NUMBER,10X,12H AUTOMOBILES)
        600 FORMAT(1H0,30X,I9,15X,I3)
        END
```

Typical output obtained from the program is shown on the next page. Notice that the program has found the ID numbers of both salespersons who have sold the largest number of automobiles.

ID NUMBER	AUTOMOBILES
111111111	2
222222222	5
723543299	2
999321002	5
555555555	0

```
222222222

999321002
```

5.4 IMPLICIT DO LOOPS

Let us consider the data input operation shown in the first DO loop of Program (5.P1):

```
        DO 20 I = 1, PERSNS
            READ(5,200) ID(I), AUTO(I)
   20   CONTINUE
```

The data input instruction in the range of the DO loop is the READ statement shown above. Every time the DO loop is executed, the READ is also executed, and every time the READ is executed, the computer starts reading a *new* card. Since a separate data card is prepared for each salesperson, this is a natural approach for this program. Suppose, however, we have an array SCORE into which we want to read 1,000 values. Following the example of Program (5.P1), we use

```
        REAL SCORE(1000)
        DO 20 I = 1, 1000
            READ(5,250) SCORE(I)
   20   CONTINUE
```

Now we must prepare one thousand data cards each containing a single number. This is obviously an enormous waste of time and cards. We can easily put many more than one number on each card. With the above READ arrangement, however, only the first of these numbers on a card will be read and the rest ignored.

What we need is an arrangement in which the READ instruction is executed only once. This will, of course, require a list of variables with a thousand elements in it:

```
        READ(5,250) SCORE(1), SCORE(2), . . . , SCORE(1000)
```

It is impractical to generate such a long list explicitly, element by element. We can, however, use an *implicit* DO loop to generate such a list of variables, i.e., without explicit enumeration as shown above. Such an implicit DO loop can be written as

READ(5,250) (SCORE(I), I=1, 1000)

The implicit DO loop (, I=1, 1000) looks very much like a DO loop except that the word DO is not mentioned explicitly. I acts as the index of this DO loop, whose parameters are as follows: starting value = 1, test value = 1000, and increment (suppressed) = 1. The array listed to the left of the implicit DO loop is expanded element by element by the DO loop. Note that the READ statement is outside the implicit DO loop and is executed only once. The implicit DO loop generates the list of variables for this READ statement. Upon execution of the READ, the computer will continue reading data cards until all one thousand values have been read. Hence we can put more than one value on each card.

The choice of the parameters of the implicit DO loop must observe the same restrictions as those of a regular DO loop. Suppose we want to read N values into the array SCORE where N ≤ 1000. We can use

REAL SCORE(100)
READ(5,300) (N, SCORE(I), I=1,N)

The first number on the first data card must be the value of N. The rest of the values following N must be arranged in the following order SCORE(1), SCORE(2), SCORE(3), . . . , SCORE(N). Note that in this approach, the value of N remains unchecked.

Implicit DO loops can be used with WRITE statements as well as READ statements. The following WRITE statement

WRITE(5,400) (SCORE(I), I=3, 20, 5)

is equivalent to

WRITE(5,450) SCORE(3), SCORE(8), SCORE(13), SCORE(18)

and will print the values of those elements of the array SCORE. Note that this implicit DO loop illustrates the use of a starting value, a test value, and an increment for the index variable. As another example consider

WRITE(5,450) N, (Y(I), X(I), I=2,20,7)

which will print the following list

N, Y(2), X(2), Y(9), X(9), Y(16), X(16)

the general form of an implicit DO loop is

(List of Array Name (Index), Index=Starting value, Test value, Increment)

If we want to read or print *every* element of an array, we can simplify our instruction even further to:

> READ(5,250) SCORE
> WRITE(5,450) SCORE

In other words, when we want to input or output an entire array, we can suppress the DO loops (implicit or explicit) and simply use the name of the array in the list of variables after the READ or WRITE statement.

5.5 SMOOTHING A TIME-SERIES

Problem Description

Suppose the temperature of a system is recorded at discrete instants of time over a given time period. The data obtained from such a recording are called a time-series. The recorded values of the temperature are subject to random observational errors. We want to reduce the effects of these random errors by a three-point averaging technique, called *smoothing*. Let T_{k-1}, T_k, and T_{k+1} denote the recorded values of the temperature at time instants t_{k-1}, t_k, and t_{k+1}, respectively. The smoothed value of the temperature at t_k is then

$$ST_k = \frac{(T_{k-1} + T_k + T_{k+1})}{3} \tag{5.4}$$

Problem Solution

Level 1

First we store the temperature data into an array and then smooth them using Eq. (5.4), storing the smoothed data into another array. Note that Eq. (5.4) is not defined for terminal values of k which we assume to be $k = 1$ and $k = N$. In other words, if the given values of temperature are T_1, T_2, . . . , T_N, then since T_0 and T_{N+1} are not available, Eq. (5.4) cannot be used for $k = 1$ and $k = N$. As is shown below, this peculiarity of Eq. (5.4), unless properly handled, can give rise to bounds violations for the arrays.

Level 2

(i) Declare the dimensions of the arrays used for processing:

> REAL DATA(50), SMDATA(50)

Here DATA stores the values to be smoothed and SMDATA stores the smoothed values. Note that the problem description does not tell us the maximum number of data values to be smoothed and so we have arbitrarily used a dimension of fifty. We can, of course, add this information to our problem description, but in this case, that will be no less arbitrary. The important point is that problem specifications are often incomplete, and the programmer must ask for further clarification whenever necessary.

(ii) Read the exact number of values (NUMVAL) to be processed and check for bounds violations. If a violation occurs, print an error message and terminate execution.

```
READ(5,100) NUMVAL
IF(NUMVAL.GT.50) WRITE(6,400) NUMVAL
IF(NUMVAL.GT.50) STOP
```

(iii) If bounds violations have not occurred, read the values to be smoothed into DATA.

```
READ(5,200) (DATA(I), I=1, NUMVAL)
```

(iv) Since the first and the last values cannot be smoothed by Eq. (5.4), initialize these elements of SMDATA by the corresponding values read into DATA.

```
SMDATA(1) = DATA(1)
SMDATA(NUMVAL) = DATA(NUMVAL)
```

(v) We can now start the smoothing operation using Eq. (5.4). Obviously, we must use a DO loop to pick successive elements of DATA, such as DATA(K−1), DATA(K), and DATA(K+1). However, the starting value and the final value of K, the index of the DO loop, should be chosen carefully to avoid the possibilities of K−1 = 0 or K+1 = NUMVAL+1. In the first case, the arithmetic expression will require DATA(0) and cause a bounds violation of DATA. In FORTRAN the lowest element of an array is its *first* element [i.e., DATA(1) in this case] and there is no zeroth element. In the second case, it will be necessary to use DATA(NUMVAL+1), but nothing has been read into this element of DATA in step (iii) and consequently its use is improper. We can avoid these two problems by fixing the range of values of K to be [2, LIMIT] where LIMIT = NUMVAL−1. The smoothing process in FORTRAN therefore becomes

```
      LIMIT = NUMVAL−1
      DO 50 K=2, LIMIT
          SMDATA(K)=(DATA(K−1)+DATA(K)+DATA(K+1))/3.0
 50   CONTINUE
```

(vi) To verify the proper execution of the program, we can now print out the contents of SMDATA:

WRITE(6,300) (SMDATA(I), I=1, NUMVAL)

Level 3

The FORTRAN program for smoothing a time-series is as follows:

```
C
C          *** SMOOTHING A TIME SERIES
C
           INTEGER LIMIT,NUMVAL
           REAL DATA(50),SMDATA(50)
           READ(5,100) NUMVAL
C
C          *** CHECK FOR ARRAY BOUNDS VIOLATION ***
C
           IF(NUMVAL.GT.50) WRITE(6,400) NUMVAL
           IF(NUMVAL.GT.50) STOP
C
C          *** DATA RECEIVES INPUT TIME-SERIES; SMDATA
C          *** STORES SMOOTHED VALUES OF DATA ***
C
           READ(5,200) (DATA(I),I=1,NUMVAL)
           WRITE(6,300) (DATA(I),I=1,NUMVAL)
C
C          *** INITIALIZE SMDATA ***
C
           SMDATA(1)=DATA(1)
           SMDATA(NUMVAL)=DATA(NUMVAL)
C
C          *** START THREE-POINT AVERAGING ***
C
           LIMIT=NUMVAL-1
           DO 50 K=2,LIMIT
              SMDATA(K)=(DATA(K-1)+DATA(K)+DATA(K+1))/3.0
50         CONTINUE
           WRITE(6,300) (SMDATA(I),I=1,NUMVAL)
           STOP
100        FORMAT(I3)
200        FORMAT(8F10.2/)
300        FORMAT(1H0,5X,12F10.2)
400        FORMAT(1H0,20X,23H ARRAY BOUNDS VIOLATION,I5)
           END
```

(5.P2)

Typical output obtained from this program is shown below:

Original data:

| 3.29 | 2.71 | 0.52 | 1.78 | 2.54 | 4.38 | 3.27 |

Smoothed data:

| 3.29 | 2.17 | 1.67 | 1.61 | 2.90 | 3.40 | 3.27 |

5.6 BASIC SORTING TECHNIQUES

Sorting is an important operation in many data processing applications. In its simplest form, sorting means rearranging the elements of a given set of numbers into a preassigned order based on their numerical values. For example, starting with a set of numbers such as

$$1.25 \qquad -3.17 \qquad 2.94 \qquad 5.71 \qquad 0.05 \qquad 1.57$$

we obtain the following set after some rearrangements:

$$-3.17 \qquad 0.05 \qquad 1.25 \qquad 1.57 \qquad 2.94 \qquad 5.71$$

The numbers in the second set are ordered according to their numerical values in the sense that for every pair of numbers, the one with the higher value is to the right of the one with the lower value. We call this arrangement the *ascending order,* and the process of going from the first set to the second set is called *sorting.*

There are at least three fundamentally different approaches to sorting. In *exchange sort,* whenever a pair of numbers are found not in the ascending order, they are exchanged. In *selection sort,* the largest number is selected and separated from the rest, followed by the next largest and so on, until the smallest one is processed. In *insertion sort,* the numbers are considered one at a time, and each new number is inserted into its appropriate position among the previously sorted subset of numbers. Various sorting methods have been designed based on these three fundamental approaches to sorting. In this section, we describe the simplest sorting schemes in each of these three categories. We caution the reader that although these sorting schemes are simple to program, they are among the poorest in performance and should never be used to sort large sets of numbers (over fifty elements in the set). Better sorting schemes such as Shell sort and Quick sort are discussed in the following chapter. The main reason for discussing these sorting schemes is to compose simple programs using one-dimensional arrays.

5.6.1 Exchange Sort (Bubble Sort)

Level 1

We assume that the numbers to be sorted are stored in a one-dimensional array. To rearrange the numbers in the ascending order with the largest number stored in the highest element of the array, we scan the array comparing the values of two successive elements at a time. If the higher element has a smaller value, we exchange the values. After the first such scan, the largest number in the array is moved into the highest element of the array (the reader should verify this by hand calculations). Each successive scan puts one more number in its proper position in the array. Hence, if there are N numbers, we can sort them completely in N−1 such scans at most. If some of the numbers are already in the ascending order, we need fewer than N−1 scans for complete sorting.

Level 2

(i) Read the numbers in an array called SCORE.
(ii) Scan the array two elements at a time until completely sorted.
   (a) *If* SCORE (K+1) ≥ SCORE(K), *then* increment K by one and continue with pairwise comparison.
   (b) *If* SCORE(K+1) < SCORE(K), *then* store the value of SCORE(K+1) in a temporary storage variable called SAVE, and move the value of SCORE(K) into SCORE(K+1). Next move the value of SCORE(K+1) from temporary storage SAVE into SCORE(K). Increment K by one and continue with pairwise comparison. Figure 5.7 shows an example of the exchange of values described here.

Level 3

We add two details to the scan phase of Level 2 to make it more efficient. First of all, each scan puts one number in its proper position in the array. Thus there is no need to scan the entire array every time since part of the array has already been sorted. The range of the scan can therefore be reduced by one element every time. Secondly, if there is no exchange of data within the array during a scan, the array is completely sorted and we can stop any further scanning. Since the exchange sort scheme is very inefficient to begin with, these added features can perhaps be ignored. They do, however, provide us with simple opportunities for exercising our programming skills as beginners.

Level 4

The scan and exchange phase of the program can be implemented in FORTRAN as follows:

```
LIMIT = LIMIT − 1
EXCHNG = 0
DO 100 K = 1, LIMIT
   If (SCORE(K) .LE. SCORE(K+1)) GO TO 100
   EXCHNG = 1
   SAVE = SCORE(K+1)
   SCORE(K+1) = SCORE(K)
   SCORE(K) = SAVE
100 CONTINUE
```

The DO loop shown above carries out a scan of the SCORE array comparing values of successive elements and exchanging them if necessary. The value of LIMIT determines the last element of SCORE included in the scan and is decreased by one

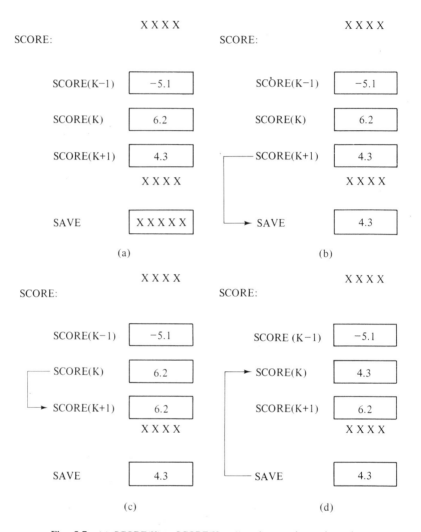

Fig. 5.7 (a) SCORE(K) > SCORE(K − 1) and no exchange is made. SCORE(K + 1) < SCORE(K) and an exchange is needed. (b) The value of SCORE(K + 1) stored in SAVE. (c) The value of SCORE(K) is moved into SCORE(K + 1). (d) The value of SAVE is moved into SCORE(K).

every time a new scan is started. The value of the variable EXCHNG, declared to be an integer variable in the completed program, helps us to determine whether the array is already sorted and no further scans are necessary. The value of EXCHNG is set to zero before a scan begins. Within the range of the DO loop while the scan is in progress, if values are ever exchanged, EXCHNG is set to one. Thus by testing the value of EXCHNG after each scan, we can determine whether any exchange of values took place during the scan. If EXCHNG = 0, then no exchanges occurred and the array is completely sorted.

Level 5

The complete exchange sort program is shown below. SCORE is declared to be an integer array in order to follow the output easily; it can be a real array if need be.

This sorting method is rather inefficient and should be limited to a small number of data values; we therefore selected the dimension of SCORE to be twenty.

```
C
C          *** EXCHANGE SORT ***
C
           INTEGER SCORE(20),EXCHG,NUMVAL,LIMIT,SAVE,NUMSCN
C
C          *** NUMVAL IS THE NUMBER OF VALUES TO BE SORTED ***
C
           READ(5,280) NUMVAL
C
C          *** CHECK FOR ARRAY BOUNDS VIOLATION ***
C
           IF(NUMVAL.GT.20) WRITE(6,400) NUMVAL
           IF(NUMVAL.GT.20) STOP
C
C          *** STORE THE VALUES TO BE SORTED IN SCORE ***
C
           READ(5,300) (SCORE(K),K=1,NUMVAL)
           WRITE(6,351) (SCORE(K),K=1,NUMVAL)
C
C          *** INITIALIZE RANGE OF SCAN & NUMBER OF SCAN ***
C
           LIMIT=NUMVAL
           NUMSCN =NUMVAL-1
C
C          *** BEGIN EXCHANGE SORT SCANS ***
C                                                            (5.P3)
           DO 200 J=1,NUMSCN
           LIMIT=LIMIT-1
           EXCHNG=0
C
C          *** BEGIN SCAN OF DATA ARRAY ***
C
           DO 100 K=1,LIMIT
           IF (SCORE(K).LE.SCORE(K+1)) GOTO 100
C
C          *** VALUES OUT OF ORDER; EXCHANGE VALUES ***
C
           EXCHNG=1
           SAVE=SCORE(K+1)
           SCORE(K+1)=SCORE(K)
           SCORE(K)=SAVE
100        CONTINUE
C
C          *** EXCHNG=0 MEANS NO MORE SCANS NEEDED ***
C          *** GOTO 250 FOR OUTPUT ***
C
           IF(EXCHNG.EQ.0) GOTO 250
           WRITE(6,351) (SCORE(K), K=1,NUMVAL)
200        CONTINUE
250        WRITE(6,350) (SCORE(K),K=1,NUMVAL)
           STOP
```

```
280    FORMAT(I3)
300    FORMAT(16I5/)
350    FORMAT(1H0,12(5X,I5)/)
351    FORMAT(2H0*,12(5X,I5)/)
400    FORMAT(1H0,20X,23H ARRAY BOUNDS VIOLATION,I5)
       END
```

Typical output obtained from this program demonstrates the step-by-step execution of the exchange sort scheme.

*	317	254	-309	752	591
*	254	-309	317	591	752
*	-309	254	317	591	752
	-309	254	317	591	752

Note that the outputs generated by FORMAT 351 are intermediate outputs marked by * and should be eliminated from the final version of the program.

5.6.2 Selection Sort

Level 1

Let us assume that the values stored in the array SCORE, from the $(K+1)$st to the Nth elements, are already in the ascending order. We then find the largest value stored among the first K elements of the array and exchange it with the value stored in the Kth element. This results in the values stored in the array from the Kth to the Nth elements to be in ascending order (see Fig. 5.8). This procedure is started with $K=N$ and terminated when $K=1$.

Level 2

This is essentially Level 1 with a refinement added to make the technique a little more efficient. While finding the largest value stored in the first K elements of the array, we note the location of this value in the array. If the largest value happens to be stored in the Kth element, we skip the exchange of values, which becomes unnecessary in this case.

Level 3

(i) Read the values to be sorted in an array called SCORE.
(ii) Initialize variables.
(iii) Find the largest value in the unsorted part of the array. *If* this value is located in the right place as explained in Level 2, *then* go to step (iv). *Else*

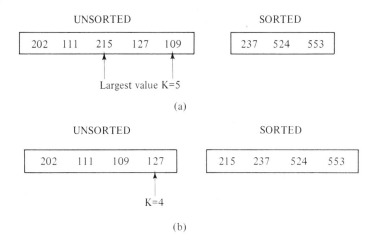

Fig. 5.8   (a) The selection sort. For K = 5, the sorted portion of SCORE
contains 237, 524, and 553. The largest value 215 in the unsorted part of
SCORE is stored in SCORE(3). (b) The value of SCORE(3) is exchanged
with the value of SCORE(5). Now K = 4 and the sorted portion of SCORE
contains 215, 237, 524, and 553.

move this value to its proper position as explained in Level 1 and go to step
(iv).

(iv) *If* the array is completely sorted, *then* print the result. *Else* go to step (iii).

Level 4

```
C
C          *** SELECTION SORT ***
C
           INTEGER SCORE(20),POINTR,SCORMX,NUMVAL,LOCATN
C
C          *** POINTR ALWAYS POINTS TO THE END OF ***
C          *** THE UNSORTED PART OF THE SCORE ARRAY ***
C
           READ(5,280) NUMVAL
C                                                              (5.P4)
C          *** CHECK FOR ARRAY BOUNDS VIOLATION ***
C
           IF(NUMVAL.GT.20) WRITE(6,400) NUMVAL
           IF(NUMVAL.GT.20) STOP
C
C          *** STORE THE VALUES TO BE SORTED IN SCORE ***
C
           READ(5,300) (SCORE(K),K=1,NUMVAL)
           WRITE(6,500) (SCORE(K),K=1,NUMVAL)
C
C          *** INITIALIZE POINTR TC FOINT AT LAST VALUE ***
C
           POINTR=NUMVAL
C
```

```
C               *** SCORMX STORES THE MAX VALUE IN THE
C               *** UNSORTED PART OF SCORE; LOCATN STORES
C               *** THE LOCATION OF SCORMX IN SCORE
C               *** INITIALIZE LOCATN AND SCORMX ***
C
10      LOCATN=POINTR
        SCORMX=SCORE(LOCATN)
C
C               *** SEARCH FOR THE MAX-VALUE IN THE
C               *** UNSORTED PART OF THE SCORE ***
C
        DO 50 I=1,POINTR
          IF(SCORMX.GE.SCORE(I)) GOTO 50
          SCORMX=SCORE(I)
          LOCATN=I
50      CONTINUE
C
C               *** EXCHANGE SCORE(LOCATN)=SCORMX WITH
C               *** SCORE(POINTR) IF NECESSARY. ELSE UPDATE POINTR ***
C
        IF(LOCATN.EQ.POINTR) GOTO 100
        SCORE(LOCATN)=SCORE(POINTR)
        SCORE(POINTR)=SCORMX
        WRITE(6,501) (SCORE(I),I=1,NUMVAL)
C
C               *** UPDATE POINTR TO POINT AT THE END OF THE
C               *** UNSORTED PART ***
C
100     POINTR=POINTR-1
C
C               *** IF UNSORTED PART CONTAINS MORE THAN ONE VALUE
C               *** THEN GO TO 10 & PROCESS THE UNSORTED PART AGAIN ***
C
        IF(POINTR.GT.1) GOTO 10
C
C               *** SELECTION SORT COMPLETE
C
        WRITE(6,500) (SCORE(I),I=1,NUMVAL)
        STOP
280     FORMAT(I3)
300     FORMAT(16I5/)
400     FORMAT(1H0,20X,23H ARRAY BOUNDS VIOLATION,I5)
500     FORMAT(2H0*,12(5X,I5)/)
501     FORMAT(2H0*,12(5X,I5)/)
        END
```

Typical output obtained from this program is shown below, where the intermediate outputs are marked by *:

*	25	-70	52	46	-39	37
*	25	-70	37	46	-39	52
*	25	-70	37	-39	46	52
*	25	-70	-39	37	46	52
*	-39	-70	25	37	46	52
*	-70	-39	25	37	46	52
*	-70	-39	25	37	46	52

5.6.3 Insertion Sort

Consider a set of files in a filing cabinet where each file is identified by a number. We want to sort this set of files by sorting the numbers on them in the ascending order.

Level 1

Assume that the set of files is divided into two parts, the sorted part and the unsorted part. We pick up the first file from the unsorted part and hold it in our hand. Then we thumb through the sorted files and look at the numbers on them until we find the proper position for the file in our hand. We insert the file in our hand into its proper position and repeat this sequence of operations until the unsorted part becomes empty. This method of sorting is called the insertion sort (see Fig. 5.9).

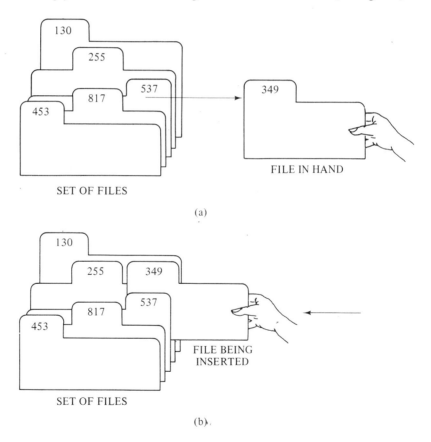

Fig. 5.9 (a) The insertion sort. Files 130, 225, and 537 are already in ascending order. File 349 has been pulled out by hand. (b) File 349 is inserted in its proper position in the sorted portion of the set of files which now contain the files 130, 255, 349, and 537 in ascending order.

Level 2

We store the identification numbers (assumed to be integers) of the files into an array called FILEID. A pointer, called POINTR, is used to point always to the first ID of the unsorted portion of FILEID. The pointer initially points to the second element of FILEID. We transfer the value stored in FILEID(POINTR) into a variable called HAND and make a pairwise comparison of the value in HAND with the values stored in FILEID(K) for K=(POINTR−1), . . . , 1. As long as the value stored in HAND is less than the value stored in FILEID(K), we transfer the value of FILEID(K) to FILEID(K+1). This describes the process of thumbing through the sorted part of the set of files. When the value in HAND becomes greater than or equal to the value in FILEID(K), we transfer this value from HAND to FILEID(K+1). This describes the process of inserting the file in hand to its proper position. We then increase the value of POINTR by one and repeat the entire process until the value of POINTR points beyond the range of data actually stored in FILEID.

Note that the process of going from K=(POINTR−1) to K=1 is, in essence, counting backward. This cannot be done in a straightforward manner by using a DO loop, since DO loops in FORTRAN always count forward. Thus we replaced K by a variable THUMB and set it to THUMB=POINTR−I, where I counts forward as the index of a DO loop.

Level 3

```
C
C          *** INSERTION SORT ***
C
       INTEGER FILEID(20),POINTR,HAND,THUMB,NUMVAL,LIMIT
       READ(5,280) NUMVAL
C
C          *** CHECK FOR ARRAY BOUNDS VIOLATION ***
C
       IF(NUMVAL.GT.20) WRITE(6,400) NUMVAL
       IF(NUMVAL.GT.20) STOP
       READ(5,300) (FILEID(K),K=1,NUMVAL)
       WRITE(6,500) (FILEID(K),K=1,NUMVAL)
C
C          *** INITIALIZE POINTER TO START OF UNSORTED PART. ***
C
       POINTR=2
C
C          *** PICK FIRST FILE IN UNSORTED PART IN HAND ***
C
10     HAND =FILEID(POINTR)
       WRITE(6,450) POINTR
       WRITE(6,475) HAND                                    (5.P5)
C
C          *** SET LOWER LIMIT FOR THUMBING ***
C
       LIMIT=POINTR-1
C
C          *** START THUMBING THROUGH SORTED PART. ***
C
```

```
          DO 50 I=1,LIMIT
             THUMB=POINTR-I
C
C         *** IF PROPER PLACE CF FILE FCUND,
C         *** GO TO 100 FOR INSERTICN ***
C
          IF(HAND.GE.FILEID(THUMB)) GCTO 100
C
C         *** NOT THE PROPER FLACE FCR INSERTION.
C         *** PUSH FILE FORWARD ***
C
          FILEID(THUMB+1)=FILEID(THUMB)
50        CONTINUE
C
C         *** FILE BELONGS TC THE EEGINNING OF SORTED PART
C
          THUMB=0
C
C         *** INSERT FILE FRCM HANC ***
C
100       FILEID(THUMB+1)=HAND
          WRITE(6,500) (FILEID(K),K=1,NUMVAL)
C
C         *** ONE MORE FILE INSERTED. MOVE POINTER FORWARD ***
C
          POINTR=POINTR+1
C
C         *** IF UNSORTED PART IS NOT EMPTY GO TO 10
C         *** AND CONTINUE WITH SORT ***
C
          IF(POINTR.LE.NUMVAL) GOTO 10
          WRITE(6,500) (FILEID(K),K=1,NUMVAL)
          STOP
230       FORMAT(I3)
300       FORMAT(16I5/)
400       FORMAT(1H0,20X,23H ARRAY BOUNDS VIOLATION,I5)
450       FORMAT(1H0,10X,24H UNSORTED FART STARTS AT,I5)
475       FORMAT(1H0,10X,13H FILE IN HAND,I5)
500       FORMAT(1H0,12(5X,I5)/)
          END
```

The following output illustrates the execution of Program (5.P5):

```
     537        255        130        349        817        453

        UNSORTED PART STARTS AT     2

        FILE IN HAND    255

     255        537        130        349        817        453

        UNSORTED PART STARTS AT     3

        FILE IN HAND    130

     130        255        537        349        817        453

        UNSORTED PART STARTS AT     4

        FILE IN HAND    349

     130        255        349        537        817        453
```

```
        UNSORTED PART STARTS AT      5

        FILE IN HAND   817

  130        255        349       537       817       453

        UNSORTED PART STARTS AT      6

        FILE IN HAND   453

  130        255        349       453       537       817

  130        255        349       453       537       817
```

Programs (5.P3), (5.P4), and (5.P5) illustrate the three basic approaches to sorting: exchange, selection, and insertion. These programs are the simplest versions of these sort schemes and are not recommended for sorting large quantities of data. Better sorting schemes based on these three basic concepts are discussed in the following chapter.

5.7 TWO-DIMENSIONAL ARRAYS

A one-dimensional array or vector consists of a string of values assigned to a single variable name. By analogy a two-dimensional array or *matrix* consists of a table of values assigned to a single variable name. A two-dimensional array is used in FORTRAN to store the values of double-subscripted variables or tables of numbers, an example of which is given in Fig. 5.10.

The array in Fig. 5.10 represents bimonthly rainfall data over a four-year period collected at Ranchipur. The rows of the array represent the years and the columns represent the months. Any number stored in the array can be located by its row and column positions. For example, the number 0.3 is stored in the array at the intersection of row 2 and column 3. The array is given the name RAIN, and the elements of

RAIN

COLUMNS

	YEAR	JAN	MAR	MAY	JULY	SEPT	NOV
R	1921	5.7	1.9	0.5	0.5	2.7	3.9
O	1922	6.3	2.5	0.3	0.7	3.1	4.5
W	1923	5.4	0.1	0.4	0.9	2.8	4.3
S	1924	5.3	1.2	0.9	1.5	1.2	3.7

Fig. 5.10 A table of rainfall data shown in the two-dimensional array format.

the array are addressed as RAIN(I,J), where the first index specifies the row location and the second index specifies the column location. Thus RAIN(1,3) = 0.5, RAIN(4,5) = 1.2, and RAIN(3,2) = 0.1.

In order for the compiler to secure enough storage for the array, we use a dimension declaration statement to specify the maximum size of the array being used. For the array RAIN, we can use the following declaration statement:

$$REAL\ RAIN\ (20,6)$$

The above dimension statement specifies that RAIN is a two-dimensional real array with twenty rows and six columns at most. Notice that out of a maximum of twenty rows, the array in Fig. 5.10 uses only four. The extra rows are declared in the event that more yearly rainfall data become available in the future and have to be stored. The indices of a two-dimensional array must conform to the same conventions as the index of a one-dimensional array.

5.8 DATA INPUT/OUTPUT FOR TWO-DIMENSIONAL ARRAYS

Data can be transferred in and out of two-dimensional arrays either in the row or in the column order. Since an element of a two-dimensional array is identified by two indices, we can use two DO loops with the READ and WRITE statements:

```
              INTEGER STOCK (4, 4)
              DO 50 I = 1,4
                  READ(5,200) (STOCK(I,J), J=1,4)
        50    CONTINUE
```

In the example above, STOCK is a two-dimensional integer array with four rows and four columns at most. The rows represent stores and the columns represent items available at the stores (see Fig. 5.11). Thus STOCK (4, 2) = 17 means that there are seventeen items numbered two (in this case, dryers) in store numbered four.

STOCK			COLUMNS (ITEMS)			
			WASHER	DRYER	ICEBOX	TV
			1	2	3	4
R	(STORES)	1	27	30	17	41
O		2	0	0	51	20
W		3	8	0	21	15
S		4	37	17	0	23

Fig. 5.11 A stock table showing the number of items in stock in different stores.

The external DO loop executes the READ statement four times. During each such execution, the value of I, the row index, is held constant and the implicit DO loop on the column index J expands the list of variables. Hence, the data are read in *row order,* one row at a time, and must be supplied in the following order:

STOCK(1, 1),STOCK(1, 2),STOCK(1, 3),STOCK(1, 4)
STOCK(2, 1),STOCK(2, 2),STOCK(2, 3),STOCK(2, 4)
STOCK(3, 1),STOCK(3, 2),STOCK(3, 3),STOCK(3, 4)
STOCK(4, 1),STOCK(4, 2),STOCK(4, 3),STOCK(4, 4)

We can make the data input operation independent of the number of data cards used by using nested implicit DO loops as shown below:

INTEGER STOCK(4, 4)
READ(5,100)((STOCK(I,J), J= 1, 4), I= 1, 4)

In this case we have two implicit DO loops, the one with index J being nested within the one with index I. The READ statement is outside these DO loops and is executed only once. The nested implicit DO loops generate the list of variables for the READ statement. The row index I is held constant, while the column index J is incremented over its range. Thus the data are still read in *row order;* however, more than four data values can now be put on a card. The list of input variables is

STOCK(1,1), . . . ,STOCK(1,4),STOCK(2,1), . . . ,STOCK(2,4), . . . ,STOCK(4,4)

If we invert the order of nesting of the implicit DO loops, we get

INTEGER STOCK(4,4)
READ(5, 100) ((STOCK(I,J), I= 1, 4), J= 1, 4)

The column index J is now held constant while the row index I is incremented over its range. The data are now read in *column order* and the list of input variables is

STOCK(1,1),STOCK(2,1), . . . ,STOCK(4,1),STOCK(1,2), . . . ,STOCK(4,2),STOCK(1,3),
. . . ,STOCK(4,3),STOCK(1,4), . . . ,STOCK(4,4)

In case we have a value for every element of an array as in Fig. 5.11, we can simplify our data input to

INTEGER STOCK(4,4)
READ(5,100) STOCK

Note that in this case the computer reads the data in the *column order,* i.e., the list of input variables is

STOCK(1,1,)STOCK(2,1), . . . ,STOCK(4,1),STOCK(1,2), . . . ,STOCK(4,2),STOCK(1,3),
. . . , STOCK(4,4)

Frequently we use only part of a two-dimensional array for computations. Suppose we want to use only M rows and N columns of the stock array where $1 \le M \le 4$ and $1 \le N \le 4$. We can achieve *rowwise input* of data by

READ(5,100) M,N,((STOCK(I,J), J=1,N), I=1,M)

and *columnwise input* of data by

READ(5,100) M,N,((STOCK(I,J), I=1,M), J=1,N)

Of course, with this approach, values of M and N remain unchecked. If in the previous examples we replace the READ instruction by the WRITE instruction, the values stored in the two-dimensional array will be printed out according to the list of variables set up by the DO loops. For a two-dimensional array, it is often more convenient to print out the values row by row:

```
        DO 50 I = 1, M
          WRITE(6,200) (STOCK(I,J),J=1,N)
    50    CONTINUE
```

The above instructions will print out N values in M rows, i.e., a two-dimensional array with M rows and N columns. Although the use of nested implicit DO loops makes the input process independent of the exact number of data values on a card, a freewheeling arrangement of data on cards can become a serious source of error. Thus, whenever possible, one should put a single row or single column of data on each card. At least data from different rows or columns should not be put on the same card.

5.9 STOCK MANIPULATION

In this section we compose several simple FORTRAN programs using the two-dimensional array STOCK shown in Fig. 5.11. The main purpose of these programs is to familiarize the beginner with row and column manipulations of two-dimensional arrays.

Problem Description I

Find the stock on hand of a given item which is specified by the value of the variable ITEM.

Problem Solution

Level 1

For a given value of ITEM, inspect the stock table and find the total number of that item available in all stores.

Level 2

  (i) Read the value of ITEM and check for bounds violations.
 (ii) Add the numbers stored in column numbered ITEM of the stock table.
(iii) Print the sum.

Level 3

```
C
C            *** FIND STOCK ON HAND CF GIVEN ITEM ***
C
        INTEGER STOCK(4,4),TOTAL,ITEM
C
C            *** READ DATA INTO STOCK TABLE ***
C
        READ(5,100) STOCK
C
C            *** GET ITEM NUMBER ***
C
        READ(5,200) ITEM
C
C            *** CHECK ARRAY BOUNDS VIOLATION ***
C
        IF(ITEM.GT.4) WRITE(6,250) ITEM
        IF(ITEM.GT.4) STOP                                    (5.P6)
C
C            *** ADD ALL VALUES CF THAT ITEM COLUMN
C            *** STORED IN THE STOCK ARRAY IN TOTAL ***
C
        TOTAL=0
        DO 50 J=1,4
           TOTAL=TOTAL+STOCK(J,ITEM)
50      CONTINUE
        WRITE(6,300) ITEM,TOTAL
        STOP
100     FORMAT(16I5)
200     FORMAT(I3)
250     FORMAT(1H0,20X,23H ARRAY BOUNDS VIOLATION,I5)
300     FORMAT(1H0,12H ITEM NC. = ,I3,5X,18H TOTAL IN STOCK = ,I9)
        END
```

To find the total number of TV sets in stock (see Fig. 5.11), we executed Program (5.P6) with the value of ITEM set to 4 and obtained the following output:

```
    ITEM NO. =   4      TOTAL IN STOCK =       99
```

Problem Description II

    For each store, find the items, if any, which are below a critical level and need restocking.

Problem Solution

Level 1

For each item, read the value of its critical level (threshold), and for every store, scan the corresponding row of the stock table, comparing each item in stock to its threshold value. If any item in the store is below its threshold value, print the item number.

Level 2

(i) Read the threshold value for each item.
(ii) Repeat for each store:
   Compare each item in stock with its threshold value. *If* the item is below its threshold value, *then* print item number and amount stored in stock.

Level 3

```
C
C          *** FIND ITEMS TO BE STOCKED ***
C
           INTEGER STOCK(4,4),TRSHLD(4)
C
C          *** READ DATA INTO STOCK TABLE ***
C
           READ(5,200) STOCK
C
C          *** GET THRESHOLD VALUES OF ITEMS ***                    (5.P7)
C
           READ(5,300) TRSHLD
           WRITE(6,350) TRSHLD
C
C          *** CHECK EACH STORE FOR RESTOCKING ***
C
           DO 100 I=1,4
             WRITE(6,400) I
C
C          *** CHECK EACH ITEM IN SELECTED STORE ***
C
             DO 100 J=1,4
               IF(STOCK(I,J).LE.TRSHLD(J)) WRITE(6,500) J,STOCK(I,J)
100        CONTINUE
           STOP
200        FORMAT(16I5)
300        FORMAT(4I5)
350        FORMAT(1H0,10X,21H CRITICAL LEVELS ARE:,4(5X,I5))
400        FORMAT(1H0,15X,16H STORE CHECKED =,I3)
500        FORMAT(1H0,25X,15H RESTOCK ITEM =,I3,5X,16H STOCK IN HAND =,I9)
           END
```

Typical output from Program (5.P7) is shown below:

```
CRITICAL LEVELS ARE:          10          20          30          20
     STORE CHECKED =   1
                    RESTOCK ITEM =   3     STOCK IN HAND =          17
     STORE CHECKED =   2
                    RESTOCK ITEM =   1     STOCK IN HAND =           0
                    RESTOCK ITEM =   2     STOCK IN HAND =           0
                    RESTOCK ITEM =   4     STOCK IN HAND =          20
     STORE CHECKED =   3
                    RESTOCK ITEM =   1     STOCK IN HAND =           8
                    RESTOCK ITEM =   2     STOCK IN HAND =           0
                    RESTOCK ITEM =   3     STOCK IN HAND =          21
                    RESTOCK ITEM =   4     STOCK IN HAND =          15
     STORE CHECKED =   4
                    RESTOCK ITEM =   2     STOCK IN HAND =          17
                    RESTOCK ITEM =   3     STOCK IN HAND =           0
```

Problem Description III

Given the value of a single unit of each item in dollars, find the total value of all items stocked in each store.

Problem Solution

Level 1

For each item stocked in a store, find its value by multiplying the number in stock by the value of a single unit. Add the value of each item over all items stocked in the store to obtain the total value of all items in the store.

Level 2

(i) Read the value per unit of each item for all items.
(ii) Repeat for each store:
        Initialize total value to zero.
           Repeat for each item:

Compute value of the item = (Number of item in stock)*
(Value of single unit of item).
Increment total value by the computed value of the item.
Print store number and total value of stock in store.

Level 3

```
C
C             *** FIND TOTAL VALUE(TOTVAL) OF ALL ITEMS IN EACH STORE ***
C
          REAL TOTVAL,VALUE(4)
          INTEGER STOCK(4,4)
C
C             *** READ DATA INTO STOCK TABLE ***
C
          READ(5,200) STOCK
C
C             *** STORE VALUE OF EACH ITEM ***
C
          READ(5,300) VALUE
          WRITE(6,350) VALUE
C
C             *** FOR EACH STORE COMPUTE TOTAL VALUE ***          (5.P8)
C
          DO 100 I=1,4
              WRITE(6,400) I
C
C             *** INITIALIZE TOTAL VALUE ***
C
              TOTVAL=0.0
              DO 50 J=1,4
C
C             *** COMPUTE VALUE OF EACH ITEM AND UPDATE TOTAL VALUE ***
C
              TOTVAL=TOTVAL+VALUE(J)*FLOAT(STOCK(I,J))
50            CONTINUE
              WRITE(6,500) TOTVAL
100       CONTINUE
          STOP
200       FORMAT(16I5)
300       FORMAT(4F6.2)
350       FORMAT(1H0,10X,20H VALUE OF EACH ITEM:,4(5X,F6.2))
400       FORMAT(1H0,15X,16H STORE CHECKED =,I3)
500       FORMAT(1H0,20X,15H TOTAL VALUE = ,5X,F10.2)
          END
```

Execution of Program (5.P8) resulted in the following output:

```
VALUE OF EACH ITEM:        319.89      217.07      135.00      225.17

     STORE CHECKED =   1

            TOTAL VALUE =          26676.09

     STORE CHECKED =   2

            TOTAL VALUE =          11388.40
```

```
STORE  CHECKED  =    3

         TOTAL  VALUE  =                8771.66

STORE  CHECKED  =    4

         TOTAL  VALUE  =                20705.02
```

In examining the formats of the outputs, particularly for programs using two-dimensional arrays, the reader will perhaps conclude that the use of headings for columns of numbers will produce better formats for the outputs. This is true, but we have kept the formats as simple and straightforward as possible in this chapter. Headings will be used in the next chapter for the outputs of arrays.

5.10 PROGRAM STRUCTURE AND DATA STRUCTURE

Until now, our discussion of data structures such as arrays has emphasized their passive role as containers of numerical values in a program. That, however, is not the only role and not even the most important role played by data structures in program design. Different data structures are created and used in order to facilitate different types of data manipulations required by different programs. Unfortunately, the most advanced data structure allowed in FORTRAN is an array of constant dimension, and hence, other useful data structures must be implemented by the programmer using such arrays.

First of all, let us note that a wrong choice of the underlying data structure can considerably increase the execution time of a program. Consider the basic insertion sort technique discussed earlier. The numbers to be sorted are stored in an array as shown in Fig. 5.12(a). A number to be inserted in the sorted portion of the array is transferred to a temporary storage location [see Fig. 5.12(b)]. It is then compared with each number in the sorted portion in sequence to determine its proper position in an ascending order. However, in order to guarantee that the number can be inserted in the array without destroying any other number, after every comparison, the number in the array is moved to the next higher element of the array [see Fig. 5.12(c)]. These data transfers between the elements of the array do not contribute anything toward sorting; they are needed to prevent accidental loss of data during insertion that may occur because of the way an array is organized. An array is therefore not the best data structure to be used with insertion sort.

Suppose now that the numbers are organized as beads in a chain as shown in Fig. 5.13(a). The chain is so constructed that a bead can be pulled out of it, and the chain restored, without moving the other beads [see Fig. 5.13(b)]. Similarly, a bead can be inserted into any position in the chain without moving the other beads, as shown in Fig. 5.13(c). With such a data structure, all internal movements of data within the structure can be avoided during an insertion sort. Such a data structure, called a *linked-list,* although not available in FORTRAN, is ideally suited for inser-

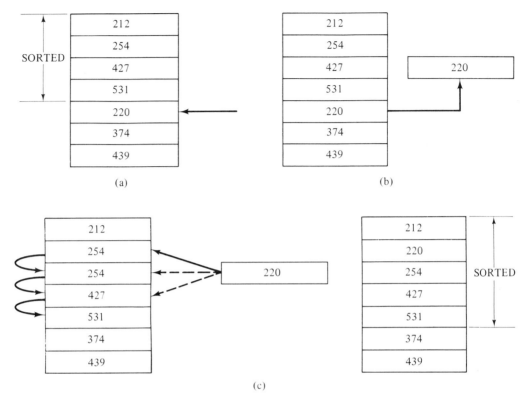

Fig. 5.12 Sequential comparison and insertion of the number 220 in its proper place in the sorted portion of the array. Note the data transfers required within the array before insertion can be carried out.

tion-type operations. A discussion of the construction of such a data structure from arrays is beyond the scope of the present chapter.

Finally, we note that the correct choice of data structures can considerably simplify the resulting program structure. As an example, let us consider the problem of counting the numbers of male and female students in a class, discussed in Chap. 4. For convenience, we repeat the problem description here.

Problem Description

A FORTRAN class has four sections, each section containing some male and some female students. A card is prepared for each student containing his/her social security number, a digit denoting section number (1, 2, 3, and 4) and a sex code (1 for male and 0 for female). We want to determine the number of male and female students in each section.

In Chap. 4 we used eight counters: MALE1, . . . , MALE4 and FEMAL1, . . . , FEMAL4, and a COMPUTED GO TO to implement a multiple branch depend-

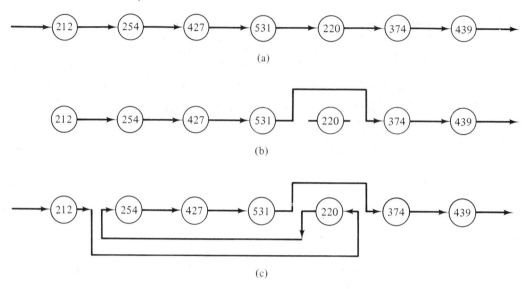

Fig. 5.13 (a) Data stored as beads on a chain. (b) A data bead removed and the chain restored without moving the other beads. (c) Data bead inserted in the chain without moving the other beads.

MCOUNT:

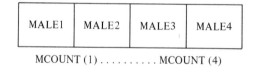

MCOUNT (1) . . . . MCOUNT (4)

FCOUNT:

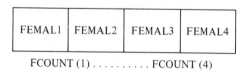

FCOUNT (1) . . . . FCOUNT (4)

Fig. 5.14 One-dimensional arrays used as counters.

ing upon the value of the variable SECTON (section) which ranges from one to four. Now that we have learned about one-dimensional arrays, we can obviously replace each set of four counters by a single one-dimensional array. The male counters are aggregated into a MCOUNT array, and similarly, the female counters are aggregated into FCOUNT. Both these arrays are of dimension four, and each element of an array represents a counter for a section as shown in Fig. 5.14. The use of these data structures for the counters eliminates the need for a multiple branch and simplifies the program structure. The resulting FORTRAN program shown on the next page should be compared with the one given in Chap. 4.

```
C
C             *** COUNTING TOTAL NUMBER OF MALE AND ***
C             *** FEMALE STUDENTS IN EACH OF FOUR ***
C             *** SECTIONS OF A CLASS ***
C
          INTEGER SOCSEC,SECTON,SEX,MCOUNT(4),FCOUNT(4),DEKEND
C
C             *** INITIALIZE COUNTERS FOR ALL SECTIONS ***
C
          DO 20 K=1,4
             MCOUNT(K)=0
             FCOUNT(K)=0
20        CONTINUE
C
C             *** READ A DATA CARD ***
C
50        READ(5,550) SOCSEC,SECTON,SEX,DEKEND
          IF(DEKEND.NE.0) GOTO 500
C
C             *** CHECK FOR BOUNDS VIOLATION ***
C
          IF(SECTON.LT.1) GOTO 450
          IF(SECTON.GT.4) GOTO 450
C
C             *** TEST FOR SEX TO SELECT BETWEEN
C             *** MCOUNT AND FCOUNT. USE VALUE
C             *** OF SECTION TO SELECT PROPER
C             *** ELEMENT OF THE COUNT ARRAY ***
C
          IF(SEX.EQ.1) MCOUNT(SECTON)=MCOUNT(SECTON)+1
          IF(SEX.EQ.0) FCOUNT(SECTON)=FCOUNT(SECTON)+1
C
C             *** GO TO 50 TO READ NEXT CARD ***
C
          GOTO 50
450       WRITE(6,650) SOCSEC,SECTON,SEX
          GOTO 50
500       WRITE(6,600)
          WRITE(6,625) (K,MCOUNT(K),FCOUNT(K),K=1,4)
          STOP
550       FORMAT(I9,2(2X,I1),64X,I1)
600       FORMAT(1H1,50X,28H COUNTS OF MALES AND FEMALES/
         1        1H0,55X,17H IN FOUR SECTIONS/
         2        1H0,40X,12H SECTION NO.,12X,
         3        6H MALES,4X,8H FEMALES)
625       FORMAT(1H0,45X,I1,19X,I3,8X,I3)
650       FORMAT(1H0,23H ERROR IN SECTION VALUE/1H0,I9,2(3X,I1))
          END
```

5.11 EXERCISES

5.1 Each card of a data deck contains a student's identification number and a score. Find the average score in the class and the total number of students who have scored higher than the average.

5.2 Given the individual weights of persons in a population and a threshold value of w, find the average weight of all persons with weights in the range of $\pm\ 10\%$ of w.

5.3 Let X be a n-dimensional vector whose n components are denoted by $x_1, x_2, \ldots, x_n$, respectively. The Euclidean length of X, denoted by $\|X\|_2$, is computed as follows: $\|X\|_2 = (x_1{}^2 + x_2{}^2 + \cdots + x_n{}^2)^{1/2}$. Let Y be another n-dimensional vector; then the scalar product between X and Y, denoted by (X, Y), is computed as follows: $(X, Y) = x_1 y_1 + x_2 y_2 + \cdots + x_n y_n$. The cosine of the angle between X and Y is given by the ratio $(X, Y)/(\|X\|_2 \cdot \|Y\|_2)$. For given vectors X and Y, find their lengths, scalar product, and cosine of the angle between them.

5.4   This and the following sequence of problems all utilize the array RAIN of Fig. 5.10. Read ten years' worth of rainfall data in RAIN and print it out in a reasonable format.

5.5   For a given month, find the maximum, minimum, and average rainfall over a ten-year period.

5.6   For a given year, find the maximum, minimum, and average rainfall.

5.7   Find the years, over a ten-year period, with maximum average rainfall.

5.8   Find the years and the months for the maximum rainfall.

5.9   Given a sequence of integers between 0 and 9 inclusive, we can sort them in ascending order in the following manner: first, we count and obtain n_0 = number of 0s in the sequence, n_1 = number of 1s in the sequence, etc.; then we write a new sequence with n_0 0s followed by n_1 1s, etc. Write a program to sort in this manner.

5.10   Write a program to solve the last problem discussed in Sec. 5.10, where the values of MALE1, FEMAL1, etc., are stored in a *two-dimensional* array. Does this approach simplify the program structure? Does your program account for errors in the value of SEX? (see Sec. 4.6 on error handling.)

5.11   Suppose we are reading data into a two-dimensional array, one row at a time. Write a program that will verify that the data cards are read in their correct order. Each card has an integer number punched in its last three columns that indicates its position in the deck. A card out of order in the deck is printed out and its contents are stored in the appropriate row of the array.

5.12   A computer dating service asks its customers twenty questions requiring simple yes-and-no answers. The yes answers are represented by ones and the no answers by zeros. The record of each customer stores his/her identification number, sex, and answers to the twenty questions. Given a data card containing a sex code and twenty answers, write a program to print the identification numbers of all persons of opposite sex whose answers match at least ten of the answers on the data card.

5.13   A travel agent has information about direct flights available among ten cities. Write a program that can find flights with the least number of intermediate stops between any two cities. Obviously, direct flights are not available among all possible pairs of cities.

6 Applications of Arrays

Arrays are the most complex form of data structures available in FORTRAN and most programs make extensive use of arrays. In this chapter we develop several FORTRAN programs to demonstrate the use of arrays. The first program implements a sorting technique that is more advanced than the basic sorting techniques discussed in the previous chapter. We then discuss the problem of generating sequences of numbers where the numbers are selected at random. This is followed by the implementation of a data structure, called stack, which is used in a later chapter in connection with another advanced technique of sorting. Finally we discuss the well-known problem of the traveling salesperson and the optimization of storage requirements.

6.1   SHELL SORT

Consider the simple insertion sort technique discussed in the previous chapter. In order to find the proper location for inserting file J, we have to compare it with about J/2 other files. For a set of N files, we need approximately $(1 + 2 + \ldots + N)/2$ or $N^2/4$ such comparisons before they are completely sorted. Since we used a one-dimensional array to store the identification numbers of the files, we also needed to move these numbers to make room for insertion. Using arguments similar to those given above, we can estimate the total number of such moves to be $N^2/4$. The time required to sort N files in this manner is therefore proportional to N^2, which increases rapidly with increasing N.

The main problem with this approach is that the file being inserted is moved, in essence, only one position at a time until its proper position is found. In order to speed up the sorting process, we must allow the file to move over larger number of files so that it can find its proper position quickly. Of course, these long leaps must be carefully controlled since our objective is to sort them and not to move them around at random. One such scheme has been devised by Donald L. Shell, and we illustrate this by means of the following example:

FILEID	1	2	3	4	5	6	7	8	9	10	11	12	13	14	15	16	
VALUES AT START	80	17	(88)	56	15	43	48	32	98	76	66	11	58	80	49	61	(A)
AFTER 8-SORT																	
	80	17	66	11	15	43	48	32	98	76	(88)	56	58	80	49	61	(B)
AFTER 4-SORT																	
	15	17	48	11	58	43	49	32	80	76	66	56	98	80	(88)	61	(C)
AFTER 2-SORT																	
	15	11	48	17	49	32	58	43	66	56	80	61	(88)	76	98	80	(D)
AFTER 1-SORT																	
VALUES AT END	11	15	17	32	43	48	49	56	58	61	66	76	80	80	(88)	98	(E)

Sixteen values for the array FILEID are shown above the values obtained by using the built-in random number generator of a hand calculator. First, we group these values into eight groups as follows: [FILEID(1), FILEID(9)], . . . , [FILEID(8), . . . , FILEID(16)]. We then sort each group separately and call this process an 8-sort. The result of the 8-sort is shown above in line B. Next we group these values into four groups as follows: [FILEID(1), FILEID(5), FILEID(9), FILEID(13)], . . . , [FILEID(4), FILEID(8), FILEID(12), FILEID(16)]. We sort each of the four groups separately and call this process a 4-sort. The result of such a sort is shown above in line C. In a similar manner, we carry out a 2-sort and finally a 1-sort where the entire array FILEID is considered as a single group.

Note that the 1-sort process performed at the last stage ensures that the files will be completely sorted. A 1-sort of the values in line D, however, is much faster than a 1-sort of the values in line A, since the values in line D are very close to their proper positions shown in line E. To obtain a better idea of the effects of the 8-sort and the 4-sort, we have divided line C into four segments. Comparing the values in line C with those in line E, we find that 62% of the values are already within their proper segments after the 4-sort. The 8- and 4-sorts allow some of the values in FILEID to take long leaps, as shown by the value 88 in FILEID(3) in line A.

Mathematical analysis of the Shell sort shows that the number of comparisons and moves are proportional to $N^{1.3}$ for reasonably large values of N and approaches $N(\ln N)^2$ as N goes to infinity. The reader should consult *The Art of Computer Programming* (vol. 3, by Donald E. Knuth) † for the mathematical analysis, which is beyond the scope of this text.

There is nothing magical about the 8-, 4-, 2-, and 1-sorts that we used in the example, and we could just as well have used 7-, 5-, 3-, and 1-sorts. The optimum choice of these increments appears to be a complex problem, and to our knowledge

---

†Donald E. Knuth, *The Art of Computer Programming,* vol. 3, *Sorting and Searching* (Reading, Mass.: Addison-Wesley Publishing Co., Inc., 1969).

is yet unsolved. One of the problems is the following: if we subdivide FILEID into a large number of groups at the start, we perform a large number of sorts and thus increase execution time. In our program for the Shell sort, we shall use the following scheme for selecting the increments h_K, suggested by Knuth:

$$h_1 = 1 \tag{6.1}$$

$$h_{K+1} = 3h_K + 1 \tag{6.2}$$

for K = 1, 2, . . . , and $h_{K+2} < N$. For N = 16 we only have $h_1 = 1$ and $h_2 = 4$, since $h_4 = 40 > N$; we therefore need to use only a 4-sort followed by a 1-sort. Applying a 4-sort directly to the values in line A, we obtain

$$
\begin{array}{cccc|cccc|cccc|cccc}
80 & 17 & 88 & 56 & 15 & 43 & 48 & 32 & 98 & 76 & 66 & 11 & 58 & 80 & 49 & 61 & \text{(A)} \\
15 & 17 & 48 & 11 & 58 & 43 & 49 & 32 & 80 & 76 & 66 & 56 & 98 & 80 & 88 & 61 & \text{(F)} \\
11 & 13 & 17 & 32 & 43 & 48 & 49 & 56 & 58 & 61 & 66 & 76 & 80 & 80 & 88 & 98 & \text{(E)}
\end{array}
$$

Now dividing line F into four segments as before and comparing the values in each segment with the corresponding values in line E, we find that 56% of the values are within their proper segments. Considering that we have saved the time required for an 8-sort, this value compares favorably with the 62% obtained earlier.

6.2 PROGRAM FOR SHELL SORT

Level 1

All the intermediate sorts (for example, 8, 4, and 2) of FILEID are carried out by means of the simple insertion sort technique discussed in the previous chapter. However, we need to modify Program (5.P5) to handle the new situation shown in Fig. 6.1. For convenience we repeat the problem description as well as the program solution (5.P5) here.

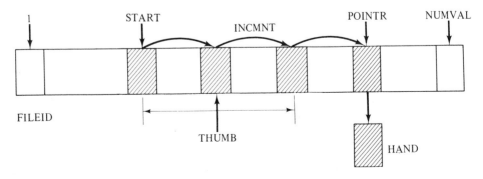

Fig. 6.1 Sorting by the insertion method a group of values in FILEID.

Problem Description

Consider a set of files in a filing cabinet where each file is identified by a number on it. We want to sort this set of files by sorting the numbers on them in ascending order.

Program (5.P5):

```
C
C          *** INSERTION SORT ***
C
           INTEGER FILEID(20),POINTR,HAND,THUMB,NUMVAL,LIMIT
           READ(5,280) NUMVAL
C
C          *** CHECK FOR ARRAY BOUNDS VIOLATION ***
C
           IF(NUMVAL.GT.20) WRITE(6,400) NUMVAL
           IF(NUMVAL.GT.20) STOP
           READ(5,300) (FILEID(K),K=1,NUMVAL)
           WRITE(6,500) (FILEID(K),K=1,NUMVAL)
C
C          *** INITIALIZE POINTER TO START OF UNSORTED PART. ***
C
           POINTR=2
C
C          *** PICK FIRST FILE IN UNSORTED PART IN HAND ***
C
10         HAND =FILEID(POINTR)
           WRITE(6,450) POINTR
           WRITE(6,475) HAND
C
C          *** SET LOWER LIMIT FOR THUMBING ***
C
           LIMIT=POINTR-1
C
C          *** START THUMBING THROUGH SORTED PART. ***
C
           DO 50 I=1,LIMIT
           THUMB=POINTR-I
C
C          *** IF PROPER PLACE OF FILE FOUND,
C          *** GO TO 100 FOR INSERTION ***
C
           IF(HAND.GE.FILEID(THUMB)) GOTO 100
C
C          *** NOT THE PROPER PLACE FOR INSERTION.
C          *** PUSH FILE FORWARD ***
C
           FILEID(THUMB+1)=FILEID(THUMB)
50         CONTINUE
C
C          *** FILE BELONGS TO THE BEGINNING OF SORTED PART
C
           THUMB=0
C
C          *** INSERT FILE FROM HAND ***
C
100        FILEID(THUMB+1)=HAND
           WRITE(6,500) (FILEID(K),K=1,NUMVAL)
```

```
C
C          *** ONE MORE FILE INSERTED. MOVE POINTER FORWARD ***
C
        POINTR=POINTR+1
C
C          *** IF UNSORTED PART IS NOT EMPTY GO TO 10
C          *** AND CONTINUE WITH SORT ***
        IF(POINTR.LE.NUMVAL) GOTO 10
        WRITE(6,500) (FILEID(K),K=1,NUMVAL)
        STOP
280     FORMAT(I3)
300     FORMAT(16I5/)
400     FORMAT(1H0,20X,23H ARRAY BOUNDS VIOLATION,I5)
450     FORMAT(1H0,10X,24H UNSORTED PART STARTS AT,I5)
475     FORMAT(1H0,10X,13H FILE IN HAND,I5)
500     FORMAT(1H0,12(5X,I5)/)
        END
```

```
537          255          130          349          817          453

        UNSORTED PART STARTS AT     2

        FILE IN HAND   255

255          537          130          349          817          453

        UNSORTED PART STARTS AT     3

        FILE IN HAND   130

130          255          537          349          817          453

        UNSORTED PART STARTS AT     4

        FILE IN HAND   349

130          255          349          537          817          453

        UNSORTED PART STARTS AT     5

        FILE IN HAND   817

130          255          349          537          817          453

        UNSORTED PART STARTS AT     6

        FILE IN HAND   453

130          255          349          453          537          817

130          255          349          453          537          817
```

First of all, the sort is started at arbitrary locations in FILEID given by the value of START. We no longer look at successive elements of FILEID while sorting, but at elements set apart by the value of INCMNT. The difference in the values of POINTR and START is some multiple of the value of INCMNT. Finally POINTR cannot be initialized to 2 as in (5.P5), but must start with the value of START +

INCMNT and stop when it goes beyond the value of NUMVAL. Using Program (5.P5) as a guide, we can now write the modified version of the most crucial segment of the insertion sort program as shown below:

```
          HAND = FILEID(POINTR)
          LIMIT = POINTR − START
          DO 50 I = INCMNT, LIMIT, INCMNT
              THUMB = POINTR − I
              IF (HAND .GE. FILEID(THUMB)) GO TO 100
              FILEID(THUMB + INCMNT) = FILEID(THUMB)
     50   CONTINUE
          THUMB = START − INCMNT
    100   FILEID(THUMB + INCMNT) = HAND
```

Comments are exactly the same as in Program (5.P5). Note that within the DO loop, the starting value of THUMB is given by the value of POINTR − INCMNT and its ending value equals the value of START. From Fig. 6.1 we see that this is the proper range of values for THUMB. In addition, every time the DO loop is executed, the value of THUMB is decreased by the value of INCMNT.

Level 2

Now let us consider how we should change the value of POINTR in the previous program segment. From Fig. 6.1, the starting value of POINTR equals the value of START + INCMNT. Its value is increased in steps by the value of INCMNT until it exceeds the value of NUMVAL. This means that we need a DO statement as follows:

```
          DO 200 POINTR = (START + INCMNT), NUMVAL, INCMNT
```

Since, however, arithmetic expressions are not allowed as parameters in a FORTRAN DO statement, we must use

```
          PSTART = START + INCMNT
          DO 200 POINTR = PSTART, NUMVAL, INCMNT
```

Figure 6.2 shows the detailed scheme of a 4-sort of a FILEID containing sixteen values. From this figure we see that the initial value of START is one. It is incremented by one until its value exceeds the value of INCMNT. We can therefore use the following DO statement for START:

```
          DO 200 START = 1, INCMNT
```

The program segment at this level now becomes

```
          DO 200 START = 1, INCMNT
              PSTART = START + INCMNT
              DO 200 POINTR = PSTART, NUMVAL, INCMNT
```

```
            HAND = FILEID(POINTR)
            LIMIT = POINTR − START
            DO 50 I = INCMNT, LIMIT, INCMNT
                THUMB = POINTR − I
                IF(HAND .GE. FILEID(THUMB)) GO TO 100
                FILEID(THUMB + INCMNT) = FILEID(THUMB)
     50     CONTINUE
            THUMB = START − INCMNT
    100     FILEID(THUMB + INCMNT) = HAND
    200   CONTINUE
```

Level 3

All that now remains is to select the proper starting value of INCMNT and to change it sequentially using Eq. (6.1) and (6.2). Using Eq. (6.2) iteratively, we find that $h_{K+2} = 9h_K + 4$. The following statements therefore compute the proper starting value of INCMNT, once the value of NUMVAL is known:

```
            INCMNT = 1
            IF(9 * INCMNT + 4 .GE. NUMVAL) GO TO 40
            DO 20 K = 1, NUMVAL
                INCMNT = 3 * INCMNT + 1
                IF (9* INCMNT + 4 .GE. NUMVAL) GO TO 40
     20     CONTINUE
```

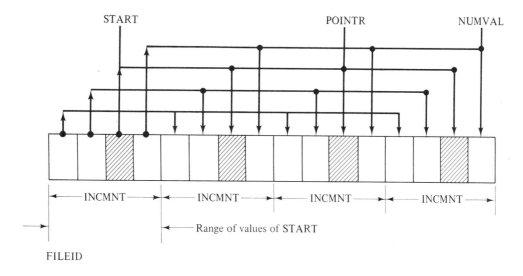

Fig. 6.2   The 4-sort of a FILEID containing sixteen values.

Statement number 40 should be assigned to the next statement in the program. The complete program for the Shell sort follows:

```
C
C          *** SORTING FILEID BY SHELL SORT ***
C
      INTEGER INCMNT,NUMVAL,BOUND,START,PSTART,POINTR,HAND,
     1          FILEID(200),LIMIT,THUMB
C
C          *** FIND TOTAL VALUES IN FILEID ***
C
      READ(5,300) NUMVAL
C
C          *** IN CASE OF BOUNDS VIOLATION GO TO 250 ***
C
      IF(NUMVAL.GT.200) GOTO 250
C
C          *** GET VALUES IN FILEID AND PRINT THEM ***
C
      READ(5,350) (FILEID(K),K=1,NUMVAL)
      WRITE(6,400) (FILEID(K),K=1,NUMVAL,10)
C
C          *** INITIALIZE VALUE OF SHELL INCREMENT ***
C
      INCMNT=1
      IF(9*INCMNT+4.GE.NUMVAL) GOTO 40
C
C          *** COMPUTE STARTING VALUE OF INCMNT. THIS VALUE
C          *** DETERMINES THE NUMBER OF GROUPS INTO WHICH
C          *** FILEID IS SUBDIVIDED AT START ***
C
      DO 20 K=1,NUMVAL
        INCMNT=3*INCMNT+1
        IF(9*INCMNT+4.GE.NUMVAL) GOTO 40
20    CONTINUE
C
C          *** BEGIN SHELL'S DECREASING INCREMENT SORT. START
C          *** POINTS TO THE FIRST FILE OF EACH * GROUP * BEING
C          *** SORTED ***
C
40    DO 200 START=1,INCMNT
C
C          *** POINTR POINTS TO THE FILE IN A GROUP TO BE INSERTED
C          *** IN ITS PROPER POSITION WITHIN THE GROUP. STARTING
C          *** VALUE=PSTART ***
C
      PSTART=START+INCMNT
      DO 200 POINTR=PSTART,NUMVAL,INCMNT
C
C          *** PICK FIRST FILE IN UNSORTED PART OF A GROUP
C
      HAND=FILEID(POINTR)
C
C          *** SET LOWER LIMIT FOR THUMBING THROUGH GROUP ***
C
      LIMIT=POINTR-START
C
C          *** START THUMBING THROUGH SORTED PART OF GROUP ***
C
          DO 50 I=INCMNT,LIMIT,INCMNT
            THUMB=POINTR-I
            IF(HAND.GE.FILEID(THUMB)) GOTO 100
```

(6.P1)

```
                   FILEID(THUMB+INCMNT)=FILEID(THUMB)
50                 CONTINUE
C
C          *** FILE BELONGS TO THE START OF THE SORTED GROUP ***
C
                   THUMB=START-INCMNT
C
C          *** INSERT FILE FROM HAND INTO FILEID ***
C
100                FILEID(THUMB+INCMNT)=HAND
C
C          *** ONE MORE FILE INSERTED. UPDATE POINTER AND REPEAT DO
C          *** LOOP. WHEN ONE GROUP IS SORTED UPDATE START IN DO
C          *** LOOP AND BEGIN SORTING NEXT GROUP ***
C
200        CONTINUE
C
C          *** DECREASE VALUE OF INCMNT. IF INCMNT EXCEEDS OR
C          *** EQUALS ONE, GO TO 40 AND SORT AGAIN. ***
C
           INCMNT=(INCMNT-1)/3
           IF(INCMNT.GE.1) GOTO 40
C
C          *** OUTPUT SORTED FILE ***
C
           WRITE(6,400) (FILEID(K),K=1,NUMVAL,10)
           STOP
C
C          *** ARRAY BOUNDS VIOLATION ***
C
250        WRITE(6,450) NUMVAL
           STOP
300        FORMAT(I5)
350        FORMAT(16(I5))
400        FORMAT(1H0,10(I5,5X)//)
450        FORMAT(1H0,42H ARRAY BOUNDS VIOLATION. NUMBER OF VALUES:,I5)
           END
```

Note that since the Shell sort is more efficient than the simple insertion sort, we have used a dimension of 200 for FILEID. The output statements do not print all the values in FILEID but only every tenth value. This is done to keep the output to within reasonable limits. Yet we do not show any typical output for this program. The reason is that before we arrive at the output, we have to find some way of generating the input data. We need at least a hundred values to perform any reasonable test. The reader may try to generate such a volume of test data using a keypunch machine. We want an automatic method, which is the topic of the next section.

6.3   GENERATION OF RANDOM NUMBERS

In testing computer programs such as a sort routine, it often becomes necessary to generate large quantities of input data. It is quite impractical to generate such large quantities of data by hand using a keypunch machine. Since a computer can produce numbers much faster than a human, we should obviously use a computer program to generate our input data. To test a sort routine, however, we would also like our input data to be random in some sense. Generating numbers at random by a computer program is by no means a simple task. Programs can generate numbers only by using some sort of mathematical relationship, and the numbers are therefore related to each other in an essentially nonrandom manner. To resolve this problem, we have to be a little more specific about what is meant by a sequence of random numbers.

For our purpose, a sequence of numbers is a random sequence, if the occurrence of every number in the sequence is unpredictable to a person who does not know how the numbers are generated. Furthermore, such sequences should pass certain traditional statistical tests of randomness. In essence what we are saying is that it does not matter how sequences of numbers are generated; as long as the sequences satisfy statistical tests, the numbers are selected at random. This is not unreasonable since statistical tests are our only dependable measures of randomness.

It may appear that to pass these statistical tests we need complex mathematical expressions for generating sequences of random numbers. Fortunately, this is not so. For a comprehensive discussion of random number generation, the reader should consult *The Art of Computer Programming* (vol. 2, by Donald E. Knuth) †. The following formula can be used iteratively to generate a set of random *integers:*

$$J_{n+1} = [(A*J_n+C)] \bmod M \tag{6.3}$$

Table 6.1 lists a set of values for A, C, and M and a dozen random integers generated by Eq. (6.3).

Table 6.1.   A typical sequence of random integers

M = 1024;   A = 371;   C = 217
$J_0 = 0$;   A mod 8 = 3
A = 371 > $(M)^{1/2}$ = 32;   M/100 < 371 < M$-$M$^{1/2}$
C = 217;   C/M = 217/1024 = .2119

n	J_n
0	0
1	217
2	635
3	325
4	767
5	115
6	681
7	747
8	657
9	35
10	697
11	539
12	289

†Donald E. Knuth, *The Art of Computer Programming,* vol. 2, *Seminumerical Algorithms* (Reading, Mass.: Addison-Wesley Publishing Co., Inc., 1969).

The choice of values for A, C, and M is critical for the proper functioning of Eq. (6.3) as a generator of sequences of random integers. The value of J_0 can be chosen arbitrarily. The value of M should be large, a possible choice being the largest positive value that can be stored in the computer. With this choice of M, no division is necessary to implement Eq. (6.3). If M is a power of 2, as is frequently the case, then A should be chosen such that A mod 8 equals three or five. The value of A should be larger than $(M)^{1/2}$; if possible, it should be larger than M/100 but smaller than $M - (M)^{1/2}$. The digits in A should not follow any simple regular pattern. When M is a power of 2, the value of C should be odd and the ratio C/M should be approximately equal to 0.2113249. These guidelines for the choice of the values of A, C, and M are obtained from the previously cited reference.

The least significant digits of J_n are usually not very random. It is therefore better to divide J_n by the largest positive number and to convert it to a number in the range [0,1]. Then to obtain an integer value between 0 and N, this value in [0,1] can be multiplied by (N+1) and the product truncated to its integer value.

6.4   PROGRAMS FOR RANDOM NUMBER GENERATION

Problem Description

Generate a sequence of 200 random numbers, each of which lies in the interval [0,99]. Assume that the largest positive integer that can be stored in the computer is $2^{31} - 1 = 2147483647$, the reciprocal of which is 0.4656613E−9.

Problem Solution

Level 1

First we use Eq. (6.3) to generate a sequence of random integers between 0 and $2^{31} - 1$. The values chosen for the parameters are $M = 2^{31}$, $A = 314159269$, and $C = 45381677$; all three values satisfy the guidelines given in the previous section. For binary computers, if the modulus M is chosen as a power of 2, no division at all need be performed; all that is necessary is to clear some of the most significant bits of the product. Because of our choice of M, the value of J_n obtained by Eq. (6.3) and stored in the computer is always less than M and the division in Eq. (6.3) need not be carried out. On occasions when the value of J_n computed by Eq. (6.3) exceeds M, the computer retains only the least significant digits of J_n since the largest integer it can store is $M - 1$. This is equivalent to a division by M except that because of the representation of integers in the computer (i.e., leading bit indicates the sign of the integer), the values of J_n may turn out to be negative. In such cases we add the value of M to J_n and assign the positive sum as the new value of J_n.

Next we divide the value of J_n by $M - 1$ to obtain a real number in the range (0,1). Actually we multiply the value of J_n by the reciprocal of $M - 1$ (only because multiplication is faster than division). Finally this value is multiplied by 100 and truncated to generate the desired random number. The starting value J_0 is arbitrary and is commonly called the seed.

Level 2

The FORTRAN program is straightforward and is shown below:

```
C
C         *** GENERATION OF RANDOM NUMBERS ***
C
      INTEGER SEED,RNDINT,NUMVAL,RNDNUM
      REAL FRACTN
C
C         *** READ THE NUMBER OF RANDOM VALUES NEEDED ***
C
      READ(5,150) NUMVAL
C
C         *** READ ARBITRARY STARTING VALUE AND PRINT SO THAT ***
C         *** THE SEQUENCE CAN BE RECREATED IF NECESSARY ***
C
      READ(5,150) SEED
      WRITE(6,175) SEED
C
C         *** INITIALIZE RANDOM INTEGER RNDINT
C
      RNDINT=SEED
C
C         *** GENERATE RANDOM NUMBERS IN DO LOOP ***
C
      DO 100 I=1,NUMVAL
C
C         *** APPLY EQUATION (6.3)                              (6.P2)
C         *** NOTE: A WARNING WILL BE GIVEN FOR OVERFLOW
C         *** ONLY IN WATFIV, NOT IN FORTRAN G ***
C
      RNDINT=314159269*RNDINT+45381677
C
C         *** IF RNDINT IS NEGATIVE ADD M TO IT
C
      IF(RNDINT.LT.0) RNDINT=(RNDINT+2147483647)+1
C
C         *** COMPUTE FRACTION IN  0,1
C
      FRACTN=FLOAT(RNDINT)*0.465661E-9
C
C         *** COMPUTE AND OUTPUT RANDOM NUMBER IN (0,99)
C
      RNDNUM=IFIX(FRACTN*100.0)
      WRITE(6,200) RNDNUM
100   CONTINUE
      STOP
150   FORMAT(I9)
175   FORMAT(1H0,24H SEED OF THIS SEQUENCE =,I9)
200   FORMAT(1H0,I4)
      END
```

Level 3

Program (6.P2) is a simple random number generator which is designed accord-ing to the guidelines given in the previous section. To our knowledge it is untested, and if the reader is planning to make extensive use of it he should first perform some statistical tests. Knuth, in the work cited previously, † shows a method for generat-ing sequences of random numbers using two random number generators. This method appears to be better than the simple technique implemented in Program (6.P2) and can be considered an improvement on it.

With this method, we use a one-dimensional array called VALUE which stores a sequence of numbers generated at random by one of the random number generators (see Fig. 6.3). The other random number generator is used to select an element of VALUE at random. The value stored in this element is then printed out as part of the sequence of random numbers needed, and a new value is put into this element by the first random number generator. In other words, we are creating a second sequence of random numbers by selecting, at random, numbers from a given random sequence.

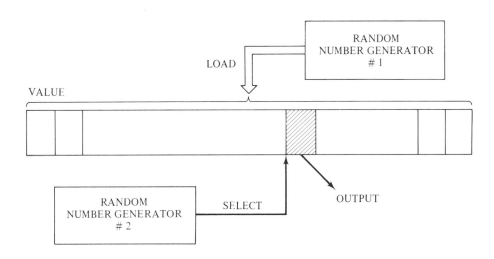

Fig. 6.3 Selecting a number at random from a random sequence.

Level 4

The FORTRAN program for the method discussed in Level 3 is as follows:

†*The Art of Computer Programming*, vol. 2.

```
C
C          *** IMPROVED METHOD FOR THE GENERATION ***
C          *** OF SEQUENCES OF RANDOM NUMBERS ***
C
        INTEGER SEED1,SEED2,RINT1,RINT2,NUMVAL,RND1,RND2,VALUE(100)
        REAL FRAC1,FRAC2
        READ(5,250) NUMVAL
        READ(5,250) SEED1,SEED2
        WRITE(6,275) SEED1,SEED2
        RINT1=SEED1
        RINT2=SEED2
C
C          *** USE FIRST RANDOM NUMBER GENERATOR ***
C          *** TO INITIALIZE DATA ***
C          *** NOTE: WARNINGS WILL BE GIVEN FOR OVERFLOWS
C          *** IN WATFIV, BUT NOT IN FORTRAN G ***
C
        DO 100 I=1,100
        RINT1=314159269*RINT1+453B1677
        IF(RINT1.LT.0) RINT1=(RINT1+2147483647)+1
        FRAC1=FLOAT(RINT1)*0.465661E-9
        RND1=IFIX(FRAC1*100.0)
        VALUE(I)=RND1
100     CONTINUE
C
C          *** BEGIN GENERATION OF RANDOM OUTPUT SEQUENCE ***
C
        DO 200 I=1,NUMVAL                                        (6.P3)
C
C          *** USE SECOND RANDOM NUMBER GENERATOR TO SELECT LOCATION
C          *** OF ELEMENT IN VALUE ***
C
        RINT2=271828189*RINT2+45381677
        IF(RINT2.LT.0) RINT2=(RINT2+2147483647)+1
        FRAC2=FLOAT(RINT2)*0.465661E-9
        RND2=IFIX(FRAC2*100.0)+1
C
C          *** OUTPUT NUMBER FROM SELECTED ELEMENT OF VALUE ***
C
        WRITE(6,300) VALUE(RND2)
C
C          *** REPLACE OLD VALUE IN VALUE(RND2) BY A NEW VALUE
C          *** GENERATED BY THE FIRST RANDOM NUMBER GENERATOR
C
        RINT1=314159269*RINT1+45381677
        IF(RINT1.LT.0) RINT1=(RINT1+2147483647)+1
        FRAC1=FLOAT(RINT1)*0.465661E-9
        RND1=IFIX(FRAC1*100.0)
        VALUE(RND2)=RND1
200     CONTINUE
        STOP
250     FORMAT(I9,6X,I9)
275     FORMAT(1H0,32H FOLLOWING SEEDS ARE USED.FIRST:,I9,9H SECOND: ,I9)
300     FORMAT(1H0,50X,I4)
        END
```

The outputs of neither one of the random number generators described above have been statistically tested. The following simple test can be tried by the reader. Generate 2,000 random values in the range (0,99) and count the number of values in the ten intervals (0,9), (10,19), . . . , (90,99). These counts should be close to 200

for an ideal random number generator. If the reader is not satisfied with the perform-
ances of these generators, he/she can always consult the reference cited and design a
new one.

Let us now consider the problem of testing a program, such as a random number
generator, for possible errors. Since the outputs of such programs are designed to be
random in nature, it is very difficult to detect *programming errors* by inspecting these
outputs. Such errors can only be detected by paying careful attention to the structure
of the program and the individual statements. The best approach is to use the formal
mathematical technique for proving programs correct; these techniques, however,
are beyond the scope of an elementary text in FORTRAN.

As a concrete example, suppose that by error the statement

$$RND2 = IFIX(FRAC2 * 100.0) + 1$$

in (6.P3) is written as

$$RND2 = IFIX(FRAC2 * 100.0)$$

This is quite possible because of its similarity to the assignment statement for
RND1. Then the use of RND2 as an index for VALUE will result in a bounds violation when RND2 equals zero. Such an error may remain undetected for a long
time, even with a check for bounds violations, because of its infrequent occurrence.

Program (6.P4) is an example of how the random number generator (6.P2) output was used to check out the Shell sort program (6.P1).

```
C
C        *** RANDOM NUMBERS GENERATED AND THEN SORTED BY USING
C        *** A SHELL SORT.
C
C
C        *** GENERATION OF RANDOM NUMBERS ***
C
      INTEGER SEED,RNDINT,NUMVAL,RNDNUM
      INTEGER INCMNT,BOUND,START,FSTART,POINTR,HAND
      INTEGER FILFID(200),LIMIT,THUMB
      REAL FRACTN
C
C        *** READ THE NUMBER OF RANDOM VALUES NEEDED ***
C
      READ(5,450) NUMVAL
C
C        *** READ ARBITRARY STARTING VALUE AND PRINT SO THAT ***
C        *** THE SEQUENCE CAN BE RECREATED IF NECESSARY ***
C
      READ(5,450) SEED
      WRITE(6,475) SEED
C
C        *** INITIALIZE RANDOM INTEGER RNDINT
C
      RNDINT=SEED
C
C        *** GENERATE RANDOM NUMBERS IN DO LOOP ***
C
      DO 100 I=1,NUMVAL
```

(6.P4)

```
C          *** APPLY EQUATION (6.3)
C          *** NOTE: A WARNING WILL BE GIVEN FOR OVERFLOW
C          *** IN WATFIV, BUT NOT IN FORTRAN G ***
C
           RNDINT=314159269*RNDINT+45381677
C
C          *** IF RNDINT IS NEGATIVE ADD M TO IT
C
           IF(RNDINT.LT.0) RNDINT=(RNDINT+2147483647)+1
C
C          *** COMPUTE FRACTION IN  0,1
C
           FRACTN=FLOAT(RNDINT)*0.465661E-9
C
C          *** COMPUTE AND OUTPUT RANDOM NUMBER IN (0,99)
C
           RNDNUM=IFIX(FRACTN*100.0)
           FILEID(I)=RNDNUM
100     CONTINUE
C
C          *** SORTING FILEID BY SHELL SORT ***
C
C          *** INITIALIZE VALUE OF SHELL INCREMENT ***
C
        INCMNT=1
        IF(9*INCMNT+4.GE.NUMVAL) GOTO 300
C
C          *** COMPUTE STARTING VALUE OF INCMNT. THIS VALUE
C          *** DETERMINES THE NUMBER OF GROUPS INTO WHICH
C          *** FILEID IS SUBDIVIDED AT START ***
C
        DO 200 K=1,NUMVAL
           INCMNT=3*INCMNT+1
           IF(9*INCMNT+4.GE.NUMVAL) GOTO 300
200     CONTINUE
C
C          *** BEGIN SHELL'S DECREASING INCREMENT SORT. START
C          *** POINTS TO THE FIRST FILE OF EACH * GROUP * BEING
C          *** SORTED ***
C
300     DO 350 START=1,INCMNT
C
C          *** POINTR POINTS TO THE FILE IN A GROUP TO BE INSERTED
C          *** IN ITS PROPER POSITION WITHIN THE GROUP. STARTING
C          *** VALUE=PSTART ***
C
        PSTART=START+INCMNT
        DO 350 POINTR=PSTART,NUMVAL,INCMNT
C
C             *** PICK FIRST FILE IN UNSORTED PART OF A GROUP
C
           HAND=FILEID(POINTR)
C
C             *** SET LOWER LIMIT FOR THUMBING THROUGH GROUP ***
C
           LIMIT=POINTR-START
C
C             *** START THUMBING THROUGH SORTED PART OF GROUP ***
C
           DO 325 I=INCMNT,LIMIT,INCMNT
              THUMB=POINTR-I
              IF(HAND.GE.FILEID(THUMB)) GOTO 340
              INDX=THUMB+INCMNT
              FILEID(INDX)=FILEID(THUMB)
325        CONTINUE
```

```
C
C                    *** FILE BELONGS TO THE START OF THE SORTED GROUP ***
C
                     THUMB=START-INCMNT
C
C                    *** INSERT FILE FROM HAND INTO FILEID ***
C
340                  INDX=THUMB+INCMNT
                     FILEID(INDX)=HAND
C
C                    *** ONE MORE FILE INSERTED. UPDATE POINTER AND REPEAT DO
C                    *** LOOP. WHEN ONE GROUP IS SORTED UPDATE START IN DO
C                    *** LOOP AND BEGIN SORTING NEXT GROUP ***
C
350        CONTINUE
C
C                    *** DECREASE VALUE OF INCMNT. IF INCMNT EXCEEDS OR
C                    *** EQUALS ONE. GO TO 300 AND SORT AGAIN. ***
C
           INCMNT=(INCMNT-1)/3
           IF(INCMNT.GE.1) GOTO 300
C
C                    *** OUTPUT SORTED FILE ***
C
           WRITE(6,400) (FILEID(K),K=1,NUMVAL)
           STOP
400        FORMAT(1H0,29(I3,1X))
450        FORMAT(I9)
475        FORMAT(1H0,24H SEED OF THIS SEQUENCE =,I9)
           END

       SEED OF THIS SEQUENCE =987654321

        0    3   11   12   12   14   19   25   30   33   44   49   52   57   61

            62   65   67   71   71   82   84   84   88   92   95   96   97   99
```

6.5   IMPLEMENTATION OF A STACK

In the previous chapter we demonstrated, using examples, the important role played by data structures in program design. Unfortunately the most complex data structures available in FORTRAN are arrays of constant dimensions. We can implement other data structures by using arrays, although such implementations are not always as flexible as we would like them to be. Arrays in FORTRAN are *static* data structures, i.e., their sizes are fixed throughout the execution of a program. *Dynamic* data structures, on the other hand, can grow or shrink in size during execution, depending upon the demands made by the program. An example of such a dynamic structure is the linked-list mentioned in the previous chapter. Implementation of dynamic data structures by static ones is always cumbersome, since we have to estimate the maximum size before execution begins. However, we have no other choice in FORTRAN.

A stack is an example of a simple dynamic data structure which is central to many aspects of programming in general. Figure 6.4 shows a simple stack. A stack has a bottom and a top, and normally data items are stored or retrieved only from the top of the stack on a last-in/first-out basis. We can think of the bottom of the stack as fixed and the top as moving, in response to demands on the stack. In FORTRAN a simple stack called SCORE that can store five integer numbers at most can be imple-

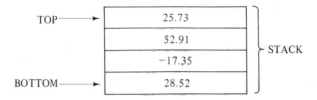

TOP ———▶

25.73

52.91

−17.35

BOTTOM ———▶

28.52

STACK

Fig. 6.4 Example of a stack. Storage and retrieval of data is done only at the top of the stack.

mented by a one-dimensional integer array of dimension five (see Fig. 6.5). The top of such a stack is pointed out by the value of an integer variable, called TOP. When TOP = 0, the stack SCORE is empty. When TOP > 5 we have *stack overflow* and no more values can be stored in this stack. The programs developed below implement the operations of storing and retrieving data from such a stack. These operations are also known as the *push* and the *pop* operations, respectively.

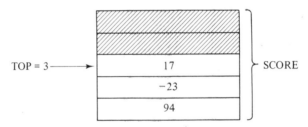

TOP = 3 ———▶

17

−23

94

SCORE

Fig. 6.5 Partially full integer stack SCORE of fixed size (5).

Problem Description

Write a FORTRAN program for pushing and popping integer numbers from a stack that can store forty values at most.

Problem Solution

Level 1

Before pushing a value on the top of the stack, we increment the value of TOP by one. If this value is greater than the maximum value of forty, the stack is full and we print an error message indicating a stack overflow and abort the push operation. Otherwise we store the value in the array at the location pointed to by TOP.

Before popping a value from the stack, we test the value of TOP. If this value is zero, the stack is empty and we print an appropriate error message. Otherwise we retrieve the value pointed to by TOP and decrease the value of TOP by one.

Level 2

```
C          ***CREATE AN INTEGER STACK CALLED SCORE
           INTEGER SCORE(40), MAXTOP, TOP, VALUE
           DATA TOP/0/MAXTOP/40/
C          ***PUSH VALUE ON STACK OPERATION
           READ(5,200) VALUE
           TOP = TOP + 1
C          ***TEST TOP FOR STACK OVERFLOW
           IF(TOP .GT. MAXTOP) WRITE (6,250) TOP
           IF(TOP .GT. MAXTOP) STOP
C          ***IN CASE STACK DID NOT OVERFLOW
C          ***STORE VALUE ON TOP OF STACK
           SCORE (TOP) = VALUE                                    (6.P5)
C ****************END OF PUSH OPERATION
C          ***POP VALUE FROM TOP OF STACK. TEST TOP FOR EMPTY STACK
           IF(TOP LE. 0) WRITE(6,260)TOP
           IF(TOP .LE. 0) STOP
C          ***RETRIEVE VALUE FROM TOP OF STACK
           VALUE = SCORE(TOP)
C          ***DECREMENT TOP BY ONE TO POINT AT THE NEW TOP OF STACK
           TOP = TOP − 1
C ****************END OF POP OPERATION
           STOP
    200    FORMAT(I5)
    250    FORMAT(1H0, 22H STACK OVERFLOW. TOP:, I3)
    260    FORMAT(1H0,20H STACK EMPTY. TOP:,I3)
           END
```

The above program segments are not complete and must be incorporated in other programs that use a stack. A program for sorting and using a stack is discussed in Chap. 8.

6.6   TRAVELING SALESPERSON

Problem Description

A traveling salesperson has to travel to ten cities at most. He/she wants a round-trip tour, visiting each city *once and only once,* and the strategy is always to visit the *nearest unvisited* city. Find the total length of such a round-trip tour.

Problem Solution

Level 1

Since we want a round-trip tour, we can start from any city, say city k. At city k, we inspect a set of distance values from city k to other *unvisited* cities. We pick any one of the *nearest* unvisited cities and move to that one. Then we scratch city k from our list of unvisited cities. At the next city we repeat the same procedure and move again to the nearest unvisited city. When we have no more cities to visit, we return to the city we started from.

Level 2

We now describe one possible method for keeping track of all the unvisited cities and the round-trip tour as it is built up by adding one city after another. We use an array called CITY whose kth element represents the kth city. By definition, if CITY(K) = 1, then it has already been visited. Otherwise, if CITY(K) = 0, the kth city is unvisited. We store the sequence of city numbers in which the cities are visited into another array called TOUR and thus keep track of the round-trip tour being created. We can combine the two arrays into one, thereby saving storage, but we keep them separate for the sake of clarity.

Level 3

We use the following variables in the procedure described below:

(1) CTNUM stores the number of remaining cities to be toured.

(2) CTNOW points to the current city we are in.

(3) NEXTCT points to the city we should visit next.

(4) TOTAL stores the total distance traveled so far.

(5) DSTMIN stores the minimum distance from the current city to the next unvisited city.

The procedure is as follows:

(i) Read the number of cities, distances between pairs of cities, and the city to start from.

(ii) Initialize CTNOW, TOUR(1), and CITY.

(iii) Find the *first* unvisited city from array CITY and set NEXTCT to this one and DSTMIN to the distance between CTNOW and NEXTCT.

(iv) Using array CITY and distance data, find by pairwise comparison the *nearest* unvisited city and store it in NEXTCT.

(v) Scratch current city from the list of unvisited cities. Set CTNOW to NEXTCT and decrease CTNUM by one. Store NEXTCT in TOUR and update TOTAL. If the value of CTNUM (the number of cities remaining to be toured) is greater than or equal to 2, then go to step (iii).

(vi) Update TOTAL, print results, and stop.

Level 4

We use a two-dimensional array called DISTNC to store the distance data between pairs of cities as shown in Fig. 6.6. The (I,J)th element of the array DISTNC stores the value of the distance *from* city I *to* city J. Whenever I = J, DISTNC(I,J) = 0 for obvious reasons. In Fig. 6.6, DISTNC (2,3) = 1E60 represents the fact that city 3 cannot be reached from city 2. Note that although the distance between cities

DISTNC		TO CITY			
	1	2	3	4	5
1	0	10.5	7.2	12.0	3.7
2	10.5	0	1E60	5.0	11.7
FROM CITY 3	7.2	1E60	0	13.5	4.6
4	12.0	5.0	13.5	0	8.7
5	3.7	11.7	4.6	8.7	0

Fig. 6.6 Distance data between pairs of cities stored in a two-dimensional array.

I and J in Fig. 6.6 is the same regardless of the direction of travel [i.e., DISTNC(I,J) = DISTNC(J,I)], this need not always be true.

```
C
C          *** TOUR OF A TRAVELING SALESMAN ***
C
       REAL DSTMIN,DISTNC(10,10),TCTAL
       INTEGER CITY(10),TOUR(10),CTNUM,CTNOW,NEXTCT,START,
      1        FIRST,LIMIT
       DATA TOTAL/0.0/
C
C          *** GET NUMBER OF CITIES TC BE TOURED ***
C
       READ(5,500) CTNUM
C
C          *** CHECK FOR BOUNDS VIOLATION ***
C
       IF(CTNUM.GT.10) WRITE(6,525) CTNUM
       IF(CTNUM.GT.10) STOP
C
C          *** GET DATA ON DISTANCES ***
C
       DO 100 I=1,CTNUM
          READ(5,550) (DISTNC(I,J),J=1,CTNUM)
100    CONTINUE
C
C          *** GET STARTING CITY OF TOUR ***
C
       READ(5,500) START
```
                                                    (6.P6)

```
C
C          *** INITIALIZE VARIABLES ***
C
      CTNOW=START
      TOUR(1)=START
      DO 150 I=1,CTNUM
         CITY(I)=0
150   CONTINUE
C
C          *** SCRATCH CURRENT CITY FROM LIST OF UNVISITED CITIES
C
      CITY(CTNOW)=1
C
C          *** REPEAT PROCESSING SHOWN BELOW AS LONG AS THERE ARE
C          *** UNVISITED CITIES ***
C
      LIMIT=CTNUM-1
      DO 400 K=1,LIMIT
C
C          *** FIND FIRST UNVISITED CITY BY INSPECTING CITY ARRAY
C          *** FOR THE FIRST ZERO
C
         DO 200 I=1,CTNUM
            FIRST=I
            IF(CITY(I).EQ.0) GOTO 250
200      CONTINUE
C
C          *** EXIT FROM DO LOOP AT THIS POINT MEANS AN ERROR SINCE
C          *** THERE SHOULD ALWAYS BE CTNUM-K ZEROES AND SINCE
C          *** K<=CTNUM-1 THERE IS ALWAYS AT LEAST 1 ZERO.
C
      GOTO 475
C
C          *** INITIALIZE NEXTCT AND DSTMIN ***
C
250   NEXTCT=FIRST
      DSTMIN=DISTNC(CTNOW,NEXTCT)
C
C          *** SEARCH FOR THE NEAREST UNVISITED CITY BY PAIRWISE
C          *** COMPARISON ***
C
      DO 300 I=1,CTNUM
         IF(CITY(I).NE.0) GOTO 300
         IF(DISTNC(CTNOW,I).GE.DSTMIN) GOTO 300
         NEXTCT=I
         DSTMIN=DISTNC(CTNOW,NEXTCT)
300   CONTINUE
C
C          *** IF MINIMUM DISTANCE EQUALS 1E60 THE ALGORITHM
C          *** FAILS. GO TO 475, PRINT ERROR MESSAGE AND STOP
C
      IF(DSTMIN.EQ.1E60) GOTO 475
C
C          *** UPDATE TOTAL DISTANCE TRAVELED. ***
C
      TOTAL=TOTAL+DSTMIN
C
C          *** BUILD UP ROUND TRIP ***
C
      TOUR(K+1)=NEXTCT
```

```
C
C           *** MOVE TC NEXT CITY ***
C
        CTNOW=NEXTCT
        CITY(CTNOW)=1
C
C           *** CONTINUE IN DO LCCP UNTIL ALL UNVISITED CITIES ARE
C           *** VISITED ***
C
400     CONTINUE
C
C           *** ALL CITIES HAVE BEEN VISITED. UPDATE TOTAL FOR THE
C           *** RETURN TRIP TO THE STARTING CITY. ***
C
450     TOTAL=TOTAL+DISTNC(CTNOW,START)
C
C           *** OUTPUT RESULTS ***
C
        WRITE(6,600) START
        WRITE(6,650) (TOUR(K), K=1,CTNUM)
        WRITE(6,700) TOTAL
        STOP
475     WRITE(6,725) CTNOW,NEXTCT,CITY
        STOP
500     FORMAT(I3)
525     FORMAT(1H0,32H ARRAY BOUNDS VICLATION. CTNUM: ,I5)
550     FORMAT(5E16.7)
600     FORMAT(1H0,50X,16H STARTING CITY: ,I5)
650     FORMAT(1H0,50X,16H TOUR SECUENCE: ,10I5)
700     FORMAT(1H0,50X,17H TOTAL DISTANCE: ,F10.3)
725     FORMAT(1H0,21H** ALGORITHM FAILS **/1H0,13H CURRENT CITY,
       1         I5,10H NEXT CITY ,I5/1H0,8H CITY = ,10I3)
        END
```

Typical output from this program, with input data given in Fig. 6.6, is as follows:

```
        STARTING CITY:      3

        TOUR SEQUENCE:      3     5     1     2     4

        TOTAL DISTANCE:     37.300
```

6.7 OPTIMIZING STORAGE REQUIREMENTS

In many programs we find that part of the data stored in a two-dimensional array is redundant. For example, in Fig. 6.6 we note that $DISTNC(I,J) = DISTNC(J,I)$ and the array is symmetric about its diagonal storing zeros. In such cases, we can reduce our requirements for data storage by storing the same data without redundancy in a one-dimensional array as shown in Fig. 6.7. In this figure we have stored only the top part of the columns of the two-dimensional array in a one-dimensional array. A value stored in any element of $DISTNC(I,J)$ can be obtained from $DIST(K)$ of the one-dimensional array where

| 0 | 10.5 | 0 | 7.2 | 1E60 | 0 | 12.0 | 5.0 | 13.5 | 0 | 3.7 | 11.5 | 4.6 | 8.7 | 0 |

DIST

Fig. 6.7 Distance data stored in a one-dimensional array DIST after removal of redundancy.

$$K = \text{Min(I,J)} + \frac{\text{Max(I,J)}(\text{Max(I,J)} - 1)}{2}$$

For example, when I = 1 and J = 4,

$$\text{DISTNC}(1,4) = 12.0$$

$$K = 1 + \frac{4(4-1)}{2} = 7$$

and

$$\text{DIST}(7) = 12.0$$

and in a similar manner, when I = 5, J = 2,

$$\text{DISTNC}(5,2) = 11.5$$

$$K = 2 + \frac{5(5-1)}{2} = 12$$

and

$$\text{DIST}(12) = 11.5$$

Note that if the dimension of the two-dimensional array is N, the dimension of the one-dimensional array shown in Fig. 6.7 is N(N + 1)/2.

6.8 EXERCISES

6.1 Write a program for *bucket sorting* as explained below.
DATA denotes an array of integer numbers to be sorted.

DATA: 17   60   31   25   08   50   21   37   55   34
            48   18   61   07   05

A *BUCKET* is a *two-dimensional array* with rows numbered from 0 to 9. If the least significant digit of the value stored in DATA(K) is d_i, we put this value in the ith row of BUCKET. The figure below shows the nonempty rows of BUCKET.

Row

0	60	50	
1	31	21	61
4	34		
5	25	55	05
7	17	37	07
8	08	48	18

We now take the values from the rows of BUCKET and put them back in DATA with the $(i + 1)$st row following the ith row:

DATA:	60	50	31	21	61	34	25	55	05	17
			37	07	08	48	18			

We repeat the same procedure except that if the next most significant digit of the value in DATA(K) is d_i, we put this value in the ith row of BUCKET. The figure below shows the nonempty rows of BUCKET.

Row

0	05	07	08
1	17	18	
2	21	25	
3	31	34	37
4	48		
5	50	55	
6	60	61	

Again we take the values from the rows of BUCKET and put them back in DATA as before:

DATA: 05   07   08   17   18   21   25   31   34   37
                  48   50   55   60   61

As can be seen from the above, the values in DATA are all sorted.

6.2 For N cities, let $d_{i,j}$ denote the distance from city i to city j. We want to find the shortest routes from every city to city N. Let $f_{k,i}$ denote the distance of the shortest route from city i to city N *passing via at most k cities*. Then

$$f_{k,i} = \frac{\text{Min}}{j}\,(d_{i,j} + f_{(k-1),j})$$

and $f_{0,i} = d_{i,N}$. Write a program to find the shortest routes.

6.3 In a multiple-choice test, there are five questions and each question is followed by four probable answers. The correct answer is marked by a one and the wrong answers are marked by zeros. This information can be stored in a two-dimensional array as shown below.

· Questions

		1	2	3	4	5
A	1	0	1	0	0	1
n						
s	2	0	0	1	0	0
w						
e	3	1	0	0	0	0
r						
s	4	0	0	0	1	0

The answers given by a student are punched in data cards; a typical data card is shown below.

Question Number	Answer Marked by Student
3	0 0 1 0

Each correct answer adds 10 and each wrong answer subtracts 5 from a student's total score. If a student does not answer a question at all, then the data card corresponding to that question contains only zeros for answers. In this case, 2 is subtracted from his total score. Write a program to compute a student's total score in such a test.

6.4 When two sequences of numbers in ascending order are combined to form a single sequence such that the new sequence is also in ascending order, the process of combination is called *merging*. For example,

$$\text{Sequence X:} \quad -2, \ 0, \ 3, \ 7, \ 9$$
$$\text{Sequence Y:} \quad -1, \quad 4, \ 5, \ 11, \ 16$$
$$\text{Merged Sequence Z:} \quad -2, \ -1, \ 0, \ 3, \ 4, \ 5, \ 7, \ 9, \ 11, \ 16$$

Write a FORTRAN program to implement the following procedure for a two-way merging scheme:

(i) Initialize variables i, j, and k to one.

(ii) If $X_i > Y_j$, then go to step (v).

(iii) Set $Z_k = X_i$ and increment i and k by one. If i is less than or equal to the number of elements in X, then go to step (ii).

(iv) Transfer all the remaining values in Y into Z, starting at Z_k, and stop.

(v) Set $Z_k = Y_j$ and increment j and k by one. If j is less than or equal to the number of elements in Y, then go to step (ii).

(vi) Transfer all the remaining values in X into Z, starting at Z_k, and stop.

6.5 Consider a collection of cities such that every city in the collection is directly connected by air or by road (but not by both) to some of the other cities. The road connections are given by a two-dimensional array called ROAD such that if there is a direct road connection from city I to city J, then ROAD(I,J) = 1, else ROAD(I,J) = 0. A similar two-dimensional array called AIR gives the air connections between pairs of cities. Given cities I and J, compute the total number of ways of traveling from city I to city J, passing through at most one other city, such that the first part of the journey is by air and the second part is by road. (*Hint:* Compute the matrix product AIR * ROAD.)

6.6 With the data given in array ROAD, write a program to output all possible ways of traveling from city I to city J by road only and the route that goes through the least number of intermediate cities. Note that it may be impossible to go from city I to city J by roads alone. The program should terminate with an appropriate message if the same intermediate city shows up a second time during the search.

6.7 Write a program to simulate the random drawing of a card from a deck of cards. The card deck can be represented as shown below.

	A	1	2	3	4	5	6	7	8	9	10	J	Q	K
Spades	A	1	2	3	4	5	6	7	8	9	10	J	Q	K
Clubs	.													.
Diamonds	.													.
Hearts	.	.	.	.	.	.	.	.	.	.	.	.	.	.

6.8 Write a program to shuffle such a deck of cards and output the contents of the shuffled deck. Note that in a shuffled deck, the rows as well as the columns are mixed up. Is the above data structure sufficient for representing a shuffled deck?

6.9 Write a program to simulate the random throw of a pair of dice and print the sum of the dots that show up.

6.10 Suppose a shuffled deck of cards is represented by the data structure shown below

Suit	H	S	H	C	D	D	. . . .
Value	10	3	J	5	A	3	

where H, S, C, and D represent Hearts, Spades, Clubs, and Diamonds, respectively. How do we sort this deck so that the suits will be in the S, C, D, and H order, and within each suit, the cards will be in the order shown in Exercise 6.7?

7 Subprograms

A subprogram, as the name implies, is a program that can be used as a building block for writing a larger and more complex program. In FORTRAN, a subprogram is essentially a collection of executable FORTRAN statements identified as a single unit by a unique name attached to it. The FORTRAN statements implement some numerical procedure in its entirety, and the user of a subprogram can use this procedure simply by calling its name in an appropriate manner.

There are two important reasons for using subprograms. First of all, many programs are frequently utilized by many different users — for example, programs for sorting, statistical computations, solutions of equations, and vector/matrix manipulations. In this situation, it is reasonable to code these programs as subprograms and store them in a library to be shared by all users. This approach saves a user the effort of generating commonly used code from scratch. Secondly, it is difficult to develop and code a large and complex program as a single unit. The effort is considerably reduced if the large program is decomposed into modules and each module is coded and tested separately as a subprogram. The complete program is then generated by statements that link together these subprograms by calling them in a sequence dictated by the logic of the larger program.

In FORTRAN, a subprogram may call, or invoke, another subprogram during its execution. A chain of such calls may link together several subprograms at any point during execution. A subprogram cannot, however, call itself directly or indirectly through a chain of other subprograms. A program that calls another program is called a *calling program*. A program that calls other subprograms, but is never called by any other program, is commonly called a *main program*.

In FORTRAN we have two classes of subprograms: the *function subprograms* and the *subroutines*. The main characteristic of a function is that it has a value, and according to our definition in Chap. 2, a function is simply the name of a procedure that computes a value for it. Such procedures for computing values of functions, written as FORTRAN programs and identified by unique names, are called function subprograms and return the calculated value via the name of the function subprogram.

Subroutines, on the other hand, are different from functions in that they do not return a single value via the name of the subroutine, but rather, all interactions occur through parameters passed via argument lists. Other than that, they are also complete procedures for processing data in FORTRAN identified by unique names. These names are merely identifying labels with no values attached to them.

7.1 BUILT-IN FUNCTIONS

Functions in algebra and trigonometry and some special purpose functions commonly used in numerical computations are provided in FORTRAN as built-in functions. Examples of such functions are: ABS, SQRT, EXP, SIN, COS, AMAX1, AMIN1, IFIX, FLOAT, and MOD; a partial list is given in Table 7.1. The reader should consult his/her computer installation to obtain a complete list of such built-in FORTRAN functions.

The built-in FORTRAN procedures for computing the value of any of these functions can be invoked, at any point within an executable FORTRAN statement, by using the name of the function followed by an appropriate list of variables within parentheses. For example,

SQRT(DATA)
and   EXP(TIME)

will invoke the square root and the exponential functions, respectively, with DATA and TIME as input variables. Simple variable names can be replaced by arithmetic expressions when appropriate; for example,

SQRT(A**2 + B**2)
EXP(– TIME/CONST)

For our purpose it is useful to note that most FORTRAN built-in functions accept either real or integer input variables but not both, and the computed function value is of the same type as the type of the input variables. For example, the SQRT function accepts only real variables or real mathematical expressions as input. AMAX1 accepts only real input variables, while MAX0 accepts only integer variables.

Some built-in functions do provide a change of type going from the input to the output value. Arithmetic expressions used as inputs to built-in functions may use built-in functions; for example,

SQRT(ABS(VALUE1 – VALUE2))
SQRT(SQRT(ABS(DATA)))

Array elements can be used as input variables to built-in functions; for example,

AMAX1(DATA(2), DATA(4), DATA(6))

Table 7.1   Partial list of built-in functions in FORTRAN

Function	Name	Type of	
		Input Variable(s)	*Output Value*
Absolute value	ABS	Real	Real
	IABS	Integer	Integer
Square root	SQRT	Real	Real
Exponential	EXP	Real	Real
Natural logarithm	ALOG	Real	Real
Common logarithm	ALOG10	Real	Real
Sine	SIN	Real	Real
Cosine	COS	Real	Real
Tangent	TAN	Real	Real
Largest value	MAX0	Integer	Integer
	AMAX1	Real	Real
	AMAX0	Integer	Real
	MAX1	Real	Integer
Smallest value	MIN0	Integer	Integer
	AMIN1	Real	Real
	AMIN0	Integer	Real
	MIN1	Real	Integer
Type conversion	INT or IFIX	Real	Integer
	FLOAT	Integer	Real
Remainder function	MOD	Integer	Integer
	AMOD	Real	Real

Logically we may think of a built-in function as being evaluated at the point of its invocation in a FORTRAN statement and ignore the specific mechanism used to link with the function.

7.2   STATEMENT FUNCTIONS

Recall that in Chap. 2, while introducing the concept of a function, we said that a function is defined by a mathematical expression which is used to compute its value. This is not the most general definition of a function but a very useful one. Statement functions in FORTRAN are examples of functions that satisfy our rather limited definition of a function. The general form of the *defining statement* of a statement function in FORTRAN is as follows:

Name of function (list of input variables) = Any logical or arithmetic expression
involving the input variables.

The name of a statement function must satisfy the same conventions satisfied by FORTRAN variable names and can be declared to be either integer or real. The variables listed as input variables are *local* to a statement function and are used only to evaluate the expression used to compute the value of the function. The same variable names can be used in the rest of the program with no implied relationship to the variables in the defining statement of a statement function, but it is better and clearer not to do so. The defining statement of a statement function is placed before the first executable statement of the program that uses it. The expression may use any variable defined in the program itself, built-in functions, and other statement functions *defined earlier*. A statement function must have at least one input variable and cannot use subscripted variables in its defining statement. Examples of statement functions are shown below:

POLY(A, B, C, X) = A * X ** 2 + B * X + C
RANGE(A, B, C) = AMAX1(A, B, C) − AMIN1(A, B, C)
AREA(RADIUS) = 3.14159 * RADIUS ** 2

The following is an example of a statement function that employs a variable (BONUS) created in the program that uses it:

PAY(HOURS, RATE) = HOURS * RATE + BONUS

We would like to caution the reader about problems that may be created by defining statement functions the way we defined PAY above. This statement function uses BONUS without explicitly listing it as an input variable. If at a later time when PAY is being used in a program, the programmer forgets to assign proper values to BONUS, incorrect results will be computed. Note that the function PAY(HOURS, RATE) does not warn the programmer that another variable BONUS is involved in the computation. This is a trivial example of a hidden interaction at the data level which is a poor programming technique. A better way to define PAY is

PAY(HOURS, RATE, BONUS) = HOURS * RATE + BONUS

An example of a statement that uses another statement function defined earlier is the following:

AREA(WIDTH, LENGTH) = WIDTH * LENGTH
VOLUME(HEIGHT, WIDTH, LENGTH) = HEIGHT * AREA(WIDTH, LENGTH)

Finally, we give an example of a statement function whose type is declared by a type declaration statement:

REAL LIGHT
LIGHT(WEGHT1, WEGHT2, WEGHT3) = AMIN1(WEGHT1, WEGHT2, WEGHT3)

Once a statement function has been defined, it can be used in the subsequent program like a built-in function. For example, suppose we want to compute the mean, the variance, and the standard deviation of twenty numbers, with appropriate rounding taking place. The following program using the statement function ROUND can do that.

```
C
C           *** PROGRAM TO DETERMINE THE MEAN, VARIANCE,
C           *** AND THE STANDARD DEVIATION OF 200
C           *** NUMBERS READ IN, AND
C           *** SUMMED IN SUM ***
C
      REAL  SUM,SUM2,MEAN,VAR,STD,VALUE
C
C           *** DEFINE STATEMENT FUNCTION ROUND(G,N)
C           *** WHERE G IS THE DUMMY ARGUMENT THAT
C           *** IS TO BE ROUNDED, AND N IS THE DUMMY
C           *** ARGUMENT THAT INDICATES THE NUMBER OF
C           *** DECIMAL PLACES WHERE THE
C           *** ROUNDING IS TO TAKE PLACE
C
      ROUND(G,N)=G+(0.5*0.1**N)*(G/ABS(G))
C
C           *** EXAMPLE OF ROUNDING
C           ***   N=0      0.5*0.1**N=0.5
C           ***    =1                =0.05
C           ***    =2                =0.005
C           ***    =3                =0.0005
C           ***
C
      SUM=0.0
      SUM2=0.0
C
C           *** READ THE NUMBERS, ACCUMULATING THE SUM
C           *** AND THE SUM SQUARED
C
      DO 100 K=1,20
        READ(5,500) VALUE
        SUM=SUM+VALUE
        SUM2=SUM2+VALUE**2
100   CONTINUE
C
C           *** CALCULATE MEAN VARIANCE AND STANDARD
C           *** DEVIATIONS WITH APPROPRIATE ROUNDING
C
      MEAN=SUM/20.
      VAR=SUM2/20.-MEAN**2
      STD=ROUND(SQRT(VAR),2)
      MEAN=ROUND(MEAN,2)
      VAR=ROUND(VAR,2)
C
C        *** FINALLY ADJUST THE ROUNDED RESULT
C
      WRITE(6,550) MEAN,VAR,STD
      STOP
500   FORMAT(F10.0)
550   FORMAT(1H ,3(F10.2,5X))
      END
```

(7.P1)

The above program shows the following points about the use of statement functions in a program:

(i) Statement functions must be defined before the first executable statement of the program that uses it.

(ii) Statement functions are invoked, like built-in functions, by using their names followed by an appropriate list of variables.

(iii) The list of variables used at the point of invocation, in this case (SQRT(VAR),2), establishes a one-to-one correspondence with the variables listed in the definition (G,N). When we used (MEAN,2) at the point of invocation, ROUND computed the value of

$$MEAN + (0.5 * 0.1 ** 2) * (MEAN/ABS(MEAN))$$

(iv) The numbers and the types of the variables in both lists must match.

(v) Although the defining statement of a statement function cannot use array elements, it can be invoked with array elements in the list of input variables.

Statement functions, like built-in functions, can also be used as subexpressions in more complex arithmetic expressions; for example,

ROOT(A,B,C) = (−B+SQRT(B ** 2 −4.0 * A * C))/(2.0 * A)
PROD = ROOT (X(1), 3.0, W+1.0) * ROOT (X(I), 4.0, W+2.0)

7.3 FUNCTION SUBPROGRAMS

In general, a function is a name that identifies a procedure for computing its value. In FORTRAN, such functions are implemented as function subprograms and compiled separately from the programs that use them. Function subprograms are invoked by using their names followed by appropriate lists of input variables. Control then passes to the subprogram invoked, which computes the value of the function. At the termination of this computation, the value of the function is returned along with the control back to the point of invocation. Figure 7.1 describes this sequence of transfers. The program invoking a function subprogram is normally called a calling program. A program that invokes other subprograms, but is never invoked by any other program, is often called a main program.

The general form of the *defining statement* of a function subprogram is as follows:

[Type] FUNCTION Name of function (list of input variables)

The key word FUNCTION in the defining statement of a function subprogram identifies it as a function subprogram. The name of a function subprogram must satisfy

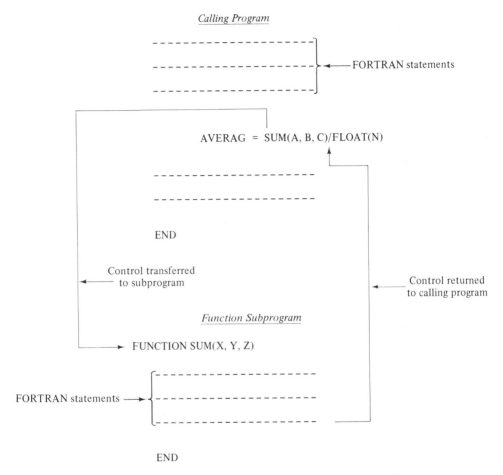

Fig. 7.1 The sequence of transfers involved in the invocation of a function subprogram.

the same conventions satisfied by FORTRAN variable names and can be declared to be either INTEGER or REAL. The optional type statement shown above is used for the explicit declaration of the type of the name of the function. The list of input variables serves the same purpose here as in the case of statement functions. This list, also called a list of parameters, may contain names of simple variables, arrays, and other functions, but not constants or subscripted variables.

The defining statement of a function subprogram is followed by other FOR-TRAN statements which implement the procedure for computing the value of the function. Since logically a function subprogram must return a value, it does not make sense to terminate the execution of a function subprogram with the STOP statement. Instead, when the value has been computed, we execute a RETURN statement to return the value and the control to the main program. Of course, if for any reason the subprogram cannot correctly compute the function value, it must take some special action. The simplest thing to do is to return some improbable number as the value of the function. It is then left up to the main program to verify the proper execution of the subprogram by testing this value. An example of a simple function subprogram that rounds at the appropriate decimal position (see previous section) is the following:

```
        REAL FUNCTION ROUND (G,N)
C
C   ***THE FUNCTION ROUND ROUNDS THE INPUT
C   ***VARIABLE G AT DECIMAL POSITION GIVEN BY N
C
C   ***FOR EXAMPLE
C   ***N=0                          0.5*0.1**N=0.5
C   ***  =1                                  =0.05
C   ***  =2                                  =0.005
C   ***  =3                                  =0.0005
        REAL G
        INTEGER N
        ROUND = G + (0.5 * 0.1 ** N) + (G/ABS(G))
        RETURN
        END
```

Another example of a function subprogram which includes a check on the validity of the input variables is a subprogram for computing the average of test scores.

```
        REAL FUNCTION AVRAGE(SCORES,TESTS)
C          ***FIND AVERAGE SCORE FROM A GIVEN
C          ***NUMBER OF TEST SCORES
        REAL SCORES(50),TOTAL
        INTEGER TESTS
C          ***CHECK FOR BOUNDS VIOLATION.GO TO 200
C          ***AND RETURN IMPROPER VALUE FOR AVRAGE
        IF(TESTS .GT. 50)GO TO 200
        IF(TESTS .GT. 1)GO TO 200
C          ***INITIALIZE TOTAL SCORE TO ZERO
        TOTAL=0.0
C          ***SUM THE VALUES IN SCORES AND STORE IN TOTAL
        DO 100 K=1,TESTS
            TOTAL=TOTAL+SCORES(K)
100     CONTINUE
C          ***COMPUTE AVERAGE SCORE AND RETURN NORMALLY
        AVRAGE=TOTAL/FLOAT(TESTS)
        RETURN
C          ***BOUNDS VIOLATION DETECTED.SET AVRAGE
C          ***TO A NEGATIVE VALUE AND RETURN
200     AVRAGE=-1.0
        RETURN
        END
```

The name of this function subprogram is AVRAGE, and to avoid any misunderstanding as to its type, we have explicitly declared it to be real. The function computes an average score from a given set of test scores. The test scores are stored in SCORES and the number of tests is given as the value of TESTS. Thus SCORES and TESTS are listed as input variables or parameters.

Since SCORES is an array, its dimension is declared in the statement REAL SCORES (50),TOTAL. The method of computing the average score should be obvious. Note that the subprogram *uses its name as a variable* for storing the value of the average score to be returned to the main program.

The subprogram checks the value of TESTS against the specified dimension of SCORES for possible array bounds violations. If no such violation occurs, the value of average score is computed and a *normal* return takes place via the first RETURN statement in the subprogram. Otherwise statement 200 sets the value of AVRAGE to − 1.0 (an improbable value for an average test score) and an *abnormal* return takes place via the second RETURN statement. Note that the two RETURN statements are identical in their effects; it is only the logic of the program that imparts the labels of normal and abnormal returns to them.

Of course, this test for the array bounds violation can be left out of the subprogram on the assumption that it will be carried out by the calling program before it invokes the subprogram. Since, however, a subprogram can be used by different users, and because errors in data or the main program can occur, it is perhaps safer to carry out such a test in the subprogram itself.

Since SCORES is an array, we have declared its dimension in a type declaration statement. The question naturally arises as to how we select the values to be used for declaring dimensions of arrays in subprograms. Our choice of the number fifty in this case is completely arbitrary, and we could have used forty or sixty or any other number. As we shall see in the following chapter, in the top-down, modular approach to program development, the calling program dictates the functions and the structures of subprograms. We shall therefore be able to use the dimension declarations in the calling program as our guides for declaring the dimensions in a subprogram.

According to the rules of standard FORTRAN, the dimensions of arrays in a subprogram must be identical to the dimensions of the corresponding arrays in the calling program. Suppose, however, that we are writing a subprogram that may be used by different users. We have no way of knowing the values that will be used in dimensioning arrays by these users. The problems of dimensioning in such a situation can be solved by using *variable dimensions* in subprograms, discussed in a later section.

In both these subprograms, it has been rather simple to select an improper value for return when the correct value could not be computed. In general, however, this may not be so. One approach is to use special variables in the list of input variables whose values can be set by the subprogram to denote various error conditions. The main program assigns arbitrary values to these special variables at the point of invocation. For example, consider the following function subprogram:

```
          REAL FUNCTION AVRAGE(SCORES,TESTS,ERROR)
          INTEGER ERROR, TESTS
          REAL SCORES(50),TOTAL
          ERROR=0
          IF(TESTS .GT. 50)GO TO 200
          IF(TESTS .LT. 1)GO TO 200
          TOTAL=0.0
          DO 100 K=1,TESTS
             TOTAL=TOTAL+SCORES(K)
      100 CONTINUE
          AVRAGE=TOTAL/FLOAT(TESTS)
          RETURN
      200 ERROR=1
          AVRAGE=0.0
          RETURN
          END
```

This subprogram uses a special input variable called ERROR. The calling program should use a corresponding variable in its list of variables at the point of invocation and assign an arbitrary value to it. Upon normal return from the subprogram, the value of ERROR is set to zero. An abnormal return will be indicated if the value of ERROR is set to one. The calling program can test the value of the corresponding variable in its list to determine whether the function value is correct. A main program as a calling program that uses this subprogram is shown below.

```
C
C      *** COMPUTE THE AVERAGE HEIGHT OF A POPULATION
C      *** FLAG IS USED IN THE MAINPROG PROGRAM
C      *** CORRESPOND TO ERROR IN SUBPROGRAM
C
       REAL HEIGHT(50),AVRHGT,AVRAGE
       INTEGER FLAG,PERSNS
       READ(5,200) PERSNS
C
C      *** IN CASE OF BOUNDS VIOLATION GO TO 100
C
       IF(PERSNS.GT.50)GO TO 100
C
C      *** READ AND PRINT VALUES OF HEIGHT
C
       READ(5,250) (HEIGHT(K),K=1,PERSNS)
       WRITE(6,300)
       WRITE(6,350) (HEIGHT(K),K=1,PERSNS)
C
C      *** SET ARBITRARY INITIAL VALUE OF FLAG
C
       FLAG=5
C
C      *** INVOKE FUNCTION SUBPROGRAM AVRAGE
C
       AVRHGT=AVRAGE(HEIGHT,PERSNS,FLAG)
C
C      *** IF FLAG=1 OUTPUT ERROR MESSAGE
C
       IF(FLAG.EQ.1) WRITE(6,400)
C
```

```
C      *** IF FLAG=0 OUTPUT VALUE OF AVRHGT
C
       IF(FLAG.EQ.0) WRITE(6,450)AVRHGT
       STOP
C
C      *** BOUNDS VIOLATION.STOP WITH ERROR MESSAGE
C
  100  WRITE(6,500) PERSNS
       STOP
  200  FORMAT(I3)
  250  FORMAT(8(F5.2,5X))
  300  FORMAT(1H1,50X,20H HEIGHT DISTRIBUTION)
  350  FORMAT(1H0,60X,F5.2)
  400  FORMAT(1H0,35H ERROR IN EXECUTION OF SUBPROGRAM  )
  450  FORMAT(1H0,30X,16H AVERAGE HEIGHT:,F6.2)
  500  FORMAT(1H0,50X,34H ARRAY BOUNDS VIOLATION.PERSONS:   ,I5)
       END


       REAL FUNCTION AVRAGE(SCORES,TESTS,ERROR)
       INTEGER ERROR,TESTS
       REAL SCORES(50),TOTAL
       ERROR=0
       IF(TESTS.GT.50)GO TO 200
       IF(TESTS.LT.1)GO TO 200
       TOTAL=0.0
       DO 100 K=1,TESTS
          TOTAL=TOTAL+SCORES(K)
  100  CONTINUE
       AVRAGE=TOTAL/FLOAT(TESTS)
       RETURN
  200  ERROR=1
       AVRAGE=0.0
       RETURN
       END
```

In the card deck, the function subprogram is placed directly after the END statement of the main program and before the data cards containing the values of HEIGHT.

Note that both the main program and the function subprogram check for possible array bounds violations. Two similar tests are admittedly superfluous, but they also illustrate a good defensive programming strategy.

A function subprogram is invoked by using its name, followed by an appropriate list of input variables. This list, also called a list of arguments, establishes a one-to-one correspondence between the variables in the calling program and the variables used to define the function subprogram. The number and the types of these variables in both lists must match. The list of arguments at the point of invocation in the calling program may contain names of simple variables, arrays, or functions, as well as constants or subscripted variables. When a function subprogram is executed, it can alter the values of variables used in the calling program and included in the list of arguments at the point of invocation.

Another example of a function subprogram which finds the location of the largest value stored in an array is shown below.

```
       REAL FUNCTION LOCATN(VALUE,LIMIT)
       INTEGER LIMIT
       REAL VALUE(20)
```

```
C
C              *** CHECK FOR ARRAY BOUNDS VIOLATION
C              *** IN CASE OF VIOLATION SET LOCATION
C              *** TO AN IMPROPER VALUE AND RETURN
C
       IF(LIMIT.GT.20) LOCATN=-1
       IF(LIMIT.GT.20) RETURN
C
C              *** INITIALIZE VALUE OF LOCATION
C
       LOCATN=1
C
C              *** SEARCH FOR THE FUNCTION OF
C              *** THE LARGEST VALUE
C
       DO 100 K=1,LIMIT
            IF(VALUE(LOCATN).LT.VALUE(K)) LOCATN=K
100    CONTINUE
C
C              *** RETURN WITH CORRECT VALUE OF LOCATION
C
       RETURN
       END
```

An example of a selection sort using the subprogram LOCATN follows.

```
C
C              *** SELECTION SORT OF AGES OF A POPULATION
C              *** USING SUBPROGRAM LOCATN
C
       INTEGER LIMIT,NUMSCN,PERSNS,POINTR
       REAL AGES(20),SAVE,LOCATN
C
C              *** READ NUMBER OF PERSONS IN POPULATION
C
       READ(5,250) PERSNS
C
C              *** CHECK FOR ARRAY BOUNDS VIOLATION
C              *** GO TO 150 IN CASE OF VIOLATION
C
       IF(PERSNS.GT.20) GOTO 150
       READ(5,275) (AGES(K),K=1,PERSNS)
C
C              *** INITIALIZE NUMBER OF SCANS OF
C              *** ARRAY AGES AND VALUE OF LIMIT OF SCAN
C              *** LIMIT POINTS TO THE END OF SCAN
C
       NUMSCN=PERSNS-1
       LIMIT=PERSNS
C
C              *** DO LOOP SELECTS LARGEST VALUE
C              *** AND EXCHANGES IT WITH AGES(LIMIT)
C
       DO 100 K=1,NUMSCN
C
C              *** POINTR POINTS TO LOCATION OF LARGEST
C              *** VALUE. INVOKE SUBPROGRAM LOCATN
C
           POINTR=LOCATN(AGES,LIMIT)
C
```

```
C            *** POINTR=-1 INDICATES ERROR IN FUNCTION
C            *** LOCATN. GO TO 200 PRINT ERROR MESSAGE AND STOP
C
             IF(POINTR.EQ.-1) GOTO 200
C
C            *** EXCHANGE LARGEST VALUE WITH AGES(LIMIT)
C
             SAVE=AGES(LIMIT)
             AGES(LIMIT)=AGES(POINTR)
             AGES(POINTR)=SAVE
C
C            *** DECREASE LIMIT BY CNE AND REPEAT
C
             LIMIT=LIMIT-1
100     CONTINUE
C
C            *** SORTING ENDED WITH NO FROBLEMS
C
        WRITE(6,400) (AGES(K),K=1,PERSNS)
        STOP
C
C            *** ARRAY BOUNDS VIOLATION CETECTED
C
150     WRITE(6,300) PERSNS
        STOP
C
C            *** SUBPROGRAM LOCATN ENDED ABNORMALLY
C
200     WRITE(6,350) POINTR,LIMIT
        STOP
250     FORMAT(I3)
275     FORMAT(8(F5.2,5X))
300     FORMAT(1H0,32H ARRAY BCUNDS VICLATED. PERSNS: ,I5)
350     FORMAT(1H0,38H SUBPROGRAM ENDED ABNORMALLY. POINTR: ,I5,
       1        5X,7H LIMIT:,I5)
400     FORMAT(1H0,10(F5.2,5X)//)
        END
```

Note that the dimensions of the arrays used in the function subprograms are identical to the dimensions of the corresponding arrays in the calling programs. The main program for the selection sort also indicates why it may be a good idea to check for array bounds violations in a subprogram. The value of LIMIT, passed to the function subprogram LOCATN, is initialized with the value of PERSNS and decremented by one every time the DO loop is repeated. The number of repetitions of the DO loop is controlled by the value of NUMSCN. Simple errors here can very easily initialize LIMIT with a wrong value or decrement its value to a negative number, and thereby cause LOCATN to malfunction.

7.4 SUBROUTINES

A subroutine in FORTRAN is a named procedure for processing data that do not generate a single number that can be identified or labeled as its "value," as in the case of a function subprogram. To illustrate the need for subroutines, let us consider the problem of computing the average test scores of a class of students. The data for this problem can be organized as shown in Fig. 7.2. We can solve this problem by the repeated application of our function subprogram AVRAGE, in a DO loop, to the scores of each individual student. A different approach, however, is to write a FORTRAN program for computing all the average scores as a single unit and invoking this program only once. Such a program is no longer a function subprogram since it does not compute a function value. But like a function subprogram, we identify it by a name and provide it with a list of input and output variables at the point of invocation.

The general form of the *defining statement* of a subroutine is shown below:

SUBROUTINE Name of subroutine (list of input and output variables)

SCORES   AVERAGE
                                                                                            SCORE

Number of students in class	55.0	27.0	63.0	44.0	75.0	52.8
	X	X	X	X·	X	X
	X	X	X	X	X	X
	X	X	X	X	X	X
	X	X	X	X	X	X
	X	X	X	X	X	X

◄───────── Number of tests ─────────►

Fig. 7.2 Data for computing the average of test scores of students in a class.

The key word SUBROUTINE identified the following program segment as a subroutine with the name specified in the defining statement. The name of a subroutine is merely a label that identifies it. There is no value associated with this name, but it must satisfy the same conventions of name formation as all FORTRAN names do. Since a subroutine name has no value, it makes no sense to declare its type. The list of input and output variables, also called a list of parameters, may contain names of simple variables, arrays, and functions, but not constants and subscripted variables. The defining statement is followed by a FORTRAN program that implements the data processing procedure. Execution of these programs is terminated by RETURN statements. During its execution, a subroutine can alter the values of variables in the calling program included in the list of arguments at the point of its invocation.

A subroutine is invoked by a calling program by using a special *call statement* as follows.

CALL Name of subroutine (list of input and output variables)

The list of input and output variables at the point of invocation, also called a list of arguments, may contain names of simple variables, arrays, and functions, as well as constants and subscripted variables. This list establishes a one-to-one correspondence between the variables in the calling program and the variables used to define the subroutine. The numbers and the types of these variables in both lists must match.

Upon return from a subroutine, control passes to the statement immediately after the CALL statement in the calling program (see Fig. 7.3). The following example of a subroutine computes the average test scores of an entire class of students.

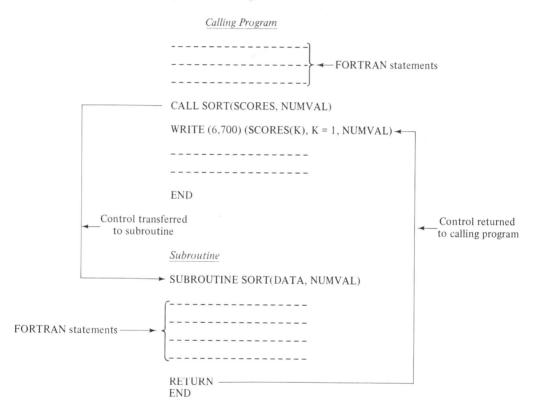

Calling Program

FORTRAN statements

CALL SORT(SCORES, NUMVAL)

WRITE (6,700) (SCORES(K), K = 1, NUMVAL)

END

Control transferred to subroutine

Control returned to calling program

Subroutine

SUBROUTINE SORT(DATA, NUMVAL)

FORTRAN statements

RETURN
END

Fig. 7.3 The sequence of control transfers involved in the invocation of a subroutine.

```
      SUBROUTINE CLASAV(SCORES,STUMAX,TESTS,AVSCOR,ERROR)
      REAL AVSCOR(40),SCORES(40,6),TOTAL
      INTEGER ERROR,STUDNT,STUMAX,TESTS
C
C        *** STUMAX IS THE MAXIMUM NUMBER OF STUDENTS
C        *** ENROLLED IN THE CLASS.LIMIT IS FORTY.
C        *** ERROR=0 INDICATES NORMAL RETURN FROM
C        *** SUBROUTINE.INITIALIZE ERROR
C
      ERROR=0
C
C        *** IN CASE OF BOUNDS VIOLATION GO TO 300
C        *** FOR ABNORMAL RETURN
```

```
C
        IF(STUMAX.GT.40)GO TO 300
        IF(TESTS.GT.6)GO TO 300
C
C         *** COMPUTE AND STORE AVERAGE SCORE OF EACH STUDENT
C
        DO 200 STUDNT=1,STUMAX
          TOTAL=0.0
          DO 100 K=1,TESTS
             TOTAL=TOTAL+SCORES(STUDNT,K)
  100     CONTINUE
          AVSCOR(STUDNT)=TOTAL/FLOAT(TESTS)
  200   CONTINUE
C
C         *** AVERAGE SCORES STORED IN AVSCOR
C         *** EXECUTE NORMAL RETURN
C
        RETURN
C
C         *** BOUNDS VIOLATION. SET ERROR TO -1
C         *** AND RETURN
C
  300   ERROR=-1
        RETURN
        END
```

A main program as a calling program that uses this subroutine is shown below. It computes the average test scores of a group of students in an art class.

```
C
C           *** CLASS AVERAGES ***
C
        REAL ARTCLS(40,6),AVRAGE(40)
        INTEGER FLAG,NUMSTU,NUMTST
C
C         *** READ NUMBER OF STUDENTS AND TESTS
C
        READ(5,250) NUMSTU,NUMTST
C
C         *** IN CASE OF BOUNDS VIOLATION GO TO 200
C
        IF(NUMSTU.GT.40)GO TO 200
        IF(NUMTST.GT.6)GO TO 200
C
C         *** READ SCORES OF STUDENTS IN CLASS
C         *** ONE STUDENT AT A TIME
C
        DO 100 K=1,NUMSTU
          READ(5,300) (ARTCLS(K,J),J=1,NUMTST)
  100   CONTINUE
C
C           *** INVOKE SUBROUTINE CLASAV
C
        CALL CLASAV(ARTCLS,NUMSTU,NUMTST,AVRAGE,FLAG)
C
C         *** FLAG=1 MEANS MALFUNCTION OF SUBROUTINE ***
C         *** PRINT ERROR MESSAGE
C
        IF(FLAG.EQ.1) WRITE(6,400) NUMSTU,NUMTST
C
```

```
C         *** FLAG=0 MEANS NORMAL RETURN FROM
C         *** SUBROUTINE. PRINT AVERAGE AND STOP ***
C
          IF(FLAG.EQ.0) WRITE(6,450) (AVRAGE(K),K=1,NUMSTU)
          STOP
C
C         *** BOUNDS VIOLATION.PRINT ERROR MESSAGE
C         *** AND STOP.
C
  200     WRITE(6,500) NUMSTU,NUMTST
          STOP
  250     FORMAT(I3,5X,I2)
  300     FORMAT(6(F5.1,5X))
  400     FORMAT(1H0,40H SUBROUTINE FAILED.NUMBER OF STUDENTS:
         $,I5,18H NUMBER OF TESTS :,I5)
  450     FORMAT(1H0,F5.1)
  500     FORMAT(1H0,40H BOUNDS VIOLATION.NUMBER OF STUDENTS:
         $,I5,18H NUMBER OF TESTS :,I5)
          END
```

Note that the subroutine performs its own test for array bounds violations in the event that the user fails to do so in the calling program. The dimensions of the arrays in the subroutine are identical to those of the corresponding arrays in the calling program. In the preparation of the program deck, the subroutine is placed immediately after the END statement of the calling program and in front of the data cards.

7.5 VARIABLE DIMENSIONS

The rules of standard FORTRAN require that the dimensions of arrays in subprograms be identical to the dimensions of the corresponding arrays in the calling program. This requirement creates no problems as long as the subprograms can be written with complete knowledge of the calling program that uses them. We run into difficulties, however, when we write subprograms that are destined to be shared by many users. If we use constant dimensions in our subprograms, the user will be forced to use the same dimensions in his/her calling programs even if they have different needs. This problem can be eliminated by using *variable dimensions* for arrays in subprograms. We caution the reader that the variable dimensions feature is not available in standard FORTRAN.

As an example, if we use variable dimensions for the array SCORES in the subroutine CLASAV, the subroutine will begin as follows:

```
SUBROUTINE CLASAV(SCORES, ROWMAX, COLMAX, STUMAX, TESTS,
$      AVSCOR, ERROR)
INTEGER ROWMAX, COLMAX, ERROR, STUDNT, STUMAX, TESTS
REAL AVSCOR(ROWMAX), SCORES(ROWMAX, COLMAX), TOTAL
```

As the type declaration statement REAL clearly indicates, the arrays AVSCOR and SCORES have variable dimensions given by the values of the variables ROWMAX and COLMAX, respectively. Since these values are integers, ROWMAX and COLMAX have been declared to be integer variables. These variables are also listed in the list of parameters so that their values can be specified by the calling program. The CALL statement in the main program now reads as follows:

CALL CLASAV(ARTCLS, 40, 6, NUMSTU, NUMTST, AVRAGE, FLAG)

At the point of invocation, the numbers 40 and 6 are assigned as the values of the variables ROWMAX and COLMAX, respectively. Note that during the process of translation of a subprogram, a FORTRAN compiler does not use the dimension declarations for allocating storage in memory for the values of the arrays. Since these values are already stored by the calling program, it will be an obvious waste of memory to do so, not to mention the effort expended in copying values before and after the execution of a subprogram. These dimension declarations are used by a compiler to generate machine language code for accessing elements of arrays created by the calling program. The numbers specified in the dimension declarations are used as parameters by this machine language code. Thus, as long as these numbers are specified no later than the time of invocation of a subprogram, execution of a subprogram can proceed without any difficulty. Variable dimensions are a mechanism for specifying the necessary numbers in the dimension declaration statements at the time of invocation of a subprogram, and hence this approach is also known as *execution-time dimensioning*.

7.6 DATA SHARING

It should be obvious by now that a calling program and its associated subprograms in FORTRAN cooperate in processing by sharing data. So far we have discussed only one means of sharing such data, and this is by explicit lists of parameters and arguments. Another means of sharing data in FORTRAN is based on the use of the COMMON statement. A COMMON statement in a calling program declares certain memory locations to be directly accessible to all subprograms with matching COMMON statements. The names of the data structures whose values are shared in this manner need not be explicitly listed in the lists of input and output variables of these subprograms. As an example, let us use this method of data sharing between the subroutine CLASAV and the main program that uses it. The main program begins with

```
REAL ARTCLS(40,6),AVRAGE(40)
INTEGER FLAG,NUMSTU,NUMTST
COMMON FLAG,NUMSTU,NUMTST,ARTCLS,AVRAGE
```

The subroutine CLASAV begins with

```
SUBROUTINE CLASAV
REAL AVSCOR(40),SCORES(40,6),TOTAL
INTEGER ERROR,STUDNT,STUMAX,TESTS
COMMON ERROR,STUMAX,TESTS,SCORES,AVSCOR
```

All the data shared by these two programs are shared via the COMMON statements. The COMMON statements in the two programs establish one-to-one relationships among the variables listed. The list of variables following a COMMON statement may contain names of simple variables and arrays, as well as subscripted variables. The same variable, however, cannot be listed in a COMMON statement and a list of input and output variables. In addition, arrays listed in COMMON statements cannot use variable dimensions. COMMON statements create more efficient machine language code for accessing shared data.

The main program will now invoke CLASAV by

CALL CLASAV

Note that no explicit list of input and output variables is given in the CALL statement since all data are being shared implicitly via COMMON statements. Normally COMMON statements are used in FORTRAN for sharing a large number of data structures among several subprograms, where explicit lists become awkward to write or, in terms of linkage, too expensive to access.

In general, sharing of information among programs via shared data structures is a technique fraught with dangers. Undetected errors in a subprogram can destroy the contents of a shared data structure and thereby indirectly induce other subprograms to behave abnormally. Errors in subprograms, interacting through shared data structures, can be very difficult to diagnose. A better way to share information is by sharing common procedures which manipulate data structures containing shared information. Individual programs do not have *direct access* to the data structures; they can only invoke the common procedures. With this approach, if the shared procedures are carefully designed, they can prevent errant programs from destroying shared data. Such shared procedures are commonly called *monitors,* although FORTRAN does not have the ingredients necessary for building such monitors.

If data must be shared, the safest approach is to share explicitly, i.e., through lists of input and output variables. An invocation such as

CALL CLASAV(ARTCLS,NUMSTU,NUMTST,AVRAGE,FLAG)

immediately tells us which data structures in the calling program are open to the onslaught of CLASAV. But an invocation such as

CALL CLASAV

gives us very little information about shared data. COMMON statements in all subprograms must be examined carefully to ascertain the full extent of data sharing. Hence we advise caution and care in the use of COMMON statements as a means of data sharing.

COMMON statements as described above create an environment in which all subprograms share the same data. We can be somewhat more cautious and share data among subprograms only on a need-to-know basis. With this approach we divide shared data into classes and a subprogram is given access only to those classes it needs for its execution. This can be achieved by means of *labeled* COMMON statements, an example of which is:

```
REAL SALARY(50)
INTEGER ID(50),RACE(50),SEX(50)
COMMON CLASS1/SALARY/CLASS2/ID/CLASS3/RACE,SEX/
```

Information about the employees of a company is divided into three classes where CLASS1, CLASS2, and CLASS3 are called labels. The first class contains only SALARY, the second only ID, and the third RACE and SEX. A subprogram with the following labeled COMMON statement

```
REAL WAGES(50)
INTEGER SOCSEC(50)
COMMON CLASS1/WAGES/CLASS2/SOCSEC/
```

cannot access the shared data stored in CLASS3. Similarly, a subprogram with

```
REAL WAGES(50)
INTEGER RACE(50),SEX(50)
COMMON CLASS1/WAGES/CLASS3/RACE,SEX/
```

cannot access individual ID's. The labeled COMMON statement therefore provides a rudimentary security system for shared data. The security attained is minimal, since the subprograms still have free access to any of the classes of shared data. The COMMON statement introduced earlier is called *blank* COMMON to distinguish it from the *labeled* COMMON statements. Any name that satisfies FORTRAN conventions can be used as a label in a labeled COMMON statement.

7.7 EQUIVALENCE STATEMENT

The EQUIVALENCE statement in FORTRAN can be used to assign more than one name to the same data structure. For example,

```
EQUIVALENCE(LOW,MIN),(LARGE,MAX,MAXVAL)
```

declares that LOW and MIN are different names for the same variable, and that similarly LARGE, MAX, and MAXVAL are synonyms. Names that are declared to be equivalent must be of the same type. The EQUIVALENCE statement follows all declaration statements but must precede the first executable statement of a program. EQUIVALENCE can be established among arrays as shown below:

```
REAL DIET(10,5),FOOD(10,5),AGE(20),DATA(20)
EQUIVALENCE(DIET,FOOD),(AGE,DATA)
```

More complex forms of equivalences can be created as shown below, but we hardly ever find them to be necessary or desirable:

```
REAL FOOD(10,5),EAT(10),DRINK
EQUIVALENCE(FOOD,EAT),(FOOD(3,2),DRINK)
```

Let us now consider some of the reasons mentioned in the literature for the use of the EQUIVALENCE statement. Occasionally a programmer writes a very long program and, at the end, finds that he/she has used two or more names for the same variable, perhaps by accident. He/she can avoid the effort of rewriting the program by resorting to the EQUIVALENCE statement. We believe that such a state of affairs shows lack of organization on the part of the programmer and recommend that the programmer abandon his/her programming effort.

The EQUIVALENCE statement also comes to the rescue in cases where two or more programmers working independently on program segments use different names for the same variable. Perhaps a better solution is for the program manager to throw a party and introduce these recluses to each other. The EQUIVALENCE statement allows a programmer to use the same memory locations for storing different arrays in sequence that may otherwise be used only once in a program. In other words, an array no longer needed in a program can be replaced by another array. If storage is at a premium, this application of the EQUIVALENCE statement may be justified.

7.8 EXTERNAL STATEMENT

In FORTRAN, a subroutine or a function subprogram may invoke another subprogram during its execution. A chain of such invocations may link together several subprograms at any point during execution. A subprogram cannot, however, invoke itself directly or indirectly through a chain of other subprograms. If subprogram A invokes subprogram B, the name of B may be listed in the list of input and output variables for A. For example, suppose subroutine AREA computes the area under a curve where the equation of the curve is given by a function subprogram called CURVE. Then AREA has to invoke CURVE, and its defining statement may list CURVE as shown below:

SUBROUTINE AREA(CURVE, ...)

The calling program that invokes AREA will do so by

CALL AREA(CURVE, ...)

Now in order to differentiate between the name of a subprogram in a CALL statement and the names of the other variables, the calling program must declare the subprogram name to be external to itself. This is done as follows:

EXTERNAL CURVE

An EXTERNAL statement in a calling program lists the names of all the subprograms which appear in CALL statements within the calling program. The EXTERNAL statement appears before the first executable statement of the calling program.

7.9 BLOCK DATA SUBPROGRAM

Variables used in a FORTRAN program, especially those defining constants, are often initialized during compilation by a DATA statement. Variables listed in a labeled COMMON statement are initialized in a different manner by using a BLOCK DATA subprogram. Let us assume that the following labeled COMMON statement appears in a program along with the declaration statements shown:

```
REAL MAXVAL,MINVAL,HEIGHT(5)
INTEGER PERSNS
COMMON AREA1/PERSNS,MAXVAL,MINVAL/ARRAYS/HEIGHT
```

Then to initialize some of the variables in the labeled COMMON statement, we use the following BLOCK DATA subprogram:

```
BLOCK DATA
REAL MAXVAL,MINVAL,HEIGHT(5)
INTEGER PERSNS
COMMON AREA1/PERSNS,MAXVAL,MINVAL/ARRAYS/HEIGHT
DATA MAXVAL,MINVAL/2*0.0/
END
```

The first statement in a BLOCK DATA subprogram consists of the key words BLOCK DATA. It further contains all the declaration statements and the labeled COMMON statements whose variables are being initialized. The initialization is done by means of a DATA statement and the subprogram ends with the standard END statement. Note that not every variable in the labeled COMMON statement needs to be initialized.

The BLOCK DATA subprogram is not invoked in the usual manner during the execution of the main program. It does not have a name and contains no executable statements. Its sole purpose is to initialize variables in labeled COMMON statements at the time of compilation. More than one labeled COMMON statement can be processed by the same BLOCK DATA subprogram. Variables in a blank COMMON statement cannot be initialized during compilation.

7.10 EXERCISES

7.1 Write a program to compute the values of $a_0 + a_1x + a_2x^2 + a_3x^3$ without using any subprograms. The values of x and a_0, a_1, a_2, and a_3 are read in as input data.

7.2 Write a main program using a statement function to compute the values of $a_0 + a_1x + a_2x^2 + a_3x^3$ for different values of x. The values of x and a_0, a_1, a_2, and a_3 are read in as input data.

7.3 Write a function subprogram called POLY that will accept a_0, a_1, . . . , a_n, n, and x as input data and compute the value of $a_0 + a_1x + . . . + a_nx^n$. The values of a_0, a_1,

..., a_n are stored in an array called COEF. The values of POLY can be computed in more than one way. Find an efficient scheme.

7.4 Consider a deck of playing cards where numerical values of 1, 11, 12, and 13 are assigned to the aces, jacks, queens, and kings. Some of the cards in the deck are missing. Write a subroutine that can find the missing cards by checking the numerical values of the cards. (This problem can be solved in more than one way; see if you can improve on your first program.)

7.5 The velocity necessary to keep a satellite in a circular orbit h feet above the surface of a spherical planet of radius R is

$$V_s = \frac{(V_o(R)^{1/2})}{(R + h)^{1/2}}$$

where V_o is a parameter. The velocity necessary for a projectile to go into a parabolic escape orbit from a satellite is

$$V_p = V_s(h)^{1/2}$$

Given that $V_o = 25{,}830$ ft/sec and $R = 20{,}903{,}520$ ft for earth, compute V_s and V_p for different values of h using statement functions.

7.6 Write a subroutine that can search through a one-dimensional array for a specific value. If this value is located, the subroutine returns the location of this value to the array. If the value is not found, the subroutine attempts to insert this value at the end of all the other values stored in the array. If the array is full, the subroutine sets an error indicator and returns.

7.7 Write subroutines for the PUSH and POP operations on a stack.

7.8 Write a subroutine for the simple insertion sort that can sort any section of an array, starting and ending at arbitrary elements.

7.9 Write a subroutine to sort a shuffled deck of cards as explained in Exercise 6.10.

8 Top-down Design of Modular Programs

In this chapter we make systematic use of subprograms to design modular programs by the top-down method. Modular programs are easier to understand, debug, and modify. As a consequence of using the top-down approach, we find that the calling program, or the main program, has to be designed first. The calling program dictates the number and the nature of the subprograms to be called and, more importantly, the list of input and output variables for each such subprogram, the so-called module interface. We also demonstrate top-down methods for the testing and modification of modular programs.

8.1 SALESPERSONS OF THE MONTH

This problem, discussed in Sec. 5.3, is repeated for the convenience of the reader.

Problem Description

An automobile dealer has twenty-seven salespersons. The dealer decides to give bonuses each month to the persons who sold the largest number of automobiles that month. Every month the dealer prepares a set of cards, each containing a salesperson's social security number and the number of automobiles sold by that person. Write a program to find the salespersons of the month who receive the bonuses.

Problem Solution

Level 1

We store the input data in two one-dimensional arrays called ID and AUTO, respectively. Next we search the AUTO array for the largest number of automobiles sold. We then compare this value with the values stored in AUTO one at a time, and whenever the two values match, we print the social security number of the corresponding salesperson from the ID array.

Level 2

As the description in Level 1 indicates, the solution of this problem involves three major tasks: the first is to obtain input data and check its validity; the second is to find the largest number in the AUTO array; and the third is to search the AUTO and ID arrays jointly for the eligible salespersons. We can use three subprograms to carry out each of these three tasks.

The first subprogram is a subroutine to read data into AUTO and ID. It is called INPUT and it uses AUTO, ID, and PERSNS as parameters. A second subprogram searches AUTO and returns the largest value stored in it. The simplest way to implement this subprogram is to use a function subprogram and name it LARGST. This subprogram needs as input the array AUTO and the exact number of salespersons involved. The third subprogram searches ID and AUTO jointly for the eligible salespersons and prints their social security numbers. The most straightforward way to implement this subprogram is to use a subroutine, called SEARCH, with ID, AUTO, the largest value in AUTO, and the exact number of salespersons as input. The main program can now be written as follows:

```
      INTEGER AUTO(30), AUTOMX, ID(30), LARGST, PERSNS
C        ***CALL INPUT SUBROUTINE
C        ***TO READ INPUT DATA
      CALL INPUT(AUTO, ID, PERSNS)
C        ***INVOKE LARGST TO FIND                        (8.P1)
         ***LARGEST VALUE IN AUTO
      AUTOMX = LARGST(AUTO, PERSNS)
C        ***CALL SEARCH SUBROUTINE
C        ***TO FIND THE ELIGIBLE SALESPEOPLE
      CALL SEARCH (ID, AUTO, AUTOMX, PERSNS)
      STOP
      END
```

Note that we created the subprograms on the basis of the tasks clearly defined by the main program. The main program explicitly specifies its input/output interfaces with the subprograms. It says nothing, however, about the way codes for the subprograms are to be designed (see Fig. 8.1). The choice of the subprograms depend on the tasks they carry out. Those that return a value to the main program are designated to be functions and the others are characterized as subroutines. The functions are implemented either as statement functions or as function subprograms, depending on their complexity.

Level 3

The next step in the design process is to implement the three subprograms. By now the reader should have learned enough to realize that the actual implementations

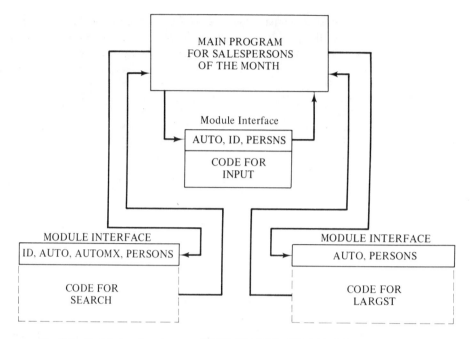

Fig. 8.1 Module interfaces between INPUT, SEARCH, AND LARGST and the main program for salespersons of the month. The codes for the subprograms are unspecified.

of these subprograms are trivial. The function of each subprogram has been clearly spelled out, as well as the input data. The dimensions of the arrays to be used in the subprograms are known exactly from the dimension declarations in the main program. Thus, before completing this straightforward task, let us pause a moment and consider the problem of testing our completed program.

In general, when a complex program is modularized by means of the top-down approach, the calling program invokes a large number of subprograms. Each subprogram in turn may invoke other subprograms. The most common approach to test such a program for errors is first, to code all the subprograms in detail, and then to test the whole assemblage as a single unit. Since errors in subprograms can interact in an unpredictable manner via shared data, diagnosis of errors becomes a difficult task with this approach.

An alternate approach is to use the method of *top-down testing,* where subprograms are coded selectively at each level and the partially assembled system is tested concurrently with its development process. Each such test increases our confidence in the program's proper execution and errors can be quickly isolated to newly designed subprograms. Admittedly, the current program is simple, but we can still use it to illustrate top-down testing.

Before proceeding further, suppose we want to test the proper execution of Program (8.P1). We can code it and execute it, but since the subprograms have not yet been designed, execution will lead to improper termination. To avoid this problem, we first design a test scheme that can at least partially test the proper execution of

(8.P1). Using this test scheme as a guide, we selectively code some of the subprograms in detail. The other subprograms are either simulated by *dummy subprograms* — i.e., subprograms with proper defining statements and returns but no real code — or their invocation statements are replaced by simple assignment statements. Next we test this partially assembled system, and if no errors are detected, we proceed to the next level of the design process. A partial test for (8.P1) is discussed at the next level.

Level 4

As a partial test of (8.P1), we want to verify whether the program generates the correct output when AUTOMX is assigned a specific value. We replace the invocation statement

$$AUTOMX = LARGST(AUTO, PERSNS)$$

by

$$AUTOMX = AUTO(i)$$

In general, it is better to create dummy subprograms than to alter statements in the main program. However, we find the later approach more convenient at this point. Next we code the SEARCH subroutine as shown below:

```
        SUBROUTINE SEARCH(ID, AUTO, AUTOMX, PERSNS)
        INTEGER ID(30), AUTO(30), PERSNS, AUTOMX
        DO 100 K = 1, PERSNS
          IF(AUTOMX .EQ. AUTO(K)) WRITE(6,200) ID(K)          (8.P2)
100     CONTINUE
        RETURN
200     FORMAT(1H0, I9)
        END
```

Clearly, the INPUT subroutine must also be coded and we leave this as an exercise for the reader. Upon execution of (8.P1) with the above mentioned modification and the INPUT and SEARCH subroutines, we obtained the following output:

ID NUMBER	AUTOMOBILES
111111111	2
222222222	5
723543299	2
999321002	5
555555555	0

```
111111111
723543299
```

This test tells us that the main program along with the INPUT and SEARCH subroutines are performing their designated functions. To make the complete program function properly, we only need to assign the largest value in AUTO to AUTOMX. This is done by the LARGST subprogram which is designed at the next level.

Level 5

```
        INTEGER FUNCTION LARGST(AUTO, PERSNS)
        INTEGER AUTO(30), PERSNS
        LARGST = AUTO(2)                              (8.P3)
        DO 100 K = 2, PERSNS
          LARGST = MAX0(LARGST, AUTO(K))
100     CONTINUE
        RETURN
        END
```

If the complete program now fails to perform under a final test, we can be reasonably certain that the cause of the malfunction has something to do with the code in LARGST or the position of its invocation statement in (8.P1). As a matter of fact, the LARGST subprogram does have an error, which will go undetected *if we use the previous input data*. The diagnosis of this error is left to the reader.

8.2   PLOTTING GRAPHS

Graphs of functions are often very useful visual aids, and in this section we show how graphs can be drawn using a line-printer. In using a line-printer for drawing graphs, the simplest approach is to plot the function values along horizontal lines and the corresponding values of the independent variable along a vertical line. Figure 8.2 shows a general graph where the function has both positive and negative values. In order to plot such a graph of a function, we have to estimate accurately the location of its zero value so that the vertical axis (see Fig. 8.2) can be properly positioned on

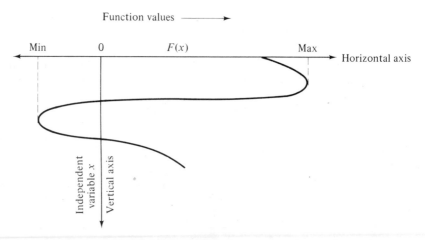

Fig. 8.2   A general graph showing both positive and negative function values.

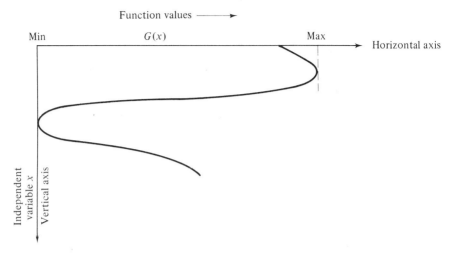

Fig. 8.3 Uniform frame of reference for all graphs.

the paper. To avoid this difficulty we plot all graphs in a uniform manner, as shown in Fig. 8.3. In this figure, the vertical axis, showing the direction of the independent variable, does not intersect the horizontal axis at the function value zero. Rather, it intersects the horizontal axis at the smallest function value denoted by MIN. A simple transformation of coordinates takes us from Fig. 8.2 to Fig. 8.3. This transformation is given by the following equation:

$$G(x_k) = \frac{F(x_k) - \text{MIN}}{(\text{MAX} - \text{MIN})} \tag{8.1}$$

Note that the shape of the graph of G remains identical to that of F.

It is impossible to plot smooth continuous graphs, such as those shown in Figs. 8.2 and 8.3, using a line-printer. The graphs we shall plot will be discrete, as shown in Fig. 8.4(a), where each function value on the graph is identified by a character, such as an asterisk. Note that Fig. 8.4(b) shows an even better graph since the nature of the variations in the function values can be spotted immediately. The smooth curve (or envelope) shown in Fig. 8.4(b) need not be drawn *explicitly*.

Problem Description

Given at most one hundred function values and the corresponding values of the independent variable, draw a graph as shown in Fig. 8.4(b).

Problem Solution

Level 1

We assume that the function values and the corresponding values of the independent variable are stored in arrays called CURVE and VARIBL, respectively. The

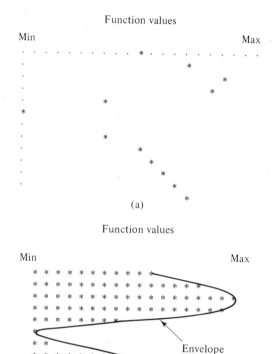

Fig. 8.4 (a) Discrete graph generated by a line-printer. (b) Envelope of the asterisks output by the line-printer shows the nature of the function at a glance.

graph is plotted by a subroutine, called GRAPH, which accepts as input CURVE, VARIBL, and the exact number of values to be plotted, called NUMVAL. This subroutine uses Eq. (8.1) to transform coordinates. The denominator $\overline{(\text{MAX} - \text{MIN})}$ of Eq. (8.1) as well as MIN are computed by a subroutine called RANGE, which is invoked by GRAPH and whose inputs are CURVE and NUMVAL. The outputs of RANGE are FRANGE and FMIN. Finally GRAPH invokes a subroutine called PLOT to do the plotting on the line printer. The input to PLOT consists of CURVE, VARIBL, NUMVAL, and the values computed by RANGE. The reader can consult Fig. 8.5 for a functional description of GRAPH. The subroutine GRAPH is shown below.

```
C
C          *** GRAPH DRIVER PROGRAM ***
C
       REAL CURVE(100),VARIBL(100)
       INTEGER NUMVAL,ERROR
C
C          *** READ NUMBER OF DATA VALUES ***
C
       READ(5,1000) NUMVAL
C
C          *** READ DATA VALUES INTO CURVE VECTOR ***
C
       DO 100 I=1,NUMVAL
          READ(5,1100) CURVE(I),VARIBL(I)
100    CONTINUE
C
C          *** CALL GRAPH PLOTTING ROUTINE ***
C
       CALL GRAPH(CURVE,VARIBL,NUMVAL,ERROR)
C
C          *** CHECK ERROR CODES ***
C
       IF(ERROR.EQ.0) GOTO 300
       IF(ERROR.EQ.1) WRITE(6,1300) ERROR
       IF(ERROR.EQ.2) WRITE(6,1400) ERROR
300    STOP
1000   FORMAT(I3)
1100   FORMAT(2(4X,F6.2))
1300   FORMAT('0',5X,'ARRAY BOUNDS VIOLATION, ERROR CODE = ',I2)
1400   FORMAT('0',5X,'FUNCTION RANGE TOO SMALL, ERROR CODE = ',I2)
       END

       SUBROUTINE GRAPH(CURVE,VARIBL,NUMVAL,ERROR)
       REAL CURVE(100),VARIBL(100),FRANGE,FMIN
       INTEGER NUMVAL,ERROR
       ERROR=0
C
C
C          *** CHECK FOR ARRAY BOUNDS VIOLATION. IN CASE OF
C          *** VIOLATION GO TO 200
C
       IF(NUMVAL.GT.100) GOTO 200
C
C          *** COMPUTE RANGE OF FUNCTION VALUES, FRANGE. INVOKE
C          *** RANGE PROGRAM
C
       CALL RANGE(CURVE,NUMVAL,FRANGE,FMIN)
C
C          *** IF RANGE IS SMALL, DIVISION IN (8.1) MAY FAIL
C          *** THEN GO TO 250
C
       IF(ABS(FRANGE).LT.(1.0E-5)) GOTO 250
C
C          *** INVOKE PLOT FOR DRAWING GRAPH
C
       CALL PLOT(CURVE,VARIBL,NUMVAL,FRANGE,FMIN)
C
C          *** RETURN AFTER PLOTTING GRAPH
C
```

(8.P4)

```
        RETURN
C
C        *** BOUNDS VIOLATION. SET ERROR TO ONE AND RETURN
C
200     ERROR=1
        RETURN
C
C        *** FRANGE SMALL. SET ERROR TO TWO; RETURN
C
250     ERROR=2
        RETURN
        END
```

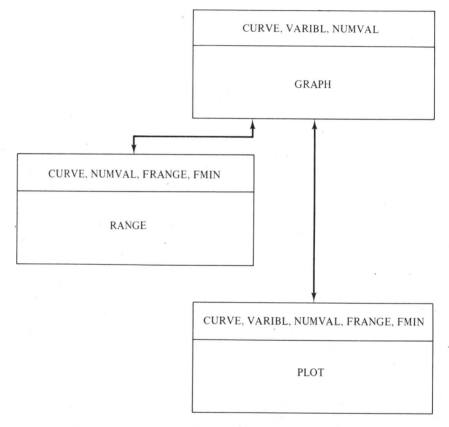

Fig. 8.5 Functional description of GRAPH with modules RANGE and PLOT.

Level 2

Now we carry out a partial test of GRAPH before coding PLOT in detail. The calling program assigns some arbitrary values to NUMVAL, CURVE, and VARIBL, and invokes GRAPH. The test is designed to verify the proper execution of GRAPH and RANGE. The subroutine RANGE is coded as follows.

```
      SUBROUTINE RANGE(CURVE,NUMVAL,VALRNG,VALMIN)
      REAL CURVE(100),VALMAX,VALMIN,VALRNG
      INTEGER NUMVAL
      VALMAX=CURVE(1)
      VALMIN=CURVE(1)
      DO 100 K=1,NUMVAL
         VALMAX=AMAX1(VALMAX,CURVE(K))
         VALMIN=AMIN1(VALMIN,CURVE(K))                (8.P5)
100   CONTINUE
      VALRNG=VALMAX-VALMIN
      RETURN
      END
```

The subroutine PLOT is simulated by the following dummy subroutine.

```
      SUBROUTINE PLOT(CURVE,VARIEL,NUMVAL,FRANGE,FMIN)
      REAL CURVE(100),VARIBL(100),FRANGE,FMIN
      INTEGER NUMVAL
      WRITE(6,100) FRANGE,FMIN
      RETURN
100   FORMAT(1H0,26H COMPUTED VALUE OF RANGE: ,F10.3,
     1   27H COMPUTED VALUE OF MINIMUM:,F10.3)
      END
```

With suitable output statements in the calling program, we can now test to determine whether GRAPH detects an array bounds violation and a small value of FRANGE, and whether RANGE performs as it should.

Level 3

We now begin to design PLOT. A regular page of computer printout can display a maximum of 132 characters on a line. We shall use 100 of these positions to draw our graph, and this will leave at most 32 positions per line for any other types of output we may want. To print the asterisks as shown in Fig. 8.4(b), we use a one-dimensional array, called LINE, of dimension 100 and store asterisks in it as shown in Fig. 8.6.

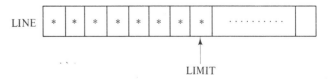

Fig. 8.6 Printing asterisks using a one-dimensional array called LINE.

There are two problems to be solved here. One is to find the value of LIMIT shown in Fig. 8.6 which controls the number of asterisks stored in LINE. The value of LIMIT must lie in the range of 1 to 100 and be *proportional to the function value* stored in CURVE that is being printed on the line of the page. This is done by means of the ROUND function defined in Sec. 7.3 and the following statement,

$$\text{LIMIT} = \text{IFIX}(\text{ROUND}((\text{CURVE}(K) - \text{FMIN})/\text{FRANGE} * 99.0, 2))$$

which is based on Eq. (8.1). In this case the value of the IFIX function lies between 0 and 99, and consequently the value of LIMIT is in the appropriate range.

The next problem is to store and output the asterisks. This can be done in a straightforward manner by using the A format discussed in Chap. 3. However, we use a programming trick to avoid handling character data. This does not mean that we recommend the use of such programming tricks. In a later section we shall discuss the difficulties introduced by this trick. First of all, we assign values to LINE in a DO loop shown below:

```
        DO 150 K = 1, 100
          LINE(K) = 22
150   CONTINUE
```

The important point to note is that the value (22) assigned to all the elements of LINE contains *more than one digit*. Next we use the following output statement:

```
      WRITE(6,300)(LINE(K), K= 1,LIMIT)
300   FORMAT(1H0,16X,100I1)
```

The net result is a series of asterisks on the output line; the exact number of asterisks is given by the value of LIMIT. If the reader is wondering why this is so, he/she should examine the FORMAT statement carefully. A little reflection will convince the reader that LINE need not even be an array for this trick to work; however, we do not want to go to that extreme with tricks like this. The PLOT subroutine, designed on the basis of the above discussion, is shown below. Also included is the main "test" program, as well as all the associated subprograms.

```
C
C         *** GRAPH DRIVER PROGRAM ***
C
        REAL CURVE(100),VARIBL(100)
        INTEGER NUMVAL,ERROR
C
C          *** READ NUMBER OF DATA VALUES ***
C
        READ(5,1000) NUMVAL
C
C          *** READ DATA VALUES INTO CURVE VECTOR ***
C
        DO 100 I=1,NUMVAL                                    (8.P6)
          READ(5,1100) CURVE(I),VARIBL(I)
100     CONTINUE
        WRITE(6,1200)
C
C          *** CALL GRAPH PLOTTING ROUTINE ***
C
        CALL GRAPH(CURVE,VARIBL,NUMVAL,ERROR)
C
C          *** CHECK ERROR CODES ***
C
```

```
        IF(ERROR.EQ.0) GOTO 300
        IF(ERROR.EQ.1) WRITE(6,1300) ERROR
        IF(ERROR.EQ.2) WRITE(6,1400) ERROR
300     STOP
1000    FORMAT(I3)
1100    FORMAT(2(4X,F6.2))
1200    FORMAT('1',25X,'GRAPH DRAWING PROGRAM'//)
1300    FORMAT('0',5X,'ARRAY BOUNDS VIOLATION, ERROR CODE = ',I2)
1400    FORMAT('0',5X,'FUNCTION RANGE TOO SMALL, ERROR CODE = ',I2)
        END

        SUBROUTINE GRAPH(CURVE,VARIBL,NUMVAL,ERROR)
        REAL CURVE(100),VARIBL(100),FRANGE,FMIN
        INTEGER NUMVAL,ERROR
        ERROR=0
C
C
C       *** CHECK FOR ARRAY BOUNDS VIOLATION. IN CASE OF
C       *** VIOLATION GO TO 200
C
        IF(NUMVAL.GT.100) GOTO 200
C
C       *** COMPUTE RANGE OF FUNCTION VALUES, FRANGE. INVOKE
C       *** RANGE PROGRAM
C
        CALL RANGE(CURVE,NUMVAL,FRANGE,FMIN)
C
C       *** IF RANGE IS SMALL, DIVISION IN (8.1) MAY FAIL
C       *** THEN GO TO 250
C
        IF(ABS(FRANGE).LT.(1.0E-5)) GOTO 250
C
C       *** INVOKE PLOT FOR DRAWING GRAPH
C
        CALL PLOT(CURVE,VARIBL,NUMVAL,FRANGE,FMIN)
C
C       *** RETURN AFTER PLOTTING GRAPH
C
        RETURN
C
C       *** BOUNDS VIOLATION. SET ERROR TO ONE AND RETURN
C
200     ERROR=1
        RETURN
C
C       *** FRANGE SMALL. SET ERROR TO TWO; RETURN
C
250     ERROR=2
        RETURN
        END

        SUBROUTINE RANGE(CURVE,NUMVAL,VALRNG,VALMIN)
        REAL CURVE(100),VALMAX,VALMIN,VALRNG
        INTEGER NUMVAL
        VALMAX=CURVE(1)
        VALMIN=CURVE(1)
        DO 100 K=1,NUMVAL
            VALMAX=AMAX1(VALMAX,CURVE(K))
            VALMIN=AMIN1(VALMIN,CURVE(K))
100     CONTINUE
        VALRNG=VALMAX-VALMIN
        RETURN
        END
```

```
           SUBROUTINE PLOT(CURVE,VARIBL,NUMVAL,FRANGE,FMIN)
           REAL CURVE(100),VARIBL(100),FRANGE,FMIN,FMAX
           INTEGER NUMVAL,LIMIT,LINE(100)
    C
    C         *** OUTPUT HEADING ON A NEW PAGE ***
    C
           WRITE(6,600)
           FMAX=FRANGE+FMIN
           WRITE(6,650) FMIN,FMAX
    C
    C         *** ASSIGN VALUES TO LINE ***
    C
           DO 150 K=1,100
              LINE(K)=22
    150    CONTINUE
    C
    C         *** DO LOOP PLOTS CURVE ONE VALUE AT A TIME ***
    C
           DO 200 K=1,NUMVAL
              IF((CURVE(K)-FMIN).NE.(0.0)) GOTO 190
              WRITE(6,675) VARIBL(K)
              GOTO 200
    190       LIMIT=IFIX(ROUND((CURVE(K)-FMIN)/FRANGE*99.0,2))
              IF(LIMIT.GT.100) LIMIT=100
              WRITE(6,700) VARIBL(K),(LINE(I),I=1,LIMIT)
    200    CONTINUE
           RETURN
    600    FORMAT(1H1,50X,26H GRAPH OF USER'S FUNCTION )
    650    FORMAT(1H0,12X,5HMIN =,F10.4,59X,5HMAX =,F10.4)
    675    FORMAT(1H0,5X,F10.4)
    700    FORMAT(1H0,5X,F10.4,1X,100I1)
           END


           REAL FUNCTION ROUND(G,N)
           REAL G
           INTEGER N
           ROUND=G+(0.5*0.1**N)+(G/ABS(G))
           RETURN
           END
```

A typical plot of the function $f(x) = x^2$ for $-0.2 \leq x \leq 0.6$ at increments of 0.1 using GRAPH is shown on page 179.

8.3 MODIFICATION OF GRAPH

After a subroutine has been developed and used for a while, one often meets new ideas and/or requirements related to the function of the subroutine which often lead to the modification of the existing subroutine. For example, now that we can plot the graph of a single function, we may want to plot the graphs of several functions simultaneously over the same range of values of the independent variable.

This means that we shall have to modify the GRAPH subroutine in some manner. In attempting to do so, we learn that well-designed programs are easier to mod-

GRAPH OF USER'S FUNCTION

MIN =   0.0000   MAX =   0.3600

-0.2000 ***************
-0.1000 ***
 0.0000
 0.1000 ***
 0.2000 *************
 0.3000 *******************
 0.4000 ***********************
 0.5000 ******************************
 0.6000 **

ify than poorly designed ones. If a program is developed using many specialized programming tricks, it may be impossible to modify it to meeet the new requirements. In that case it becomes necessary to develop a new program from scratch.

In our case, we assume that the function values to be plotted are stored in a two-dimensional array, called CURVES, where each column stores the values of a single function. To be specific, we assume that there are at most ten such functions to be plotted. Now to plot the graphs of ten functions simultaneously we must use ten different symbols; a single asterisk is no longer sufficient. We allow the user to select his own symbols and store them in a one-dimensional array called SYMBOL. The subroutine PLOT will make use of these symbols to plot the graphs. The user should specify two extra symbols, a blank and a dot, to aid in plotting; these symbols are assumed to be stored in SYMBOL as well.

Equation (8.1) is still used to transform coordinates, except that now MAX and MIN denote the largest and the smallest of *all* the values of *all* functions. Finally, the exact number of functions stored in CURVES is assumed to be given by the value of NUMFUN. The modified subroutine GRAPH, called GRAPH1, is as follows:

```
      SUBROUTINE GRAPH1(CURVES, VARIBL, NUMVAL, NUMFUN, SYMBOL, ERROR)
      REAL CURVES(100,10), VARIBL(100), FRANGE, FMIN
      INTEGER SYMBOL(12), NUMVAL, NUMFUN, ERROR
C        ***SYMBOL(11)CONTAINS A BLANK AND SYMBOL(12) IS A DOT
      ERROR = 0
      IF(NUMVAL .GT. 100) GO TO 200
      IF(NUMFUN .GT. 10) GO TO 200                               (8.P7)
      CALL RANGE1(CURVES, NUMVAL, NUMFUN, FRANGE, FMIN)
      IF(ABS(FRANGE) .LT. 1.0E-5) GO TO 250
      CALL PLOT1(CURVES, VARIBL, NUMVAL, NUMFUN, SYMBOL, FRANGE,
     $    FMIN)
      RETURN
  200 ERROR = 1
      RETURN
  250 ERROR = 2
      RETURN
      END
```

Comparing GRAPH1 with GRAPH, we can see that the changes required are minimal and have been incorporated with very little effort. All the comments in GRAPH are relevant to GRAPH1 and are suppressed above; only additional comments needed by GRAPH1 are included.

8.4   MODIFICATION OF RANGE

Next we modify the subroutine RANGE so that it now finds the largest and the smallest values of *all* the function values stored in CURVES. The modified subroutine, called RANGE1, is shown below:

```
      SUBROUTINE RANGE1(CURVES, NUMVAL, NUMFUN, VALRNG, VALMIN)
      REAL CURVES(100,10), VALMAX, VALMIN, VALRNG
```

```
      INTEGER NUMVAL, NUMFUN
      VALMAX = CURVES(1,1)
      VALMIN = CURVES(1,1)                          (8.P8)
      DO 100 L = 1, NUMFUN
        DO 100 K = 1, NUMVAL
          VALMAX = AMAX1(VALMAX, CURVES(K,L))
          VALMIN = AMIN1(VALMIN, CURVES(K,L))
100   CONTINUE
      VALRNG = VALMAX − VALMIN
      RETURN
      END
```

Comparing RANGE1 with RANGE, the reader can verify that the modifications are minimal and require little effort.

8.5 MODIFICATION OF PLOT

We now come to the modification of PLOT, the most crucial subroutine in this package. The first thing we note is that we now have to output anywhere from one to ten symbols selected by the user and must therefore resort to the use of the A format. The subroutine PLOT was designed using a programming trick that deliberately avoided the use of the A format. Hence PLOT cannot be easily modified to satisfy this new requirement, and we are forced to design from scratch a new subroutine, called PLOT1, with all the risks that entails.

To output a series of dots to denote the horizontal axis, we can use the following FORTRAN code:

```
C               ***SYMBOL(12) IS A DOT. LOAD DOTS IN ARRAY LINE
      DO 100 I = 1, 100
          LINE(I) = SYMBOL(12)
100   CONTINUE
C               ***OUTPUT LINE IN THE A FORMAT
      WRITE(6,650)(LINE(L), L=1,100)·
650   FORMAT(1H0,16X,100A1)
```

To clear the contents of LINE we can use the FORTRAN code shown below:

```
C               ***SYMBOL(11)IS A BLANK. LOAD BLANKS IN LINE
      DO 200 I = 2,100
          LINE(I) = SYMBOL(11)
200   CONTINUE
```

Now let us consider one horizontal line of output, called line J. Various symbols are printed out along this line, representing the values of the functions stored in CURVES. The value stored in CURVES(J,K) is represented by SYMBOL(K) on line J (see Fig. 8.7), and the location of this symbol on line J is proportional to the value in CURVES(J,K). This location is given by the value of LOCATN computed as follows:

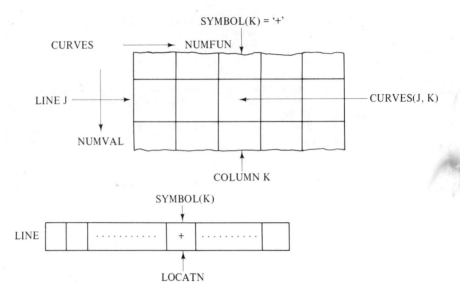

Fig. 8.7 Loading LINE with symbols from SYMBOL.

$$\text{LOCATN} = \text{IFIX(ROUND((CURVES(J,K)} - \text{FMIN)} / \text{FRANGE} * 99.0.2))$$

and the corresponding symbol is stored in LINE by

$$\text{LINE(LOCATN)} = \text{SYMBOL(K)}$$

The PLOT1 subroutine, designed on the basis of the above discussion, is as follows.

```
C
C          *** GRAPH DRIVER PROGRAM ***
C
       REAL CURVES(100,10),VARIEL(100)
       INTEGER NUMFUN,NUMVAL,ERRCF,SYMBOL(12)
       DATA SYMBOL(1),SYMBOL(2)/'*','+'/
       DATA SYMBOL(11),SYMBOL(12)/' ','.'/
C
C          *** READ NUMBER OF DATA VALUES ***
C
       READ(5,1000) NUMFUN,NUMVAL
       WRITE(6,1100) (N,N=1,NUMFUN)                    (8.P9)
C
C          *** READ DATA VALUES INTO CURVE VECTOR ***
C
       X=-1.0
       DO 100 I=1,NUMVAL
C
C          *** EVALUATE FUNCTIONS TO BE PLOTTED ***
C
       F1=X
       F2=X**2
       CURVES(I,1)=F1
       CURVES(I,2)=F2
```

```
                 VARIBL(I)=X
                 WRITE(6,1200) I,CURVES(I,1),CURVES(I,2),VARIBL(I)
                 X=X+0.2
100      CONTINUE
C
C            *** CALL GRAPH PLOTTING ROUTINE ***
C
         CALL GRAPH1(CURVES,VARIBL,NUMVAL,NUMFUN,SYMBOL,ERROR)
C
C            *** CHECK ERROR CODES ***
C
         IF(ERROR.EQ.0) GOTO 300
         IF(ERROR.EQ.1) WRITE(6,1300) ERROR
         IF(ERROR.EQ.2) WRITE(6,1400) ERROR
         WRITE(6,1500)                        .
300      STOP
1000     FORMAT(2(I3))
1100     FORMAT('1',10X,'INPUT DATA VALUES'//
        1 ' ',10X,'NUMBER',4X,2('FCN #',I2,3X),'X VALUES'//)
1200     FORMAT(1H0,10X,'(',I3,') =',3(F10.4))
1300     FORMAT('0',5X,'ARRAY BOUNDS VIOLATION, ERROR CODE = ',I2)
1400     FORMAT('0',5X,'FUNCTION RANGE TOO SMALL, ERROR CODE = ',I2)
1500     FORMAT('1')
         END

         SUBROUTINE GRAPH1(CURVES,VARIBL,NUMVAL,NUMFUN,SYMBOL,ERROR)
         REAL CURVES(100,10),VARIBL(100),FRANGE,FMIN
         INTEGER SYMBOL(12),NUMVAL,NUMFUN,ERROR
C
C            *** SYMBOL(11) CONTAINS A BLANK AND SYMBOL(12) IS A DOT
C
         ERROR=0
C
C
C            *** CHECK FOR ARRAY BOUNDS VIOLATION. IN CASE OF
C            *** VIOLATION GO TO 200
C
         IF(NUMVAL.GT.100) GOTO 200
         IF(NUMFUN.GT.10) GOTO 200
C
C            *** COMPUTE RANGE OF FUNCTION VALUES, FRANGE. INVOKE
C            *** RANGE PROGRAM
C
         CALL RANGE1(CURVES,NUMVAL,NUMFUN,FRANGE,FMIN)
C
C            *** IF RANGE IS SMALL, DIVISION IN (8.1) MAY FAIL
C            *** THEN GO TO 250
C
         IF(ABS(FRANGE).LT.(1.0E-5)) GOTO 250
C
C            *** INVOKE PLOT1 FOR DRAWING GRAPH
C
         CALL PLOT1(CURVES,VARIBL,NUMVAL,NUMFUN,SYMBOL,FRANGE,FMIN)
C
C            *** RETURN AFTER PLOTTING GRAPH
C
         RETURN
C
C            *** BOUNDS VIOLATION. SET ERROR TO ONE AND RETURN
C
200      ERROR=1
         RETURN
```

```
C
C          *** FRANGE SMALL. SET ERROR TO TWO; RETURN
C
250       ERROR=2
          RETURN
          END

          SUBROUTINE RANGE1(CURVES,NUMVAL,NUMFUN,VALRNG,VALMIN)
          REAL CURVES(100,10),VALMAX,VALMIN,VALRNG
          INTEGER NUMVAL,NUMFUN
          VALMAX=CURVES(1,1)
          VALMIN=CURVES(1,1)
          DO 100 L=1,NUMFUN
             DO 100 K=1,NUMVAL
                VALMAX=AMAX1(VALMAX,CURVES(K,L))
                VALMIN=AMIN1(VALMIN,CURVES(K,L))
100       CONTINUE
          VALRNG=VALMAX-VALMIN
          RETURN
          END

          SUBROUTINE PLOT1(CURVES,VARIBL,NUMVAL,NUMFUN,SYMBOL,
         1 FRANGE,FMIN)
          REAL CURVES(100,10),VARIBL(100),FRANGE,FMIN,FMAX
          INTEGER NUMVAL,NUMFUN,SYMBOL(12),LINE(100)
C
C          *** OUTPUT HEADING ON A NEW PAGE ***
C
          WRITE(6,600)
          FMAX=FRANGE+FMIN
          WRITE(6,625) FMIN,FMAX
C
C          *** DRAW HORIZONTAL AXIS OF DOTS. SYMBOL(12) IS A ***
C          *** DOT. LOAD DOTS IN LINE
C
          DO 100 I=1,100
             LINE(I)=SYMBOL(12)
100       CONTINUE
          WRITE(6,650) (LINE(L),L=1,100)
C
C          *** START PLOTTING GRAPH ONE LINE AT A TIME ***
C
          DO 500 J=1,NUMVAL
C
C          *** LOAD BLANKS IN LINE AND PUT A DOT IN FIRST ELEMENT ***
C
          LINE(1)=SYMBOL(12)
          DO 200 I=2,100
             LINE(I)=SYMBOL(11)  BLANK
200       CONTINUE
C
C          *** PICK ONE FUNCTION AT A TIME FROM COLUMNS OF CURVES ***
C
          DO 250 K=1,NUMFUN
C
C          *** FIND PROPER LOCATION OF SYMBOL ON LINE ***
C
             IF((CURVES(J,K)-FMIN).NE.(0.0)) GOTO 225
             GOTO 250
225          LOCATN=IFIX(ROUND((CURVES(J,K)-FMIN)/FRANGE*99.0,2))
```

```
C
C            *** LOAD SYMBOL IN LINE ***
C
             IF(LOCATN.GT.100) LOCATN=100
             LINE(LOCATN)=SYMBOL(K)
250      CONTINUE
C
C            *** PRINT LINE J OF OUTPUT
C
         WRITE(6,700) VARIBL(J),(LINE(L),L=1,100)
C
C            *** REPEAT ENTIRE PROCEDURE ***
C
500      CONTINUE
         RETURN
600      FORMAT(1H1,50X,27H GRAPH OF USER'S FUNCTIONS )
625      FORMAT(1H0,12X,5HMIN =,F10.4,59X,5HMAX =,F10.4)
650      FORMAT(1H0,16X,100A1)
700      FORMAT(1H0,5X,F10.4,1X,100A1)
         END


         REAL FUNCTION ROUND(G,N)
         REAL G
         INTEGER N
         ROUND=G+(0.5*0.1**N)+(G/ABS(G))
         RETURN
         END
```

Subroutine PLOT1 obviously has very little in common with subroutine PLOT. We could have avoided the A format here by using 0, . . . , 9 as the symbols for our graphs. This is an unnecessary restriction, and even then, PLOT would have required extensive modifications.

A major lesson to be learned here is that, by using clever programming tricks, we often force ourselves into situations where we cannot build upon our previous accomplishments. Thus, if we want to improve our programming skills progressively and build a library of useful programs, we must avoid programming tricks from the start. Clever programming tricks display our programming prowess at an infantile level; avoidance of such tricks shows maturity and foresight.

The functions plotted in the graph on page 186 are $f^*(x) = x$ and $f^+(x) = x^2$ for $-1 \le x \le 1$ at increments of 0.2. Now suppose we assume that the number of function values to be plotted is known only at execution time. How should we modify GRAPH1, RANGE1, and PLOT1 to account for this?

8.6 TOP-DOWN MODIFICATION

The previous sections demonstrated how we often need to modify existing programs to satisfy new requirements. Note that the modifications are carried out in a top-down manner. The first indications that a module may have to be modified show up

GRAPH OF USER'S FUNCTICNS

MIN = -1.0000   MAX = 1.0000

-1.0000
-0.8000
-0.6000
-0.4000
-0.2000
-0.0000
0.2000
0.4000
0.6000
0.8000
1.0000

as changes to the module interface. If the interface remains the same, then in general there is no need to modify a module. The interfaces thus act like waterproof doors in a submarine. During modifications we worry about a compartment only if its door buckles down and water pours in. Otherwise we leave the compartment alone. The top-down approach to modifications thus keeps the changes to a minimum; only those modules that suffer a change in interface are modified. Of course, well-designed modules are modified with the least effort.

We can also think of a module interface as a window in a store that hides the complexities of operations in the store. We merely place our orders at the window and get served. Thus if the code in a module is redesigned for efficiency, the users of the module do not need to know about the change as long as the interface remains the same. This idea is often called the *principle of information hiding* or communication on a need-to-know basis.

There is another aspect of the top-down, modular design of programs that is extremely helpful to the programmer during program modifications. Suppose we want to modify a program in some manner. How do we know which modules should be modified? As an example, we would like to obtain plots such as those shown in Fig. 8.4(b) but we prefer to use a symbol other than an asterisk. We can use the top levels of the program as an *index* to *guide us down* to the subroutine PLOT where extensive changes have to be made. The interface of PLOT with GRAPH remains unchanged and hides all the changes in PLOT from GRAPH.

8.7 QUICK SORT

One of the most efficient ways of sorting a large set of randomly ordered numbers was invented by C.A.R. Hoare and is known as the Quick sort. This approach uses a comparison and exchange scheme reminiscent of the simple exchange sort scheme discussed in Chap. 5. With this approach, however, the result of each comparison is used to select the next number for comparison and the number of exchanges is considerably reduced. For sorting N numbers, the average execution time of the simple exchange sort is proportional to N^2, whereas that of the Quick sort is proportional to $N \ln N$. A mathematical analysis of the Quick sort can be found in *The Art of Computer Programming,* vol. 3, by Donald E. Knuth.† We demonstrate the technique of the Quick sort by means of the following example.

Suppose an integer array SCORE stores the following 16 values generated at random:

```
        L                                                    R
        ↓                                                    ↓
SCORE:  57  82  13  25  87  93  38  15   7  91  60  58  71  43  61  72
```

We start with two pointers L and R, initialize them to 1 and 16, respectively, and store SCORE(L) in an integer variable called SAVE. Next we compare SAVE with

---

†Knuth, vol. 3, *Sorting and Searching*.

SCORE(R), and as long as SAVE < SCORE(R), we decrease R by one and continue with the comparison. When SAVE ≥ SCORE(R), we store the value of SCORE(R) in SCORE(L) and increment L by one. As a result of this process, we obtain:

```
            L                                         R
            ↓                                         ↓
SCORE:   43  82  13  25  87  93  38  15   7  91  60  68  71  43  61  72
                         SAVE=57
```

We now compare SAVE with SCORE(L), and as long as SCORE(L) < SAVE, we increase L by one and continue with the comparison. When SAVE ≤ SCORE(L), we store the value of SCORE(L) in SCORE(R) and decrease R by one. When this happens we have

```
            L                                         R
            ↓                                         ↓
SCORE:   43  82  13  25  87  93  38  15   7  91  60  68  71  82  61  72
                         SAVE = 57
```

Next we return to the previous process of comparison involving SAVE and SCORE(R) and keep on repeating these two processes until L = R. The results are shown below:

```
                L                           R
                ↓                           ↓
SCORE:   43   7  13  25  87  93  38  15   7  91  60  68  71  82  61  72
```

```
                            L           R
                            ↓           ↓
SCORE:   43   7  13  25  87  93  38  15  87  91  60  68  71  82  61  72
```

```
                                L       R
                                ↓       ↓
SCORE:   43   7  13  25  15  93  38  15  87  91  60  68  71  82  61  72
```

```
                                L  R
                                ↓  ↓
SCORE:   43   7  13  25  15  93  38  93  87  91  60  68  71  82  61  72
```

```
                                L R
                                ↓
SCORE:   43   7  13  25  15  38  38  93  87  91  60  68  71  82  61  72
```

When L = R we store the value of SAVE in SCORE(L) and obtain

```
                         SAVE = 57
SCORE:   43   7  13  25  15  38  57  93  87  91  60  68  71  82  61  72
```

Note that throughout this process the value stored in SAVE did not change. At the end, the value of SAVE is stored in STORE(7). The process is so designed that

after termination STORE(K) ≤ STORE(7) for K = 1, . . . , 6, and SCORE(K) ≥
SCORE(7) for K = 8, . . . , 16. SCORE(7) is therefore the proper position for the
value stored in SAVE. In essence we have divided SCORE into two sections, each
of which can now be sorted *independent* of the other. Applying the same process
again to each section, we can generate even smaller subsections. We can continue
this process until each subsection contains so few values that it can be sorted efficiently by a simpler method, such as an insertion sort.

Since this procedure subdivides SCORE by placing the value in SAVE in its
proper position in SCORE, the best division is obtained if the value in SAVE happens
to belong to the middle portion of SCORE, as in the above example. However, if by
chance we started out with SCORE(9) = 7 in the example above, then at the end
SCORE would have shrunk by only one element. Extending this idea further, we
can see that the worst performance of this sorting technique will occur when the
values in SCORE are already in ascending order at the start.

Various methods have been suggested in the literature for selecting the value of
SAVE from SCORE to enhance the performance of the Quick sort. One approach
selects a random integer I in (L,R) and sets SAVE = SCORE(I). Another approach
stores the median of SCORE(L), SCORE((L + R)/2), and SCORE(R) in SAVE.

Note that as score is subdivided into sections, we have to remember the first and
the last elements of every section waiting to be either further subdivided or sorted. A
convenient way of remembering this information is to push it to the top of a
stack. We process an old section by retrieving this information from the top of a
stack. The Quick sort continues as long as the stack is not empty. If SCORE has N
values and the smaller of the two sections is processed immediately, then according
to Knuth†, the stack needs to store at most $\log_2 N$ pairs of values. Recall that the
operations on a stack have been discussed in Chap. 6.

8.8 PROGRAM FOR QUICK SORT

Level 1

Description of the Quick sort procedure:

(i) Read the exact number of values in SCORE given by NUMVAL. Read
the values in SCORE. Read the value of SMALL which is used to decide
when to use insertion sort on a ''small'' section of SCORE. All input data
are read by an INPUT subprogram.

(ii) Initialize stack to store the LEFT and RIGHT endpoints of SCORE. For
convenience, this is also done by the INPUT subprogram.

(iii) Pop stack to obtain the LEFT and RIGHT endpoints of a section of
SCORE. If stack is empty, then call OUTPUT subprogram. Else, if the
section of SCORE obtained is ''small,'' then call INSERT subprogram to

†Knuth, *The Art of Computer Programming,* vol. 3, pp. 114–123.

sort this section directly. Else call DIVIDE subprogram to divide this section into two subsections, following the Quick sort scheme discussed earlier. Push the LEFT and the RIGHT endpoints of the new subsections on the stack. If stack overflows, then print error message and stop. Else repeat step (iii).

Level 2

```
C          ***TOP LEVEL PROGRAM FOR QUICK SORT
           INTEGER SCORE(500), STACK(20,2), NUMVAL, SMALL,
       $     LEFT, RIGHT, TOP, FULL, EMPTY, NEWLFT, NEWRHT
C          ***OBTAIN INPUT DATA AND INITIALIZE STACK
           CALL INPUT (SCORE,STACK,SMALL,NUMVAL,TOP)
C          ***POP STACK TO OBTAIN SECTION OF SCORE
   100     CALL POP(STACK,TOP,LEFT,RIGHT,FULL,EMPTY)               (8.P10)
C          ***IF STACK EMPTY, OUTPUT SCORES AND STOP
           IF(EMPTY .EQ. 1) CALL OUTPUT(SCORE,NUMVAL)
           IF(EMPTY .EQ. 1) STOP
C          ***IF SECTION OF SCORE IS SMALL SORT IT BY INSERTION
           IF((RIGHT − LEFT) .LE. SMALL) CALL INSERT(SCORE, LEFT, RIGHT)
           IF ((RIGHT-LEFT).LE.SMALL) GO TO 100
C          ***DIVIDE SECTION INTO SUBSECTIONS BY QUICK SORT
           CALL DIVIDE(SCORE,LEFT,RIGHT,NEWLFT,NEWRHT)
C          ***IF STACK IS NOT FULL, PUSH NEW SECTIONS
C          ***ON STACK AND GO TO POP STACK.
           IF(FULL .EQ. 0) PUSH(STACK, TOP,LEFT,NEWRHT,FULL,EMPTY)
           IF(FULL .EQ. 0) PUSH(STACK,TOP,NEWLFT,RIGHT,FULL, EMPTY)
           IF(FULL .EQ. 0) GO TO 100
C          ***OTHERWISE PRINT STACK OVERFLOW ERROR
C          ***MESSAGE AND STOP
           CALL ERROR(SCORE,NUMVAL,STACK,TOP)
           STOP
           END
```

Level 3

Let us now consider the subprograms we need for Program (8.P10). The INPUT subprogram reads all necessary data and tests for possible errors. The OUTPUT subprogram prints values from an array. These two subprograms are simple and straightforward to write, and we leave them as exercises for the reader.

The INSERT subroutine for the insertion sort must be able to sort SCORE starting at an arbitrary element pointed at by LEFT and stopping at another arbitrary element pointed at by RIGHT. We must therefore modify the simple program in Chap. 5 (5.P5) to handle this new requirement. We have previously done similar modifications to derive the Shell sort program in Chap. 6. As a matter of fact, the Shell sort program, with START=LEFT and NUMVAL=RIGHT and necessary adjustments in dimensions, can do the job of INSERT. This approach, however, may amount to using a sledge hammer to crack a peanut. In any case, we believe that the reader should be able to make these modifications and create INSERT.

Level 4

At this level we consider the PUSH and POP subprograms used to maintain the stack. Each level of the stack stores one value for the LEFT and another value for the RIGHT pointers (see Fig. 8.8). We therefore use an integer two-dimensional array

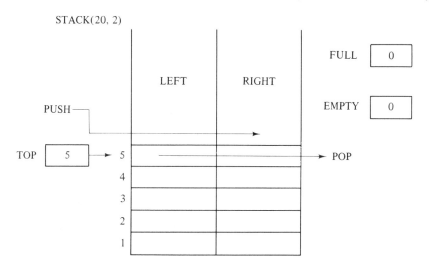

Fig. 8.8 Description of stack used in Quick sort.

for the stack. The condition of the stack is indicated by the values of the variables FULL and EMPTY. Under normal conditions, FULL = 0 and EMPTY = 0. Overflow of the stack is indicated by FULL = 1 and EMPTY = 0. When the stack is empty, we have FULL = 0 and EMPTY = 1. Using the program segments in Chap. 6 as guidelines, we have

```
      SUBROUTINE PUSH(STACK,TOP,LEFT,RIGHT,FULL,EMPTY)
      INTEGER STACK(20,2), TOP,LEFT,RIGHT,FULL,EMPTY
C          ***INITIALIZE FULL AND EMPTY
      FULL=0
      EMPTY=0
C          ***IF STACK IS NOT FULL THEN
C          ***GO TO 100 FOR PUSHING LEFT AND RIGHT              (8.P11)
      IF(TOP.GE.0.AND. TOP .LT. 20) GO TO 100
C          ***TEST FOR FULL STACK AND SET INDICATOR
      IF(TOP .GE. 20) FULL=1
C          ***RETURN BECAUSE STACK IS FULL
      RETURN
C          ***PUSH LEFT AND RIGHT ON STACK AND RETURN
  100 TOP = TOP + 1
      STACK(TOP,1) = LEFT
      STACK(TOP,2) = RIGHT
      RETURN
      END
```

In a similar manner, the POP subroutine should first test the stack to determine whether it is empty. If it is, it should set EMPTY=1 and return. Otherwise, it should assign the values on the top of the stack to LEFT and RIGHT, respectively. Using the guidelines in Chap. 6 and Program (8.P11), the reader should design this subroutine.

. We can now test Program (8.P10) and the subprograms designed so far before proceeding with the design of DIVIDE. If we set SMALL=NUMVAL, the DIVIDE subprogram is not invoked at all. Such a test can verify the operations of PUSH and POP on the stack along with that of INSERT.

Level 5

The DIVIDE subprogram accepts a section of SCORE demarcated by LEFT and RIGHT, and divides it into two subsections by the Quick sort procedure. The subsections are demarcated by LEFT, NEWRHT and NEWLFT, and RIGHT, respectively.

We copy the initial values of LEFT and RIGHT into LPOINT and RPOINT, respectively, and the value of SCORE(LEFT) in SAVE. As long as the value of SAVE is less than the value of SCORE(RPOINT), we decrease RPOINT by one. When SAVE ≥ SCORE(RPOINT), we store the value of SCORE(RPOINT) in SCORE(LPOINT) and increase LPOINT by one.

Similarly, as long as SAVE > SCORE(LPOINT), we increase LPOINT by one. When SAVE ≤ SCORE(LPOINT), we store SCORE(LPOINT) in SCORE(RPOINT) and decrease RPOINT by one.

Return from the subroutine occurs when LPOINT=RPOINT. In this case NEWLFT=LPOINT+1, NEWRHT=RPOINT and the value of SAVE is stored in SCORE(LPOINT).

```
              SUBROUTINE  DIVIDE(SCORE,LEFT,RIGHT,NEWLFT,NEWRHT)
              INTEGER  SCORE(500), SAVE,LEFT,RIGHT,NEWLFT,NEWRHT,
           $            LPOINT,RPOINT
C                    ***INITIALIZE VARIABLES
              SAVE=SCORE(LEFT)
              LPOINT=LEFT
              RPOINT=RIGHT
C             ***START QUICK SORT COMPARISONS AND EXCHANGES
       100    IF(SAVE .LT. SCORE(RPOINT)) RPOINT=RPOINT − 1
              IF(SAVE .LT. SCORE(RPOINT)) GO TO 100
              SCORE(LPOINT)=SCORE(RPOINT)
              LPOINT=LPOINT + 1
              IF (LPOINT .EQ. RPOINT) GO TO 300
       200    IF(SAVE .GT. SCORE (LPOINT)) LPOINT = LPOINT + 1
              IF(SAVE .GT. SCORE(LPOINT)) GO TO 200
              SCORE(RPOINT)=SCORE(LPOINT)
              RPOINT = RPOINT − 1
              IF(LPOINT .LT. RPOINT) GO TO 100
C             ***LPOINT=RPOINT. STORE VALUE OF
C             ***SAVE IN SCORE AND CREATE NEW SECTIONS
              SCORE(LPOINT) = SAVE
              NEWLFT = LPOINT + 1
```

```
NEWRHT = RPOINT
RETURN
END
```

All the subprograms used by Program (8.P10) are now done except for the ER-ROR subroutine. This subroutine should print an error message indicating stack overflow and the contents of SCORE and STACK, respectively. Such an output will help the programmer to understand the cause of the stack overflow situation. The reader should design ERROR as an exercise.

8.9 EXERCISES

8.1 Suppose we have a set of ID numbers of students and their scores in several exams. If we sort the ID numbers, we must also move the corresponding scores as the IDs are moved. We can reduce the amount of data that have to be moved around by using pointers. A pointer is anything that attaches an ID to its scores, and as the ID moves, the pointer is moved. For example, a pointer can be an integer number giving the location of the row of a two-dimensional array into which the scores are stored. Write a program to read the IDs and scores, and assign pointers appropriately as shown below:

IDS	POINTERS	SCORES		
4444	1	15.4	31.0	27.0
3333	2	X	X	X
8888	3	X	X	X
7777	4	X	X	X
1111	5	X	X	X
6666	6	X	X	X
2222	7	X	X	X
5555	8	X	X	X

Sort the IDs in ascending order along with the pointers as shown below, without ever moving the scores:

IDS	POINTERS	SCORES		
1111	5	15.4	31.0	27.0
2222	7	X	X	X
3333	2	X	X	X
4444	1	X	X	X
5555	8	X	X	X
6666	6	X	X	X
7777	4	X	X	X
8888	3	X	X	X

From the sorted list of IDs, using the pointers, compute and print the average score of each student.

8.2   In competitive diving, each diver makes three dives of varying degrees of difficulty. A number of judges, say nine, score the dive from 0 to 10 in steps of 0.5. The total score is obtained by discarding the lowest and highest of the judges' scores, adding the remaining scores, and then multiplying the scores by the degree of difficulty. The divers take turns, and when the competition is finished, they are ranked according to score. For example,

Name	Difficulty	1	2	3	4	5	6	7	8	9
SMITH	1.5	6.0	6.5	6.0	5.5	6.0	6.5	5.5	6.0	6.5
JONES	2.0	6.0	6.0	6.0	5.5	5.5	5.5	6.0	5.0	6.5
ADAMS	2.5	6.0	6.0	6.0	5.5	5.5	5.5	6.0	6.0	6.0
MARTIN	1.5	7.5	7.5	8.0	8.0	7.5	7.5	8.5	8.5	8.5
SMITH	2.0	6.5	6.5	7.0	7.0	6.5	6.5	6.0	7.5	7.5
JONES	2.0	6.0	6.5	7.0	6.5	7.0	7.0	7.5	6.0	6.0
ADAMS	2.0	6.5	6.0	7.5	6.0	6.0	7.0	7.0	6.0	7.0
MARTIN	1.5	7.0	7.0	6.5	6.5	6.5	6.5	6.5	7.0	7.0
SMITH	2.5	5.0	5.5	6.0	6.0	5.5	6.0	5.5	6.0	5.5
JONES	2.0	5.5	6.0	6.5	7.0	7.0	5.0	5.0	6.5	6.5
ADAMS	1.5	6.0	7.0	7.5	7.0	7.5	7.0	7.5	7.0	7.5
MARTIN	1.5	8.5	9.0	8.0	8.0	8.5	7.0	8.5	8.5	7.0

Write a program to produce the following output:

Name	Dive 1	Dive 2	Dive 3	Total
SMITH	63.75	95.00	100.00	258.75
JONES	82.00	92.00	86.00	260.00
ADAMS	102.50	91.00	75.75	269.25
MARTIN	83.25	70.50	85.50	239.25

8.3   As a continuation of Exercise 8.1, write a program that, for a given ID, will search through the sorted list of IDs and, using the pointer, print out the scores. If the given ID is not in the list, it should print a suitable error message.

8.4   Consider an intersection of two one-way streets where every 10 seconds a random number of cars (between 4 and 12) arrive on street 1 and another random number of cars (between 6 and 12) arrive on street 2. In a 10-second period, only five cars can cross the intersection on street 1 and eight cars can cross on street 2; no turning is allowed. Write a simulation program to compute the average number of cars on streets 1 and 2 over a one-minute period if the duration of the green light on street 1 is changed from 10 seconds to 40 seconds in increments of 10 seconds.

8.5   A list of IDs of students and their scores is stored in arrays as shown in the following diagram.

ID   SCORES

X

X	X	X	X	X

Write a program that can find the maximum score of a particular student given the student's ID number as input. The program should be structured as follows:

Main program uses an INPUT subroutine to read as input data the contents of the arrays shown above (maximum number of students $\leq$ 100). It uses a subprogram called CHECK to determine whether the given ID number is on the list. If the ID number is not on the list, it generates NOT ON LIST as output and stops. If the ID number is on the list, the main program calls a subprogram called SEARCH to find the maximum score of the student specified by the ID number, generates the ID number and the corresponding maximum score as output, and stops.

8.6 With the list of ID's and scores as explained above, write a subroutine called UPDATE which does the following:

Given a student's ID and a list of five new scores, UPDATE calls CHECK to determine whether the student's ID is on the list. If the ID is on the list, UPDATE replaces the student's original scores by the new scores. If the ID is not on the list, UPDATE inserts the ID at the end of the list of ID's and the new scores at the end of the list of scores. If the list is full — i.e., when we try to insert the 101st ID — UPDATE generates LIST FULL as output and stops.

8.7 A cuckoo clock counts the hour and counts once on the half-hour. After each hour is counted, a 10-second melody is played. The motive force for the pendulum is supplied by a weight suspended by a chain. A similar weight-chain system supplies the motive force for the cuckoo-music box combination.

Specifications

(1) REWIND places both weights in their topmost positions. These positions are of equal elevation.

(2) The maximum distance either weight can travel is six feet.

(3) The pendulum driving weight moves at a constant velocity and requires 30 hours to travel its maximum distance.

(4) The cuckoo-music box driving weight moves at a constant velocity only during its duty cycle.

(5) The duty cycle referred to in (4) is a function of the number of "cuckoo's" plus the melody. The cuckoo rate is one per second. The weight velocity during the duty cycle is 0.14 inches per second.

Problem

Write a FORTRAN program to do the following:

(1) Read in a REWIND card containing the hour, minute, and second of rewind.

(2) Print, with labels, the hour, minute, and second of rewind.

(3) Print and label the times of intersection of the two weights and the distance traveled from the rewind position (resolution to the nearest second).

(4) Allow time to continue until one of the weights has traveled its maximum distance.

(5) Return to (1).

(6) Process five sets of data which include the following:

    1:02:03
    5:04:03
    12:00:00

8.8 Search the matrix P, having M rows and N columns (already stored in memory), for the largest value (not absolute value), assigning it to LARGE. Print the value of LARGE, and the row number ROW and the column number COL, where this value was found.

8.9 Write a sequence of FORTRAN code that will print out a dollar value ICOST (read in as I10) ranging from zero to $10,000,000.00, floating the $ and inserting commas and the period as needed.

8.10 A certain eccentric programmer always carries two boxes of matches. The programmer starts with 50 matches in each box. Each time he/she wants a match, he/she chooses one box at random, takes out a match, and returns the box to his/her pocket. What is the probability that when he/she first finds the box he/she chooses is empty, the other will also be empty?

8.11 Let us suppose that at a certain corner in Honolulu there are two telephone booths. During any given minute, the probability is 0.3 that a person who wants to use a telephone will arrive, and the probability is 0.2 that if a person is talking, he/she will stop. We want to know:

(1) What percentage of arriving persons find a telephone available without waiting?

(2) What is the average waiting time for all persons?

9 Programming Guidelines

We know from practical experience that some programs are well-written, and we call these ''good'' programs. In the past, the quality of a program was essentially a matter of value judgment which varied from person to person. Over a number of years, however, a consensus seems to have emerged in the programming community about a set of criteria to be used to ascertain the ''goodness'' of a program. In this chapter we discuss these criteria and make suggestions for writing good programs.

9.1 CRITERIA OF GOODNESS

In judging the quality of a program, we can use various combinations of the following measures:

Simplicity: In order to understand the flow of control in a program during execution (i.e., what is *really* going on when the program is running?) and to debug, it is essential that the program be written in a simple, straightforward manner. By simplicity we mean logical clarity: avoidance of too many haphazard branches and of clever pieces of code which hide their purpose, etc.

Reliability: It is the job of a programmer to convince the user of a program that the program actually does what it claims to do. The only foolproof way of achieving this goal is to prove a program to be correct by mathematical logic. However, for complex programs this is exceedingly difficult to do, and unless *automatic* program proving systems capable of handling complex programs are designed in the future, this approach will not be very useful.

The only alternative available to a programmer to convince a user of a program's value is to explain the organization of the program and the tests used. If the user realizes the careful thinking that has gone into the organization and testing of a program, he/she may be persuaded to trust the program output.

Adaptability: the processing requirements of a program often undergo gradual but significant changes over a period of time. For example, in a program that simulates a simple queue, it may become necessary to add more than one server and/or more than one priority of service over a period of time. The simple simulation model should be written so that it can be easily modified to incorporate such changes. Programs which can be easily modified to satisfy new requirements are called adaptable. Highly efficient programs can be written by clever coding, but such programs are often complex, of unknown reliability, and difficult to modify.

Portability: A program is portable when it can be transferred from one computer system to another with very few changes or no changes at all. Clearly, portability will make a program more cost-effective and can be attained with programs written in standard source languages such as ANSI FORTRAN.

9.2 GENERAL GUIDELINES FOR PROGRAMMING

Simplicity appears to be the key in writing good programs. If a program is unncessarily complex due to poor organization, it will be difficult to test. This in turn will prevent users from ascertaining its reliability, even in a subjective manner. It is difficult to adapt a complex program to changes in requirements, and there is not much motivation for transporting a complex program of unknown quality from one system to another. Only gains in efficiency can sometimes be attained by using complex code.

One way to avoid unnecessary complexity in a program is to start with a complete picture of the overall requirements for the program. If all the requirements have not been specified, this should alert the programmer about possible adaptations that may be needed later on. In any case, an attempt to create such a list of requirements usually clears up any misunderstandings a programmer may have about a user's requirements. For example, before designing a simulation program, the programmer should determine (i) whether the system to be simulated is discrete-time or continuous-time, or both, and (ii) in case of discrete-time systems, whether they are event-driven or use fixed-time increments.

When at least the major requirements of a program are known, the programmer should design the topmost level as a functional module. Starting at this level, the programmer should always search for different methods to implement his/her ideas, always opting for the simplest approach unless grossly inefficient. Trade-offs must be made between simplicity and efficiency, and only experience can teach one how to chose among alternatives.

The top-level functional module should be decomposed into submodules forming the lower levels. The function and interface of each module should be carefully and completely described. Before any coding is started, the programmer should give some thought to the data structures in the programs since a poor choice of data structures often complicates program logic. For simplicity, each module can be conceived as a subprogram although it is not strictly necessary to implement it in that way. Simple subprograms are more efficiently implemented as integral parts of the calling program. Testing should be made an integral part of program development and not left until the end.

9.3 PROGRAM TESTING

The major problem in the reliability of a program is to determine whether it is correct. Extreme skepticism is the proper attitude to start with, until some carefully designed tests provide cause for reliance on the program as at least "right" if not "correct." Of course, a test can only demonstrate a program to be incorrect, i.e., show that the program has errors in it. Tests are still important, however, if a program is to be improved in increments, and at present that is the best we can do with complex programs.

Errors in a program can range from minor syntax errors to major errors in logic or problem specification. Trivial errors often lead to spectacular misbehavior on the part of a program, while major errors may remain hidden for a long time. It is always a good idea to involve more than one person in the development of a program. At each level of program development, one group develops the program while the other group scrutinizes the results. While one group codes, the other group prepares test cases and makes test runs. It is a particularly good idea to separate the designers from the testers, since designers tend to create test cases that reinforce their beliefs rather than question them.

9.4 SOME SPECIFIC RULES FOR PROGRAMMING

Various people have done empirical studies of programs and created specific rules for writing good programs. A collection of such rules follows.

(1) Modularize and use subprograms when necessary. Function subprograms should return only one function value, i.e., they should not change the values of the input variables. Argument lists of subroutines should be in some reasonable order, such as input, mixed input/output, and output. Any special condition arising in a subroutine should be indicated to the calling program by means of a specific value assigned to an integer variable. Except in special cases, function subprograms should not perform any input/output operations.

(2) Write programs that are easily readable. Programs that are difficult to read immediately raise psychological barriers between the user and the programmer. Some suggestions for writing easily readable programs are given below:

    (a) Format a program to help the reader understand it. Indent comments from code; use indentation to show hierarchy of logic; use blank lines to separate logically distinct blocks of code.

    (b) Use good mnemonic names for variables that are meaningful in the context of the program. Names of variables should rarely contain fewer than three characters because very little meaning can be immediately derived from so few characters.

    (c) Use short comments to explain the purpose of sections of code. Comments should explain the logic and not merely echo what is already clear from the code. Comments and code should agree, i.e., the code should do what the comments claim it does. Poorly written code should be rewritten rather than explained with numerous comments.

(d) Clarity of code should not be sacrificed for small gains in efficiency. Large gains in efficiency usually result from the use of efficient algorithms and not from diddling with code. The different methods of sorting discussed in this text illustrate this point. Do not complicate logic to reuse a section of code; duplicate code or use a subprogram. Logical patches to correct errors in poorly written code are not recommended; the code should be rewritten.

(3) Consider possible ways of testing a program as it is being developed. Think through and, if possible, test the program at different levels of development. In terms of increasing confidence in the behavior of the program, a series of tests during program development are usually more cost-effective than a single system test at the end. Schemes for detecting errors should be built into the program and eliminated only after exhaustive testing.

(4) Inspect code carefully for common errors such as (i) forgetting to initialize variables, (ii) executing loops one more or one less time than required, and (ii) going beyond dimensional limits of arrays.

Appendix

 FORTRAN Syntax

Statement	*Example*
ARITHMETIC ASSIGNMENT STATEMENT	(i) $Y = X**2 + 3.5 * X - X/7.1$ (ii) $J = J + 1$

The right-hand side is an arithmetic expression whose value is computed and assigned to the variable on the left-hand side. In Example (ii) the current value of J is used to compute $J + 1$, and the new value so obtained is assigned to J, destroying its current value.

CALL name (X,Y, . . .)	CALL SORT (DATA, NDIM, M)

The CALL statement is used to call SUBROUTINEs; "name" is the name of the SUBROUTINE followed by a list of input/output variables in parentheses.

COMPUTED GO TO	GO TO (100,25,300,200), I

COMPUTED GO TO allows us to execute a multiple-way branch. The general form of the statement is GO TO (N1,N2, . . .), I where N1, N2, etc., are statement numbers used in a program and I is an integer variable. For $I = K$, the program branches to statement number NK.

COMMON name 1,name 2,etc.	COMMON A,B,C

The COMMON statement serves to specify a list of names used in identifying successive memory locations in the unlabeled shared memory allocated to the program.

CONTINUE	200 CONTINUE

This statement has been used as the standard object statement of all DO loops.

DATA/list of names/list of values	DATA/A,B,C/ − 1, 2*0.0

The DATA statement allows a compiler to initialize variables given in the list of names with values given in the list of values.

DIMENSION name($n1,n2, \ldots$), $\ldots$	DIMENSION X(50), Y(10,5)

A DIMENSION statement is used in conjunction with ARRAYs. It declares variables as arrays and sets limits on the size of these arrays.

DO $n\, i = j, k, m$	DO 500 I = 3, 17, 2

Iterative loops are programmed by using the DO statement. "n" is the statement number of the last statement in the loop, called the object of the DO loop. The integer variable i is used as a counter to count the number of executions of the loop where j, k, and m are, respectively, the initial, final, and increment values for the counter.

END	END

The END statement denotes the physical end of a program and is used by the compiler to stop compiling.

EXTERNAL list of names	EXTERNAL FNCTN,SORT

The lists of names contain names of subprograms and are declared to be external to the calling program. These subprograms must be supplied by the user.

FORMAT(Code 1, Code 2, . . .)	FORMAT('0', I5, 3X, F10.3)

FORMAT statements are used in conjunction with READ/WRITE statements to describe the formats of input/output data.

FUNCTION name(list of input variables)	FUNCTION POLY(COEF,NDIM,N,X)

Function subprograms are defined by the FUNCTION statement. It assigns the "name" to the function defined, and the input variables for the function are listed within parentheses. The value of the function is assigned to its name.

GO TO *n*	GO TO 600

This statement is used to provide unconditional branches in a program. "*n*" is the statement number of the statement to which control is transferred.

IF(logical expression) Executable statement	IF(X.GT.0.0) SUM=SUM+X
	 IF(Y.LT.0.0) STOP
	 IF(X.GE.Y) GO TO 500

The logical IF statement is used to create two-way branches in a program. If the logical expression is true, then the listed executable statement is executed. Else the next statement is executed. The executable statement cannot be another logical IF or DO.

IF(arithmetic expression; X1, X2, X3 where X1, X2, X3 are executable statement numbers	IF(K) 10,20,20

The arithmetic IF statement is used to create a three-way branch in a program. If the arithmetic expression once evaluated is negative, control will be transferred to the executable statement at X1. If the resulting evaluation is zero, control will be transferred to X2, and if the resulting evaluation is positive, control will go to X3.

INTEGER list of variables	INTEGER A,B,C

This is a TYPE declaration statement which declares the variables listed as integer variables.

PRINT, list of variables	PRINT, A,B,I,J

An unformatted output statement prints the values of the variables listed.

READ, list of variables   READ, A,B,I,J

An unformatted input statement reads the values of the variables listed from data cards.

READ($i,n1$,END=$n2$)list of variables   READ(5,100,END=500)A,B,I,J

This statement reads the values of the variables listed according to FORMAT statement $n1$ from input device i. At the end of reading, the program branches to statement number $n2$.

REAL list of variables   REAL I,J,K

This is a TYPE declaration statement which declares the variables listed as real variables.

RETURN   RETURN

This statement replaces STOP statements in subprograms; it is used to return control to the calling program.

STOP   STOP

This statement stops the execution of a program.

SUBROUTINE name(list of I/O variables)   SUBROUTINE SORT(X,NDIM)

This statement defines a subroutine by giving it a "name" and specifying its input/output variables.

WRITE(i,n) list of variables   WRITE(5,200) A,B,I,J

This statement writes the values of the variables listed according to FORMAT statement n using output device i.

Appendix

B Bibliography

This annotated bibliography is provided to give the reader additional direction for further study. Only books published within the last ten years are listed and it is not meant to be all-inclusive. The key to the bibliography is as follows:

Reference	R
Text	T
Introductory	*
Intermediate	**
Advanced	***

R** Alexander, Daniel E., and Messer, Andrew C., *FORTRAN IV Pocket Handbook*. New York: McGraw-Hill Book Company, 1972.

> This compact guide contains a great deal of information normally found only in bulky FORTRAN texts and reference books.

T** Boillot, M., *Understanding FORTRAN*. St. Paul, MN: West Publishing Co., 1978.

> An excellent introductory text for both major and nonmajor computer science students, this book can be used as a self-teaching manual. Numerous program examples are included and the FORTRAN language, including direct access, is covered.

T** Cress, Paul, Graham, Wesley, J., and Dirksen, Paul, *FORTRAN IV with WATFOR and WATFIV*. Englewood Cliffs, NJ: Prentice-Hall, Inc., 1970.

> Designed for students entering commercial, social science, humanities, or scientific programming, this text presents fundamental concepts in comprehensible terms. It covers system features that apply to pure FORTRAN programs and gives the programmer increased flexibility, including an interface with routines written in assembly language. It includes numerous features in the language category and uses the WATFIV language to write simple compilers. Over

200 worked examples and 200 additional problems for student solution are given.

T**   Davis, Gordon B., and Hoffman, Thomas R., *FORTRAN: A Structured, Disciplined Approach*. New York: McGraw-Hill Book Company, 1978.

This programming manual is unique in its emphasis on the well-designed, complete program as the objective of programming. Because it is not oriented to a particular discipline, students from various backgrounds will find it applicable. Each topic chapter is divided into two parts: part A presents language features and self-testing exercises, and part B contains two complete sample programs and programming exercises. All exercises include problems appropriate for mathematics, engineering, social sciences, and business economics. Features include the use of the new 1977 American National Standard (ANS) FORTRAN as the basis for all material; compatibility with WATFOR, WATFIV, and MNF compilers; and easily accessible FORTRAN reference material, as well as a method for recording and referencing the unique specifications for the FORTRAN compiler used.

T*   DeTar, Delos F., *Principles of FORTRAN Programming*. Menlo Park, CA: W. A. Benjamin, Inc., 1972.

This FORTRAN primer is written in the general mold defined by McCracken primers. It is suitable as an introductory course for students other than computer science majors.

T**   Didday, R., and Page, R., *FORTRAN for Humans*. St. Paul, MN: West Publishing Co., 1974.

This is an unusually good text for a first course in FORTRAN programming. New concepts are introduced rapidly, but backed up with numerous examples and problems. A useful feature is the extensive reference section.

T*   Haag, James N., *Comprehensive Standard FORTRAN Programming*. Rochelle Park, NJ: Hayden Book Co., Inc. 1969.

This text teaches how to program effectively using the full version of FORTRAN IV as standardized by the American National Standards Institute. It covers the 32 different FORTRAN IV instructions and provides an understanding of computer capabilities and limitations.

Requiring no previous knowledge of computers or programming, the book uses examples and exercises drawn from general experience to show how to apply the complete language in solving the problems of a variety of disciplines. This book is easily adapted to specific classroom needs and is also well-suited for self-study.

T*   Hammond, Robert H., Rogers, William B., and Houck, Byard, Jr., *Introduction to FORTRAN IV*, 2nd Edition. New York: McGraw-Hill Book Company, 1978.

An introductory text to computer programming with FORTRAN IV, this book requires no mathematics beyond the college preparatory level. Suitable for a one-quarter or one-semester course, the coverage is general yet thorough. Students are taught to write computer programs early in the book, and the problems encountered increase in difficulty with each successive chapter.

T* Hirsch, Seymour C., *Essentials of FORTRAN IV*. Reston, VA: Reston Publishing Company, 1973.

This general introductory text on FORTRAN IV gives a logical presentation and progression of the material. However, structured programming techniques are not emphasized, ɩd numerous typos, minor inaccuracies, and misleading statements are contained in this first edition. On the plus side for this book: (1) it is divided into small, self-contained sections, making it easy for the student to review particular aspects of FORTRAN; and (2) it does not confuse the student with an overabundance of statement types early in the presentation — assignment, logical IF, GO TO and simple I/O are sufficient trauma for a student who is trying to learn the vagaries of keypunches and control card setup. The student is exposed to DO, computed GO TO, arithmetic IF, etc., when he will appreciate them as alternative means to an end.

T* Holt, R., and Hume, J., *Fundamentals of Structured Programming Using FORTRAN-with SF/K and WATFIV-S*. Englewood Cliffs, NJ: Prentice-Hall, Inc., 1977.

Based on examples from everyday life, this text shows the reader how to do a programming job correctly and to provide for later modifications. The authors introduce extended FORTRAN as a series of subsets called SF/K and provide a step-by-step presentation of basic programming concepts. Top-down program design and modular programming are also emphasized. This book is useful to both computer science and data processing professionals.

T* Kazmier, Leonard J., and Philippakis, Andreas, S., *Fundamentals of EDP and FORTRAN*. New York: McGraw-Hill Book Company, 1970.

This is a programmed text introducing basic data processing concepts, as well as the FORTRAN language. It is designed to enable the novice to program, key punch, and test his own problem using FORTRAN IV. One appendix explains in detail the operation of an IBM keypunch. The basic steps of program preparation, including flowcharting, are competently presented.

R,T** Kennedy, Michael, and Solomon, Martin B., *Ten Statement FORTRAN plus FORTRAN IV*. Englewood Cliffs, NJ: Prentice-Hall, Inc., 1975.

This text ranks with the best available on the subject. The authors introduce a small but programmable subset of FORTRAN early in the course; the remainder of the text expands and extends this subset. The authors anticipate and answer all of the questions students commonly ask.

T** Ledgard, Henry F., and Chmura, Louis J., *FORTRAN with Style: Programming Proverbs*. Rochelle Park, NJ: Hayden Book Co., Inc. 1978.

This FORTRAN style guide conforms to the recently proposed American Na-

tional Standard version of the FORTRAN language. It is intended for FOR-
TRAN programmers who want to write carefully constructed, readable programs. These simple rules of style enable the programmer to focus creatively
on the deeper issues in programming.

T*   Lipschutz, Seymour, and Poe, Arthur, *Theory and Problems of Programming with
FORTRAN*. New York: McGraw-Hill Book Company, 1977.

> This book is suitable as a text for an introductory course in FORTRAN or as a
> supplement to standard texts. It is available through the Schaum's Outline
> series. In addition to presenting syntax, the main aim is to teach problem solv-
> ing with FORTRAN (over 375 solved problems are included). Good program-
> ming techniques as well as practices are stressed, along with structured pro-
> gramming.

T**   Manning, William A., and Garnero, Robert S., *A FORTRAN IV Problem Solver*.
New York: McGraw-Hill Book Company, 1970.

> This is a workbook of problems (with solutions) designed as a companion text
> to conventional FORTRAN texts. The material is divided into statements and
> their uses, and practical applications, including payroll, banking, and statistical
> problems. Brief descriptions of programming errors and FORTRAN imple-
> mentations are also given.

T**   Marateck, Samuel L., *FORTRAN*. New York: Academic Press, Inc., 1977.

> This is a comprehensive text designed as an introductory treatment of FOR-
> TRAN at the freshman college level. Although a large text, over half is devoted
> to exercises, diagrams, and illustrations; one chapter deals with structured pro-
> gramming.

T*   McCameron, Fritz A., *FORTRAN IV*. Georgetown, Ontario: Irwin-Dorsey Limited,
1970.

> This is a good introductory book to FORTRAN for business-oriented students
> with no mathematical education or background beyond high school. All ex-
> amples and practice problems are drawn from the field of business administra-
> tion.

T*   McCracken, Daniel D., *A Simplified Guide to FORTRAN Programming*. New York:
John Wiley & Sons, Inc., 1974.

> An updated version of the author's previous introductory level FORTRAN text,
> this book is designed for the general, nontechnical reader.

T*   Meissner, Loren P., *Rudiments of FORTRAN*. Reading, MA: Addison-Wesley Publishing Co., Inc., 1970.

> This introductory text is excellent for instructing high-school students in such
> concepts as set, real number, and integer. Although the presentation of FOR-
> TRAN is elementary and incomplete, a clear and concise method of presenta-
> tion makes this a valuable text. Good programming practices are stressed. The

book contains numerous exercises and helpful appendices which summarize the syntactic rules of the language.

T** Mochel, Myron G., *FORTRAN Programming, Programs, and Schematic Storage Maps*. New York: McGraw-Hill Book Company, 1971.

This is a comprehensive FORTRAN text with emphasis on scientific applications. Many programs normally applicable to an introductory course in numerical analysis are included.

T* Monro, Donald M., *Computing with FORTRAN: A Practical Course*. London: Edward Arnold Ltd. 1977.

This introductory course in FORTRAN is suitable for the science-oriented upper-level undergraduate. There is strong emphasis on numerical methods, with the more advanced topics left as exercises. The text should reduce the reader's need for classroom instruction to a minimum.

T* Nickerson, Robert C., *Fundamentals of FORTRAN Programming*. Cambridge, MA: Winthrop Publishers, Inc., 1975.

This introductory-level text is suitable for nonmathematically skilled students from the social science and business fields. Although a good description of FORTRAN and a "learn by doing" approach are provided, recent trends in programming and program organization are not covered.

T*,R* Parker, James L., and Bohl, Marilyn, *FORTRAN Programming and WATFIV*. Chicago: Science Research Associates, Inc., 1973.

This textbook on FORTRAN is both tutorial and a comprehensive reference book. Students can learn the basic elements of standard FORTRAN and WATFIV quickly and use the book for self-study. Numerous examples are provided in both sections, and programming design, development, and debugging techniques are given.

T* Peterson, Wesley W., and Holz, Jean, L., *FORTRAN IV and the IBM 360*. New York: McGraw-Hill Book Company, 1971.

This clear and straightforward text gives a carefully escalated introduction to FORTRAN IV as used with the IBM S/360. The exercises are good but few.

R** Selfridge, Oliver G., *A Primer for FORTRAN IV On-line*. Cambridge, MA: The MIT Press, 1972.

This is an excellent self-teaching book on FORTRAN IV. The language is thoroughly covered, beginning with simple output and ending with tape handling. The practical details of debugging and running a program are stressed.

T* Spencer, D.D., *Problem Solving with FORTRAN*. Englewood Cliffs, NJ: Prentice-Hall, Inc., 1977.

This introductory text teaches students the two steps of solving a problem on the computer — how to formulate the problem in terms of algorithms and flowcharts, and how to express the problem-solving process in a computer language to obtain a meaningful solution. The first part of the text covers all aspects of algorithm development, flow-charting, and the FORTRAN programming language. Although FORTRAN is used, the text emphasizes a logical approach to problem solving that is independent of any specific language.

The last chapters include an extensive collection of problems in diversified areas: mathematics, business, physics, engineering, chemistry, education, statistics, game playing, number theory, and accounting. The text provides solutions to 25 problems and then gives over 75 exercises for students to do independently. Technical terminology is kept to a minimum; photographs, diagrams, flowcharts, and cartoons illustrate specific concepts, techniques, and equipment.

T*   Steingraber, Jack, *FORTRAN Fundamentals: A Short Course*. Rochelle Park, NJ: Hayden Book Co., Inc., 1975.

This text is an efficient guide to the fundamentals of FORTRAN. The main objectives are to provide an abbreviated means of learning the language, to familiarize students with their language manuals, and to instill an appreciation for the power and usefulness of FORTRAN.

Sample problems are given, along with complete solutions, although students are encouraged to try various routines and to analyze their success or failure.

Questions appearing throughout the text are designed to be answered with reference to the FORTRAN manual used. Intended for a FORTRAN class of approximately ten hours, this text is ideal for self-study.

T**   Wilf, Herbert S., *Programming for a Digital Computer in the FORTRAN Language*. Reading, MA: Addison-Wesley Publishing Co., Inc., 1969.

This text provides a problem-oriented exposition of FORTRAN in which problems are presented in advance of the needed language feature. The author views the computer essentially as a calculator and emphasizes only those language features required in numerical applications. It is limited and somewhat dated.

T*   Worth, Thomas, *Non-Technical FORTRAN*. Englewood Cliffs. NJ: Prentice-Hall, Inc., 1976.

This textbook explores all the major features of modern FORTRAN in an informal and nontechnical way. It assumes no previous exposure to the language and proceeds step-by-step to full coverage of the subject, illustrated with over 150 diagrams. Numerous questions, exercises, and problems enable students to put into practice what has been learned. The author discusses topics normally not covered or inadequately covered in other texts, such as arrays, subscripts, sorting, file usage, random number usage, character manipulations, and time-sharing FORTRAN.

T*   Wu, Nesa, *Business Programming in FORTRAN IV*. Dubuque, IO: William C. Brown Company, Publishers, 1973.

This book provides a more detailed approach to introducing FORTRAN to the beginning student than most other business-oriented texts. Eleven case studies address such areas as accounting, marketing, finance, management, and quantitative business analysis.

Index

Numbers appearing in bold type are major page references.